D0860569

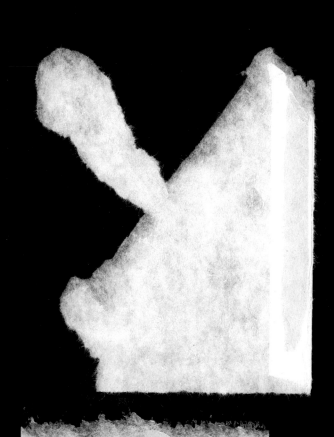

Volume 1

SPECULATIVE
CAPITAL

Volume 1

SPECULATIVE

CAPITAL

The Invisible Hand of
Global Finance

NASSER SABER

FINANCIAL TIMES
PRENTICE HALL

PEARSON EDUCATION LIMITED

Head Office:
Edinburgh Gate
Harlow CM20 2JE
Tel: +44 (0)1279 623623
Fax: +44 (0)1279 431059

London Office:
128 Long Acre, London WC2E 9AN
Tel: +44 (0)171 447 2000
Fax: +44 (0)171 240 5771

———————————————

First published in Great Britain 1999

ISBN 0 273 64155 7

British Library Cataloguing in Publication Data
A CIP catalogue record for this book can be obtained
from the British Library.

1 3 5 7 9 10 8 6 4 2

Typeset by Northern Phototypesetting Co. Ltd, Bolton
Printed and bound in Great Britain by
Biddles Ltd, Guildford & King's Lynn

*The Publishers' policy is to use paper manufactured
from sustainable forests.*

ABOUT THE AUTHOR

Nasser Saber is the general partner of Saber Partnership in New York City. He holds a masters degree in engineering from Case Western Reserve University and an MBA in quantitative analysis and finance from NYU.

CONTENTS

FOREWORD

The entire discipline of finance is driven by the fundamental conflict between the various forms of finance capital. Yet, this "portentous force of the negative" is unrecognized. Its latest creation, speculative capital, likewise remains unknown.

The effects of speculative capital – deregulation of markets, rise of derivatives, emergence of a solution to option valuation methodology, increase in market volatility, just to name a few – are all around us. Academic theorists have mistaken these effects for cause and woven a "theory" around each. The collection of theories is the bulk of "modern finance." But with the cause remaining hidden, the theories have no explanatory power. They are, furthermore, contradictory and inconsistent with one another. Only when we discover speculative capital and its central place in finance does the theoretical fog clear.

There is no mention of speculative capital in finance and economics textbooks. There is, of course, the obligatory reference to *speculation* in all of them; without that reference, their hedging argument would not work. But speculation in these books is always defined as the actions of speculators, those beneficent rascals of finance who bring liquidity to markets the way Prometheus brought fire to humans. That is their brief role on the economic stage. Then they are heard of no more.

But the subject of finance is not people. It is capital in circulation. When we shift our focus from the speculator as a person to capital as a thing, it becomes readily apparent that speculative capital – the sum total of capital in markets earmarked for speculation – is quite a different thing. In discovering speculative capital, we discover the potent force of the invisible hand in the markets and the momentous consequences of its operation.

This book is a journey, with each chapter being a stop along the way to examine a particular aspect of speculative capital. The course of the journey is historical-logical. Its driving force is dialectics: we move throughout the book by developing successive concepts from within each other in the context of material conditions which turn theoretical concepts into historical stages. The latest such condition, the collapse of the Bretton Woods system of fixed exchange rates, turned the theoretical potentiality of speculative capital into actual reality.

Like all journeys, ours also has a destination: the focal point where the consequences of operation of speculative capital in finance, law and politics come together. After penetrating financial markets and increasing their volatility, after linking markets across the globe and bringing about the dawn of "global finance," after influencing the law and politics to usher in the era of deregulation, where does speculative capital's working lead to? Our dialectical method of inquiry, moving from general to particular, facilely takes us there. That point is systemic risk, the risk of the collapse of the "system" as a result of the self-destructive movements of speculative capital.

Two general topics related to speculative capital, however, are too vast to be included in this book without disrupting its flow. One is derivatives, the shell that speculative capital assumes in the markets. We examine these products in detail in Volume 2.

The other is systemic risk, whose conditions of build-up depend on a complex set of conditions, including the size and characteristics of the "system." In that regard, the chapter titled Systemic Risk at the end of the present volume is but a broad sketch. A thorough analysis of systemic risk, time and circumstances permitting, will be Volume 3 of *Speculative Capital*.

Nasser Saber
New York, May 1999

ACKNOWLEDGMENTS

Speculative Capital began four years ago as a study of the risks of derivatives and their impact on financial markets. It was expected to take no more than one year. Indeed, the major technical parts were quickly written within the first few months. Then came the time to tie up a few "loose ends" which I had always been aware of but had not given much thought to: several inconsistencies in option valuation methods; the difficulty of defining arbitrage; and a compelling reason for the sudden rise of derivatives.

In investigating these issues, it became clear that the theories of finance were of no help. Indeed, they proved to be the source of the difficulties. The way to go was to return to basics – reading and rereading the works of classical economists for findings on which a cohesive body of explanations could be built. Thus, the side project on derivatives grew into a full-time study of economic theories which led to the discovery of speculative capital and the laws of its movement.

The study of speculative capital – the impact of its operations and the direction to which it steers the national economies – is an urgent matter. Not writing this book would be negligence. But for someone outside academia, such an open-ended excursion into the unknown would be impossible without the unqualified support of family members who, in my case, extend beyond the atomic family of contemporary Western life. Beginning with my wife, Sarina, they all did what was in their power to insulate me against the immediate demands of everyday life. Without such support, the two volumes of *Speculative Capital* could not have been written. In that regard, they are every bit as much creators of this book as I am.

Ted Ostindien graciously read the first draft of the manuscript and made valuable suggestions. A special thanks is also due to Bryan Abraham, Financial Times Prentice Hall's competent editor, whose editing skills and hundred and one "queries" went a long way toward sharpening the text and bringing out its message more clearly. Needless to say, any shortcoming in the book is solely mine. This is more than an obligatory humility on the part of the writer. Writing being action, it is a reiteration of the age-old observation that action is character.

1

A CRITIQUE OF THE THEORY OF FINANCE

The heart of economics • Influence of Knight on economic theories • The role of *Portfolio Selection* in finance • Quantification of finance • The flaw of the CAPM • The role of assumptions in a model • Uncertainty in securities law

"There is no Economics 101 which carries us through what is going on today. We're probably writing the textbooks, but we don't have them to read yet."[1]

[1] Alan Greenspan, the chairman of the Federal Reserve Board in his testimony before the Senate Banking Committee. Quoted in *New York Times*, "America's Amazing Economy," February 24, 1999, p. A20.

Introduction

Finance has no grand theory. The so-called modern theory of finance is an eclectically assembled scaffolding of individual pieces put together at different times by various theorizers. In the absence of a unifying underpinning, the pieces are inconsistent and incompatible with one another. More importantly, they fail to explain real life phenomena.

These problems do not make their way into mainstream books on finance. They usually get buried in the technical language of academic jour-

> *The so-called modern theory of finance is an eclectically assembled scaffolding of individual pieces.*

nals. Even there, when a writer feels compelled to point at some major flaw, the language is sufficiently vague to politely diffuse any tension. Sears and Trennepohl (1993, p. 421) write:

> Roll demonstrates that as long as the analyst uses a market index proxy
> … that is *ex post*, mean-variance efficient … , then the empirical tests
> of the CAPM [Capital Asset Pricing Model] should produce a linear
> relationship between betas and expected returns.

What this is saying is that Roll showed the CAPM cannot be tested and is therefore of little value. (We will examine the CAPM later in this chapter.)

Such "politeness" is not an option for us. Our goal is to develop a theory which will explain the every day occurrences in the world of finance: What caused the financial and economic crisis in Southeast Asia? What is "global finance" and where did it come from? Why were the Republicans in the US Congress blocking the Clinton Administration's funding request for the International Monetary Fund? Why did they accede? Why is the stock market volatility increasing? Why is the law of securities and derivatives uncertain? Why don't – why can't – the venerable scholars of law dispel the uncertainty with a well thought-out treatise? How do we know the Black–Scholes model is correct? Is it correct?

To a reader conditioned to regarding finance as "study of cash flows," these matters will seem to have little to do with the discipline. He would say: "The fight in the US Congress over the IMF funding is not a topic of finance. I guess you could say it is 'related' to finance in the sense that it involves allocation of money. But it surely does not belong to the same category as say, option valuation. The IMF funding is a political issue. Modern finance is a science and deals with mathematics." As we will come to see throughout this book, however, it is impossible to understand option valuation without knowing the reason for the opposition to the IMF funding. In fact, all the issues we mentioned are connected by the same thread: speculative capital. The regulator, the trader, the politician and the lawyer never imagined their paths would come so close!

Mistaking the different instances of manifestation of the same phenomenon as unrelated independent phenomena had been the fatal flaw of modern finance. Unable to offer a consistent and coherent explanation, it has remained silent on these isses.[2] But the task of theory is to explain what is happening, that is, what is changing. The theory can explain the change only if it can show the cause and direction of the change and the point to which it must lead. In that regard, theory delivers us from submissive acceptance of events just because they occur and allows us to interpret them within the body of a logically constructed system and, if need be, take action to influence them.

> *Theory delivers us from submissive acceptance of events just because they occur.*

The need for understanding and intervention has never been greater, as what is at stake is nothing short of the future of the Western economies. These economies are driven by speculative capital which, since its rise a quarter of a century ago, has steadily grown to become the main locomotive of capitalism. But the invisible hand of profit-seeking activities which propels the locomotive also sets it on a collision course of sorts. Speculative capital eliminates the arbitrage opportunities which give rise to it. In that regard, it has a built-in tendency to self-destruct, a tendency

---

[2] Theory of finance should not be mistaken with the opinion of experts. The fact that these experts commonly disagree with one another on fundamental issues is a proof that there are no generally accepted guidelines in finance.

which manifests itself every now and then in different situations. Central bankers have noticed the threat; they call it "systemic risk" – vaguely understood to be the risk of the chain reaction of defaults. Unfortunately, vague notions help little, as witnessed by the fact that the actions of the same bankers at times add fuel to systemic risk. To counter the risk, we need to gain a full understanding of the dynamics of its build-up. We need a theory that will serve as the guide for action.

This book is the journey towards developing such theory. The first step in the journey is removing the stumbling block of "modern finance" which stands in the way. The step is not incidental to the trip. It is the prerequisite for it.

The origins of modern finance

The origin of what is known as modern finance is said to date back to 1952 and the publication of Markowitz's *Portfolio Selection*. The role of *Portfolio Selection* as the pioneering work of modern finance has been extensively discussed over the past 50 years. The discussions have been marked by a religious, almost mythical bent: first there was darkness and then came Harry Markowitz and *Portfolio Selection*. Bernstein (1992, p. 41), a popular writer on the history of finance, writes:

> The most famous insight in the history of modern finance and investment appeared in a short paper titled "Portfolio Selection."… no one, including Markowitz, was aware that his paper would turn out to be a landmark in the history of ideas.

That the most famous insight in the history of modern finance went unappreciated by everyone else is conceivable. Many geniuses produced works whose significance others understood only with the passage of time. But then we learn that Markowitz himself was also unaware that his insight would be a landmark in the history of ideas. That is a curious point. How could the creator himself fail to grasp the significance of his work? The haphazard and arbitrary history of finance provides no answer.

Markowitz produced a work under the influence of powerful external forces which he neither understood nor recognized. His work, like a clock frozen at the time of an explosion, captured an instant of seismic events surrounding him. In that regard, it is a valuable clue to the history of discipline which began with the promise of embracing scientific methods but grew ever more disconnected from the real world until the advent of speculative capital and derivatives brought it to a dead end. Why a promising start led to being so marginal goes back to the heart of economics.

The heart of economics

Ever since the advent of capitalism, economists have striven to understand the nature of its laws of development. The most important question in economics was the source of profit, or productivity of capital. The discipline had to explain how it was that capital of a given sum could produce value in light of the equal exchange of values.

Take a merchant who buys a commodity for $100 and later sells it for $110. The merchant makes a profit of $10 in this purchase and subsequent sale. Where does the $10 come from?

One could argue that the merchant makes his profit by selling the commodity for more than he paid for it. This is self-evident. But what it is really saying is that the merchant "outsmarted" his trading partners and that is how the profit is generated.

This argument did not stand up well to the scrutiny of classical economists. In any economy, they pointed out, all buyers become sellers at one point and vice versa. If the agents in the economy sell commodities at a higher price than they paid, the net effect of these purchases and sales would cancel out each other, meaning that their net effect on the nation would be zero. But the "wealth of nations" was clearly increasing. The smart merchant argument, furthermore, implied that the merchant was beating the law of the equality of the exchange values in each of his transactions. But a socio-economic system could not be based on such cheating. The merchant could not pull the $10 profit out of thin air. The $10 had to be there if the merchant was to realize it as a profit. But where was it and where did it come from?

The line of inquiry to the nature of this problem that began with early economists such as William Petty, David Hume and Benjamin Franklin, led first to Adam Smith and David Ricardo and from there to Karl Marx. Marx, expanding upon Ricardo's labor theory of value, argued that the source of productivity of capital was its ability to set in motion labor power. Labor power alone created value. Indeed, Marx argued, capital itself was no more than "congealed" labor power and that fact explained the magic of capital's power to generate profit.

Knight and the source of value

Criticism of Marx's ideas began immediately. The critics offered various alternatives to explain the value-creating secret of capital. One thought which gained a foothold was the notion of risk. It was suggested that the source of the return on capital was simply compensation for the risk of investing it.

In 1921, the US economist Frank Knight (1921, p. 232) advanced the thesis that "true uncertainty," as distinct from risk, was the source of productivity of capital:

> An uncertainty which can by any method be reduced to an objective, quantitatively determinate probability, can be reduced to complete certainty by grouping cases ... but the present and more important task is to follow out the consequences of that higher form of uncertainty not susceptible to measurement and hence to elimination. It is this *true uncertainty* which by preventing the theoretically perfect outworking of the tendencies of competition gives the characteristic form of "enterprise" to economic organization as a whole and accounts for the peculiar income of the entrepreneur. To preserve the distinction ... between the measurable uncertainty and an unmeasurable one we may use the term "risk" to designate the former and the term "uncertainty" for the latter.

Knight was not the first to identify risk as an economic parameter. In his book, he credits dozens of economists who have made contributions to the study of risk in economics. He was, however, the first to associate true uncertainty with profit. As late as the mid-1960s, "proper" economic thought and talk required observing the distinction between risk and uncertainty, as exemplified by Milton Friedman (1953a, p. 21): "It seems better to use the term 'profits' to refer to the difference between actual and 'expected' results, between *ex post* and *ex ante* receipts. 'Profits' are then a result of uncertainty and ... cannot be deliberately maximized in advance."

If uncertainty and risk are different and uncertainty is the source of productivity of capital, then that difference must be the elusive capital productivity. In this way, Knight's ideas directed the research in economics towards quantitative methods. The research revealed that the boundary between true uncertainty and measurable uncertainty was at best hazy, as the addition of information turned true uncertainty into measurable uncertainty. That led to the realization that Knight's ideas explained nothing. In saying that only true uncertainty resulted in certain profits, he made a statement that, even if true, could not be expanded upon. It was of no practical or theoretical use. So the "true uncertainty" was quietly ignored. Risk and uncertainty became synonymous:

> *Knight's ideas explained nothing.*

> One tradition in economic theorizing, due to Frank Knight, distinguishes between "risk" (supposed to be a situation in which alternative outcomes exist with known probabilities) and "uncertainty" (a situation with unknown probabilities for the outcomes). Such a distinction will not be employed in this work; for our purposes, "risk" and "uncertainty" are synonymous. (Hirschleifer, 1970, p. 215)

That should have been the end of Knight's idea. But the association of risk with profit (or reward) refused to die. It hung over economics and finance and, despite its enormous contradictions, gradually became their centerpiece.

In one other, less direct way, too, Knight influenced economists: in the methodology of their research. In their efforts to measure true uncertainty, Knight's followers had embarked upon a path of quantitative analysis which shifted the focus of research in economics from traditionally normative methods to a positive method.

Normative and positive methods: "why?" vs "how?"

The normative and positive methods are not so much alternative methods of inquiry but the description of where the focus of the research lies.

The normative approach concerns itself with the *why* of events. Positive analysis focuses on the *how* aspect. The choice of method is determined by, first, the topic of the research, and then the ambition and the intellectual depth of the investigator. When Adam Smith begins his *Inquiry Into the Nature and Causes of the Wealth of Nations*, it is clear that he has more in mind than merely reporting the facts; he wants to interpret and explain them. Smith's approach, signaled by the word "inquiry," is common among classical economists. As the capitalist system developed, these economists strove to understand the laws of its dynamics; why the system behaved the way it did. Even Maynard Keynes's economic essays had a decidedly normative character.

The method of economic inquiry in the US has historically gravitated towards the positive approach.[3] Asking why things are the way they are has always been less popular than a "straightforward" explanation of how things actually work. America is the land of "how to" books and the birthplace of the Farmers Almanac: facts only, please, and no interpretations.[4] Even political economy, as developed in the US, is mostly the outgrowth of tariff considerations. Only in the works of Benjamin Franklin do we find theoretical depth and original thought.[5]

Mathematical methods are fundamentally positive. The idea of number is itself an abstraction of the highest order. In a mathematical method, all the diversity of the subject is squeezed into a numerical magnitude, which, by definition, is void of any qualitative content. The only thing important in a mathematical method is *how* to solve the puz-

---

[3] To a large extent, this "historical" gravitation is caused by economic factors and the influence of economic thoughts of the kind proposed by Knight.

[4] This tendency shows no sign of weakening. Under the heading "U.S. Pupils Score High on Science Facts but Falter on Reasoning," the *New York Times* reported: "American students have some understanding of basic scientific facts and principles, but their ability to apply scientific knowledge, design an experiment or clearly explain their reasoning is 'disappointing,' according to the latest national test of science education." May 4, 1997, p. 36.

[5] In a pamphlet titled "A Modest Enquiry Into the Nature and Necessity of a Paper Currency," the 23-year-old Franklin espouses ideas about the role of money and the nature of value that half a century later became the centerpiece of Adam Smith's *Wealth of Nations*.

zle. That is why Knight's idea about risk and the subsequent rush to measure it shifted economic research even further into positive mode.

Furthermore, in saying that true uncertainty prevented "the theoretically perfect outworking of the tendencies of competition," Knight was in effect saying that it was impossible to understand the essence of economic phenomena. The crux of economic matters – if it existed – was an impenetrable enigma. That meant that the normative approach, aiming to understand the *why* of things, was doomed.

Questionable assumptions had always been a part of flimsy economic theories.

In the normative method, one had to start with certain observations and assumptions, but it was impossible to judge one set of assumptions in a theory as more "accurate" than another because the true uncertainty in the heart of economic matters was unknowable. The best one could hope to achieve was to come as close as possible to predicting the outcome.

Questionable assumptions had always been a part of flimsy economic theories. Though officially accepted by "economists," these assumptions never failed to offend the layman's sense of logic. Here is John Dos Passos (1919, p. 478) heaping ridicule on the discipline by seeming to quote a solemn passage:

> Suppose now that into this delicate medium of economic law there is thrust the controlling factor of an owner of a third of the world's tonnage, who regards with equanimity both profit and loss, who does not count as a factor in the cost of operation the interest on capital investment, who builds vessels whether they may be profitably operated or not and who charges rates commensurate in no certain measure with the laws of supply and demand; how long would it be before the ocean transport of the whole world had broken down completely?

But questionable assumptions were always used sparingly and defensively. Economists resorted to them as a way of getting themselves out of the theoretical jams. In 1945, Milton Friedman published the "Methodology of Positive Economics," which aimed to change the theoretical conventions.

Friedman's "methodology" of positive economics

The "Methodology" is a manifesto of superficiality which has cast aside its self-conscious defensiveness and assumed an aggressive posture. It is an in-your-face crudeness of unthinking, pushing to impose itself on the unsuspecting reader under the guise of philosophical thought. In it, Friedman strove to create a theoretical framework for a "pure economics," or an economics for its own sake. The new discipline had to be independent of social constraints: He wrote (1953b, p. 4): "Positive economics is in principle independent of any particular ethical position or normative judgments."

But if ethical positions and normative judgments were to be set aside, how was one to construct or test economic theories? Economics had always been a social science. Normative issues, ethical positions and social aspects could not simply be ignored. For that, too, Friedman had an answer. He wrote: (ibid., p. 41):

> *The "Methodology" is a manifesto of superficiality.*

> Complete "realism" is clearly unattainable, and the question whether a theory is realistic "enough" can be settled only by seeing whether it yields predictions that are good enough for the purpose at hand or that are better than predictions from alternative theories. Yet the belief that a theory can be tested by the realism of its assumptions independently of the accuracy of its predictions is widespread and the source of much of the perennial criticism of economic theory as unrealistic.

By saying that the realism of assumptions did not matter in a theory, Friedman granted economists *carte blanche* to assume anything they wished as long as their theory produced "accurate predictions." But how was one to know that the predictions of a theory were accurate? Well, the prediction could be checked against what was observed, i.e., what was given – the status quo. In the highly charged ideological atmosphere of the postwar era, the implications of this reasoning went far beyond economics. Instead of starting from the observed evidence and arriving at a conclusion which could be unpleasant and controversial, Friedman espoused starting from the accepted system and then making whatever assumptions were needed to justify it.

In subordinating the realism of assumptions to predictions, Friedman turned scientific inquiry on its head. What he said, in essence, was that anything was permissible in economic theory as long as the theory produced acceptable results. The acceptable result was the confirmation of what was already in place. But if the assumptions of a theory did not matter, one could assume ghouls, ghosts and angels to explain economic phenomena. And in a way, that is what happened in the following years. Submissive acceptance of facts instead of their interpretation within logically constructed theories was to be the order of the day in economics.

Against this backdrop, *Portfolio Selection* was published.

Portfolio Selection

In practical terms, *Portfolio Selection* accomplished very little. The method was cumbersome to apply and portfolio managers generally ignored it. Elton and Gruber (1981, p. 105) write: "The reader, noting that [modern portfolio] theory is over 25 years old, might well ask ... why the theory took so long to be used by financial institutions." But the work had a profound impact on the theory of finance and its development. The impact, like Knight's theory, came from its methodology.

Portfolio Selection has a positive method. It does not concern itself with the *why* of phenomena under study. Rather, it takes the given parameters – the risk and return of stock – and proceeds to show how to construct an "efficient" portfolio that will have the highest return for a given level of risk or the lowest risk for a target return. That "how" is mathematical. This aspect of *Portfolio Selection* – its introduction of mathematics into finance – set it apart from other works. Indeed the very term *modern finance* has come to connote the employment of mathematics in finance. Bernstein (1992, p. 42) observes:

> In issues [of the *Journal of Finance*] up to 1959 I was unable to find more than five articles that could be classified as theoretical rather than descriptive. The rest contain plenty of numbers but no mathematics. No other article in the issue that carried Markowitz's paper contains a single equation.

Prior to *Portfolio Selection*, it was generally thought that investment decisions were too subjective to lend themselves to scientific analysis. For that reason, finance had remained a foster branch of economics and was generally dismissed as a not-quite-worth-pursuing discipline by more respected practitioners of mother science. *Portfolio Selection* took the theory of finance beyond the impossibly subjective attitudes of investors and presented a step-by-step, methodical approach for creating an optimum portfolio. Employing mathematics meant that finance could now be studied with the tools of scientific research.

The timing of its publication could not have been more opportune. *Portfolio Selection* came on the heels of one of the most successful periods of the application of mathematics in solving the theoretical problems of physics. The period, the years leading up to World War II and immediately following it, brought an unprecedented leap in technical and theoretical achievements that culminated in the building of the atomic bomb. Mathematics was instrumental in that success. A skillful mathematician, it was believed, could solve all problems that lent themselves to mathematical formulation. And *Portfolio Selection* had just shown that finance was one such discipline.

Pursuing mathematical finance along the lines of *Portfolio Selection* was advantageous in other ways too. It provided a respite from the contentious ideological disputes in economics between the Left and Right that in the era of McCarthyism were beginning to assume an ever sharper, and potentially career-ruining, tone. Research in mathematical finance had no downside risk. It was socially safe, it provided a perfectly respectable line of research and, with luck, it could lead to new discoveries and, from there, to fame and fortune.

That is why *Portfolio Selection* was eagerly embraced: it was not the content of the paper but its methodology which proved appealing. At the time, neither the readers of the *Journal of Finance* nor Markowitz himself could have known that.

Physicists in finance

The newly born discipline of finance required scholars with knowledge of mathematics and its methods of application.[6] One obvious place to look for such experts was the physics departments of universities. The job of physicists is applying mathematics to solve the problems of nature. Mathematics is considered to be the language of nature. In fact, a large body of mathematical theory is developed in response to needs arising from studying nature. Students of physics who knew how to apply mathematics seemed logical candidates to lead the new revolution in finance. Thus began the recruitment into finance of graduate students in physics. Some of the most well-known names in economics and finance, many of whom went on to win a Nobel Memorial Prize in Economics Science, were trained as physicists and mathematicians.

In writing his history of modern finance, Bernstein notices this phenomenon and is puzzled by it (1992, p. 2):

> The gap in understanding between insiders and outsiders in Wall Street has developed because today's financial markets are the result of a recent but obscure revolution that took root in the groves of ivy rather than in the canyons of lower Manhattan. Its heroes were a tiny contingent of scholars, most at the very beginning of their careers, who had no direct interest in the stock market and whose analysis of the economics of finance began at high levels of abstraction.

Bernstein does not see the historical and social context of the revolution, so what is in fact a very logical development – the involvement in finance of physicists with "high levels of abstraction" – to him seems a perplexing realization of an improbability which shaped the origins of modern Wall Street.

---

[6] We have not defined finance. That is intentional, so as to keep the discussion at the level transparent to the pioneers of finance. They had some vague notion that finance dealt with "money" but otherwise could not explain how it differed from economics. We define finance in the next chapter.

Like social migration, the cross-discipline migration of physicists to finance had a "cultural" component: the views of physicists about the nature of "things" and the rules governing their behavior. The "things" in physics were natural objects. Regardless of how complex the laws governing the behavior of objects turned out to be, they were decidedly void of any social content. Studying the speed and acceleration of a falling body required the invention of differential calculus. But innovative and ingenious as the discovery was, it was developed for studying the movement of falling objects and required nothing in the way of social knowledge.

Economics and finance, on the other hand, are branches of social science. As the classical economists pointed out, value itself is a social concept. Even those economists such as Karl Marx who saw economics laws developing independent of the will of individual agents, began their studies with the premise that the fundamental concept in economics – value – was a social concept because it had to be recognized by humans in the course of exchanges between them. The "sentimental value" that an individual might attach to his grandfather clock, for example, is not

Value itself is a social concept.

shared by the population at large. As such, that value is not socially recognized and the clock has a price that reflects its material and labor, the only value of concern to economists. That is the root of the disparaging saying that an economist is someone who knows the price of everything but the value of nothing.

The physicists who flocked to finance did not have a firm schooling in the principles of economics as developed by the classical thinkers. A reference to Ricardo, Smith, Marx, Franklin or even contemporary Keynes in their writings is a bibliographical rarity. More tellingly, when such references exist, they betray a profound misunderstanding of both the economist and his theories. All theoretical postulations of Adam Smith in his voluminous works, for example, are reduced to some divine "invisible hand," understood to mean that any profit-maximizing activity of any individual is beneficial to society at large.

The new recruits' ignorance of the historical developments in economics, a firm belief in the power of mathematics *per se*, and a tendency to stay away from controversial social issues, all joined forces to exorcise the social aspects of economics, and, by extension, finance, from the two disciplines. Research in finance especially took on a path long on functional aspects and short on normative investigation. The inquiring minds of scholars only wanted to know how, given the way things are, to accomplish a certain, narrow objective. Linear programming, which came to dominate the curriculum of business schools for a quarter of a century, perfectly epitomized that thinking. In linear programming, one has to mathematically maximize or minimize an "objective function" subject to given quantitative constraints. Nothing else matters.

Linear programming and its legacy

Linear programming and the role it played in shaping developments in economics and finance cannot be examined in a book on speculative capital. At the same time, the subject is pertinent to us and too important to be passed over without a comment, however brief. We merely note that the method was developed in England during World War II to improve the handling of aircraft in the airfields. After the war, it was used in similar situations, such as mapping the optimum routes for oil tankers and airlines. Then the telephone monopoly in the US, AT&T, embraced the concept and used it to determine the optimum routes for telephone calls. Its research center, Bell Labs, did some pioneering work in the field.

That deregulation in the US began with the airline industry and was soon followed by the breakup of AT&T is no accident. The impetus in both cases came from the application of linear programming: when the method showed the best way of maximizing profits and reducing costs, it bordered on madness for a company not to adopt that way. Consequently, the government rules and regulations which stood in the way also seemed irrational. So the campaign for their removal began. The ideological shift in favor of deregulation was a consequence of economic factors. Indeed, the deregulation of the airline industry took place during the presidency of Jimmy Carter, a Democrat.

Linear programming epitomized "objective" science. It seemed to be the embodiment of Friedman's (1953b) assertion that "positive eco-

nomics is in principle independent of any particular ethical position."
The solutions it offered were arrived at mathematically and were indis-
putable. There was only *one* best way of scheduling oil tankers between
a given number of ports if the profits were to be maximized or costs min-
imized. Democrats and Republicans, capitalists and communists, oil
producers and tanker owners, all had to agree on it.

But while mathematics is abstract, it
is always applied in the context of
given social conditions. And precisely
because mathematics is abstract, upon
application it assumes the characteristics of the context to which it is
applied. If the context is the Battle of

> *Because mathematics is
> abstract, upon application it
> assumes the characteristics
> of the context to which it is
> applied.*

Britain, the mathematics of linear programming shows the best way of
organizing fighter planes. If the context is the profitability of commercial
airlines, it still shows the best arrangement, which is now establishing
"hubs" and cutting services to low traffic destinations. Both solutions are
mathematically correct. In the latter case, because the purpose behind the
application of the method has changed – and that purpose is determined
by social conditions – the solution leads to a different kind of consequence: medium-sized and small communities become further isolated.
If the Nazis had learned of linear programming, they could have used it
to improve the flow of traffic in the concentration camps.

So it is nonsense of Friedman to speak of "ethical neutrality" of positive and mathematical methods. No method, indeed no act, is in itself
either ethical or unethical. That determination is made from the *consequences* of the act. And the consequences are always evaluated on social
terms. Linear programming shows the best way of allocating moveable
resources. That is "ethically neutral." But the implications and consequences of the allocation – whether of fighter planes in war, commercial
aircraft in peace or prisoners in concentration camps – involve the question of ethics. That is social. There is no escaping that fact.

Linear programming is a method of extremes; its solutions always
occur at the extreme corners of the so-called feasible region. If, in Figure 1.1, the area OABC is the universe of all possible solutions for an
optimum combination of variables X and Y, the solution will always be

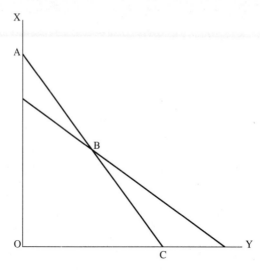

Figure 1.1 An example of "feasible region" OABC is linear programming

in one of the corners, A, B, C or O. It will never be *inside* the OABC region.

For that reason, the method tends to reinforce the existing state. In dynamic situations, it exacerbates the existing trend. This is the opposite of the much touted rational resource allocation taught in economics. In the airline example, the "hub" approach calls for increasing services to high traffic, and reducing or discontinuing services to low traffic, areas. As a result, the service is increased on the New York–Chicago and New York–London routes. Passenger fares and package delivery prices drop. Meanwhile, services to small communities are discontinued or never begin.

In the 1970s, the "strategist thinker" Herman Kahn attempted to create an "ethically neutral" approach to analyzing matters of war – especially thermonuclear war. Lewin (1996, pp. 11–12) spoofed him in his *Report From Iron Mountain*:

> What they wanted from us was a different kind of *thinking*. It was a matter of approach. Herman Kahn called it "Byzantine" – no agonizing over cultural and religious values. No moral posturing … Today it's possible … to write about … war and strategy without getting bogged down in questions of morality.

But while in a perverse sense of the word war and morality can be separated from each other – as they cannot co-exist – it is impossible to divorce the social issues from theories of economics and finance. We will see in Chapter 4, for example, that a very "neutral" device such as a currency swap reflects the circumstances of its use. When used in the context of borrowing from the International Monetary Fund in the framework of fixed exchange rates, it is a mechanism for stabilizing currencies. When used by private parties in an environment of floating exchange rates, it adds to exchange rate volatility.

Even overly mathematical option valuation models cannot rise above their social context. Behind the exotic mathematics these models stand as a social concept, namely, speculative capital; these models could not have been developed for valuing rice options in a seventeenth-century Japanese village. But speculative capital is so omnipresent in modern finance that its existence, like that of air or gravity, is taken as the natural order of things and, therefore, ignored.

The source of the vulnerability of modern economics and finance is now clear, as unwittingly explained by Professor Romer of Stanford University:

> Paul Romer, a … Stanford University economist … likens an economist's role to that of a doctor who explains what will happen if a cancer patient is taken off an aggressive [treatment] program … "You can let the pastor, the legislator, the family and the philosopher struggle with the moral question …" Mr Romer said, "but what you want from a doctor is correct scientific statement about what will happen if."[7]

The good professor is wrong on two accounts. First, doctors do not practice medicine with "moral neutrality." They are not supposed to, at any rate. The last step in becoming a doctor is reciting the Hippocratic oath, which is a moral and social declaration and not a medical one. If in recent years the moral aspects of the discipline seem to have been sidelined, the development demands an explanation.

Second, the analogy between a medical doctor and an economist is incorrect. The *mechanical* aspects of medicine are indeed independent of

---

[7] "A Challenge to Scientific Economics," *New York Times*, January 23, 1999, p. B7.

social parameters. Capitalists, communists and fascists can be equally competent surgeons. Economics and finance, on the other hand, are *per se* social disciplines. It is no more possible to separate social issues from them than it is to separate the human body from medical practice. So when, either by intention or through ignorance, social issues are driven away, what is left from economics and finance is an empty conceptual shell with no value as a roadmap for the future.

That is the peculiar legacy of *Portfolio Selection* and its positive methodology. It "rationalized" finance by opening it up to the application of mathematics. Any subject which did not lend itself to quantification was deemed subjective and, by implication, unscientific.

> *Today, this misguided objectivity is institutionalized in academia.*

Today, this misguided objectivity is institutionalized in academia. Its proponents pompously declare their views that "the scientific-mathematical outlook ... is arguably the true glory of civilization."[8] They attack the presence of any social element in economics as a sign of the intrusion of subjectivity into their discipline. In reporting about a study by the Boston Fed which showed the race of applicant to be correlated with high mortgage application rejection, the New York Times wrote that the study's critics had attacked it as "defective in its methodology and tainted by ideological preconception." One economist was quoted as saying: "I am extremely worried that economics is becoming like other social sciences – not very scientific."[9]

But the antonym of mathematical is neither subjective nor unscientific. Many scientific disciplines – medical and biological sciences readily come to mind – are objective without being mathematical. Mathematics appeared to rationalize finance but in fact it dogmatized it. Technical methods were greatly improved, but the theoretical understanding that could explain what was happening was ignored. In fact, there was no theory to speak of, so the newly arrived scholars of the discipline fell back on what they knew from physics to build their financial theories.

---

[8] "Race, Mortgages and Statistics," *New York Times*, May 10, 1996, p. D1.
[9] "Like Oil and Water: A Tale of Two Economists," New York Times, February 16, 1997, Section 3, p. 1.

The parallels between the theoretical development in physics and their replication in finance are at times quite amusing, except that crudity in

---
Crudity in finance is contemporaneous.
---

physics is associated with the earlier stages of civilization. Crudity in finance is contemporaneous. Let us look at a few examples.

Example 1: Aristotle's "Natural Place" and the "Preferred Habitat" theory

One of the earliest attempts at understanding the general laws of physics was Aristotle's explanations as to why objects fall. Aristotle maintained that the earth was the natural place of all objects. When objects were taken away from this natural place, they were eager to return to it, so they fell. The bigger objects had more "eagerness," so they fell faster.

In the late 1950s, economic theorists advanced the Preferred Habitat theory to explain the shape of the yield curve. In this theory, the word "preferred" replaced Aristotle's "natural," but the line of reasoning was Aristotle's.

The yield curve is the graph of the yield of US Treasuries plotted against their maturities. The Treasuries are issued in standard maturities of 3, 6 and 12 months and 2, 5, 10 and 30 years. Figure 1.2 shows a common shape of this curve. The curve in this instance is positively sloped, meaning that as we move along the maturity axis yields increase.

Preferred Habitat or Market Segmentation theory states, in essence, that the shape of the yield curve is positively sloped because institutions in the bond market, because of either legal requirements or their own asset–liability structure, buy bonds with only certain maturities.[10] These maturities

---

[10] There are two other theories about this common shape of the yield curve. They are Expectations Theory and Liquidity Premium Theory. According to Expectations Theory, the shape of the yield curve is formed by the expectation of market participants, so forward rates implied from the yield curve are what the market expects them to be! Liquidity Premium Theory postulates that lenders do not like risk and because longer term lending is riskier, lenders demand higher rates for longer term securities. The model does not explain why "long term" is riskier or what happens when the yield curve is inverted. Presumably, when the yield curve is inverted, the lenders change their mind and decide that short term is riskier than long term.

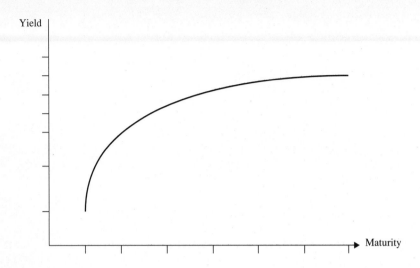

Figure 1.2 US Treasuries yield curve

are their "preferred habitat." And it is the preference of these dominant players in the bond market that gives the yield curve its positive slope.

This theory takes the most obvious manifestation of a phenomenon as its *cause* and *explanation*. It did not occur to Aristotle to take the same object, say a piece of cloth, and observe that its falling speed varied according to its shape (which would have refuted the idea of the same object always falling with the same "eagerness"). It did not, likewise, occur to the authors of this theory that the shape of the yield curve is not always positively sloped. The curve could be flat or negatively sloped, as shown in Figures 1.3(b) and 1.3(c), respectively.

The Preferred Habitat theory cannot account for these variations unless by claiming that every once in a while, large institutions inexplicably change their preferred habitat.

The reason for this theory's immense superficiality is its mechanical treatment of the interest rate, the subject it attempts to explain. The authors of the theory see the interest rate as a stand-alone "thing," – a commodity, if you will – whose value is determined by the supply and demand variations created by the actions of "big players." Interest is a deduction from profit, appropriated by credit capital. We will return to this topic in the next chapter. But even a cursory reading of daily newspapers will make the relation between the interest and profit clear. A

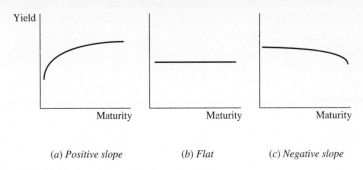

(a) Positive slope   (b) Flat   (c) Negative slope

Figure 1.3 Three shapes of the yield curve

headline in the *Wall Street Journal* about the Federal Reserve's decision to raise interest rates blurted out: "Rate Rise to Take an Early Toll on Profits."[11] The same paper reported that "the total savings in interest expenses came to about $70 billion last year [1996] over what was paid in 1989 ... Interest costs for nonfinancial corporations have fallen from $150 billion a year in 1989 to just over $80 billion last year."[12]

The longer capital is at work, the more profit it generates and, there-fore, the more claim the lenders could make on the money they have lent to the entrepreneurs. When the yield curve becomes flat or negatively sloped, i.e., when the long-term interest rate falls to the level of, or below, short-term rates, it is a sign that long-term profit on capital in industrial production is decreasing, with the result that the portion going to the lender must also decline. That is why a flattening of the yield curve, or the appearance of a negative slope, is generally and correctly interpreted as a sign of a recession.

---

[11] *Wall Street Journal*, March 27, 1997, p. A2. The article focused on the impact of the rate increase on foreign currency earnings, but that is the short-term impact. The long-term, more lasting, effect of a rate increase is that corporations must pay more in debt service. The additional payment can only come from profits.

[12] "Economists Attack 'New Era' in Profits," *Wall Street Journal*, September 23, 1997, p. A2.

Example 2: Newtonian circular motion and "Friedman deflation"

In the seventeenth century, Newton formulated his theory of the working of the universe. The theory explained the relation between gravity and circular motion. According to Newton, the same force of gravity that pulls an apple down from a tree also keeps the moon in the orbit around the earth. Specifically, the moon has an initial speed which causes it to be "thrown out" of the orbit of the earth. But the force of gravity pulls the moon "down" towards the earth. Again, the centrifugal force throws the moon "out" and gravity pulls it back towards the earth. The net effect of these counteracting forces is the circular motion of the moon around the earth, and, in fact, all circular motion.

Circular motion creates weightlessness. Objects in a circular motion – astronauts in an orbiting spacecraft, for example – experience weightlessness because they are in fact in a state of constant fall towards the earth. Weightlessness is the condition of, and requirement for, orbiting the earth.

Three hundred years later, Milton Friedman borrowed this concept to construct "Friedman Deflation." Roberds (1994, p. 7), an Atlanta Federal Reserve economist, succinctly describes the concept:

> Interest rates could be zero, Friedman argues, in a world in which prices were constantly falling at a rate equal to society's rate of time preference. "Time preference" refers to the rate at which people, on average, are willing to sacrifice future consumption of goods and services for current consumption.

Friedman Deflation is a noteworthy case because it points to, and contains the seeds of, the next stage of the intrusion of mathematics into finance. At this stage, mathematical methods developed in studying mechanics are no longer only imported into finance but *imposed* on it as well. Now, economic and financial problems are "adjusted" to fit into the Procrustean bed of ready-made mathematical solutions. So Friedman talks of a zero interest rate – the "weightlessness" of interest rate, really – in an environment of constantly falling prices. To make these absurdities hold, he is forced to invent an even

To make these absurdities hold, he is forced to invent an even greater absurdity.

greater absurdity, namely "society's rate of time preference," defined as the "rate at which people, on average [!], are willing to sacrifice future consumption … for current consumption." These assumptions do not trouble him because he has already argued that realism of assumptions in a theory is subordinate to the accuracy of its predictions. The Friedman Deflation presumably yields accurate results. (It does not occur to the Father of Monetarism that perhaps time preference exists because the interest rate exists, not the other way around. So based on his theory, the Federal Reserve responds to change in Americans' rate of time preference. And when in 1998 and then again in early 1999, the Bank of Japan pushed the interest rates to zero, it did so because 120 million Japanese had lost their time preference.)

These examples are not isolated cases. The theoretical deficiency pervades the entire discipline. The crown jewel of finance, the Capital Asset Pricing Model, offers an even clearer picture of the defect.

The Capital Asset Pricing Model: the epitome of the confusion in the theory of finance

In 1964 William Sharpe and two other researchers independently developed the Capital Asset Pricing Model (CAPM, pronounced CAP-M).[13] Their aim was to simplify the process of portfolio selection, which, as proposed by Markowitz, was cumbersome and time consuming because its application required calculating the co-variance or cross-volatility between securities in a portfolio. As the number of securities increased, the task rapidly became impractical. The CAPM proposed replacing the cross-volatility of securities in a portfolio with a single parameter β (pronounced beta), defined as the relation of the security to the market. The main CAPM relation is:

$$R_i = R_f + \beta_i \ (R_m - R_f) \hspace{2cm} \text{Eq. (1.1)}$$

In this equation, R_i is the return on the security, R_f is the risk-free rate

---

[13] The other two were John Lintner and Jan Mossin.

and R_m is the "market return."[14] In reducing the cumbersome mathematics of *Portfolio Selection* to determining a few parameters, the CAPM promised an easier adaptability to real-life applications, but the model had to be verified by empirical studies. For over a decade, researchers tested the theory. Some tests yielded good results, others were less conclusive. Finally in 1977, Richard Roll (1977, p. 130) questioned whether it was at all possible to test the predictions of the CAPM: "The theory is not testable unless the exact composition of a true market portfolio is known and used in the tests. This implies that the theory is not testable unless *all* individual assets are included in the sample."

Thus began the controversy over the CAPM that continues today. The source of the controversy, as put by Roll (1980) is: "If you don't know what the market portfolio is, you can't measure it and you can't test the theory. And if you can't test it, you don't know whether it is right or wrong." But the problem of the CAPM is far more fundamental. The ambiguity of the market portfolio is only the consequence of that flaw.

The flaw of the CAPM

The flaw of the CAPM lies with the term market return, R_m. Market return is commonly understood to mean the return on the S&P500 stock index. CAPM votaries concede that the 500 stocks which comprise the index do not constitute the "market," but if the index comprises 80 percent of the value of equities in the US, they argue, then isn't it a reasonable approximation of the market? The answer is No, because market return is a far more general concept than its adoption to the S&P 500 index implies. Sharpe himself is aware of that. As he wrote (Sharpe et al., 1995, p. 266): "Despite its [the CAPM's] widespread application, the market portfolio is suspiciously ill defined ... identifying the *true* market portfolio (or even a close approximation) is beyond the capability of any individual or organization."

---

[14] The term in parentheses in the equation clearly shows the interest to be a deduction from profit (market return minus risk-free rate).

Why is identifying the "true" market portfolio or even a close approximation of it beyond the reach? The answer is that market return in the CAPM is not the return on equities only. It is the return on *all* markets. That includes returns from real estate, venture capital, oil and gas, production lines, foreign exchange, commodities, etc. Many of these markets, as the Wall Street firms have discovered, move in opposite directions:

> Wall Street firms ... want to convince ... investors that commodity markets are legitimate places to invest... "We wanted to develop the best negative correlation with the Standard & Poor's 500 index and with the bond market and the best possible positive correlation with the U.S. Consumer Price Index," says [a] vice president ... at Bankers Trust ... "We're seeking to establish commodity investing as a set of assets distinct from stocks and bonds ..." says [a] Goldman [Sachs] partner.[15]

If the commodity indexes move in the opposite direction to stocks and bonds, how could an index capture a market return that includes stock, bonds *and* commodities?

Supporters of the CAPM have tended to dismiss this problem as a mere technicality. Sharpe (op. cit.) writes:

> What are the ramifications of not knowing the market portfolio's true composition? From a theoretical perspective, the potential problems are significant ... From a practical perspective, investors have generally been willing to overlook the market portfolio's ambiguity.

Sharpe is right when he talks of investors' willingness to "overlook the market portfolio's ambiguity." The model has become the foundation of a large industry which deals with evaluating the performance of fund managers. The distribution of billions of dollars of institutional money rides on their "risk-adjusted return" – a notion derived from the CAPM. If there is no market return, it follows that such evaluations are void of

---

[15] "Search for Better Benchmark Intensifies Index Battle," *Wall Street Journal*, August 1, 1994, p. C1.

a scientific, indeed logical, basis.[16] Academic textbooks also treat the CAPM in a "balanced" way. They praise the concept and then, in passing, mention that yes, there are some technical problems to be ironed out. In their concluding remarks discussing the CAPM, for example, Elton and Gruber (1981, p. 351) write:

> This is, perhaps, the most difficult chapter in this book to conclude. On the one hand we have a host of evidence that purports to support the CAPM. On the other hand, we have Roll's very cogent arguments questioning this evidence. Can we conclude anything positive from all this?

They then go on to conclude that (ibid.): "In summary, while the empirical work is not fully a satisfactory test of the CAPM, it produces results that are consistent with what one would expect from a test of the CAPM [!]."

Elsewhere, Professors Sears and Trennepohl (1993, p. 423) write:

> It is important to recognize that these criticisms present problems for the testing of the CAPM and that while the empirical evidence regarding the validity of the CAPM can be seriously questioned on these grounds, the CAPM has been, nevertheless, a tool widely used in the investment community.

Here, the authors imply that the controversy lies with the *testing* of the CAPM and not the model itself. They then go on to suggest that its "wide use in the investment community" is a proof of the robustness of the theory.

Finally, in his comprehensive review of the CAPM, Ross (1978, p. 898) sums up its status as follows:

> What then, is the current status of the CAPM? As a theory, its foundations have been broadened in recent years and we are closer to a rather complete understanding of the sufficient conditions for the theory to hold. But, in attempting to extend it beyond its original framework it

---

[16] "CAPM is a superficial and arbitrary construct. Any conclusion drawn from it, whether investment strategy or risk-adjusted portfolio return evaluation, can be correct only accidentally." Saber (1996), p. 37.

has proven to be somewhat less robust than might have been hoped for; the mean variance efficiency of the market portfolio is not generally sustained in broader context.

So, in an amusing case of good news-bad news reporting, Ross reports that the good news about the CAPM is that its foundation is broadened. But the bad news is that as a result of this broadening, the theory is no longer as robust as when its base was narrow!

The main reason that the CAPM controversy is not laid to rest is that no one has understood the model's real, cripping flaw.

Part of the reason for this uncertain attitude towards the CAPM in the academia is the significant position which it occupies in modern finance. The main reason that the CAPM controversy is not laid to rest is that no one has understood the model's real, crippling flaw.

A critical analysis of the CAPM

The fundamental problem of the CAPM is that it is constructed around the notion of market return, which no one seems able to define. But why did the CAPM have to be constructed around such an ambiguous and undefinable concept? Could not the creators of the CAPM have built it around some other index and thus avoided the problem? The answer is No, because the nature of the problem *forced* the concept of market return on them. The name of the model, containing the two key words *capital* and *asset*, provides a clue to the source of the difficulty.

The ambition of Sharpe, Lintner and Mossin to simplify the mathematics of *Portfolio Selection* put them face to face with the fundamental problem of economics, namely, the mystery of the productivity of capital. The problem boils down to explaining the common elements between the disparate items on the left side of the balance sheet that allows them to be classified as *assets*. To add cash, depreciation and goodwill as assets, there must be something in common between them. That common element exists; they are components of capital. But how do all these *capital assets* produce profit? Put differently, what is the source of the productivity of capital? That is the fundamental question of classical economics.

Some half-recognized the original ambition of the CAPM. In referring to the main relation of the CAPM, Eq. (1.1), Elton and Gruber (1981, p. 282) remark:

> Think about this relation for a moment. It represents one of the most important discoveries in the field of finance. Here is a simple equation … that describes the expected return for all assets and portfolios of assets in the economy. The expected return on any asset, or portfolio … can be determined from this relationship.

By way of analogy, physics, too, has as its most important discovery, a simple equation which defines the relation between the force applied to a body (F), the body's mass (m), and resulting acceleration (a). The relation is Newton's $F = ma$. Despite its deceptively simple appearance, the practical and philosophical implications of this equation are unsurpassed by any other discovery.[17] What Newton is saying is that *any* force, when applied to *any* body with a given mass, produces a precise acceleration in that body. But there are various forces in nature. The "mass," furthermore, is not defined except through this equation. We only know that it is a property of matter. Newton's equation thus brings to light two questions: what forms of force exist in nature, and what is the nature of matter? The quest for the answers to these questions *defines* the very science of physics.

The CAPM, likewise, starts with an ambitious premise. It strikes at the very source of the productivity of capital. It aims to determine the *average rate of return of capital*. That is what market return in the CAPM stands for. But investigating the answer would have required the authors of the CAPM to return to a terrain from which finance had fled on the back of mathematics. It would have required them once again to explain whether it was labor power, uncertainty, or what else, that gave the capital its special value-creating characteristics. That was not to be.

---

[17] On the importance of $F = ma$, suffice it to say that Einstein's celebrated equation, $E = mc^2$ *follows* from this elegant relation.

So while Newton's formula *begins* the questioning process and thus the discipline of physics, the CAPM begins and immediately ends the inquiry by accepting an arbitrary but convenient "proxy" to market return and calling it a day. The flight of fancy of its authors is like that of a turkey: short and low.

One is tempted to attribute this immediate retreat to a recognition of the difficulty of the task and the absence of the intellectual horsepower to tackle a problem known for its difficulty: "anyone who has tried an econometric attack on the problem of production function will know that the problem of how to deal with capital remains as formidable and challenging as ever"(Haavelmo, 1960, p. 14).

While the difficulty of the subject no doubt contributed to the aborted attempt to construct a *capital asset* pricing model, it was primarily the *methodology* of research in finance which stood in the way of taking a deeper look into the heart of the matter. In fact, a discipline with more rigorous standards would have discouraged and rejected the publication of the half-baked ideas contained in the CAPM. Witness the defensive language of Sharpe in the original CAPM paper (1964, p. 434):

> Since the proper test of a theory is not the realism of its assumptions but the acceptability of its implications, and since the assumptions imply equilibrium conditions which form a major part of classical financial doctrine, it is far from clear that this formulation [CAPM] should be rejected – especially in view of the dearth of alternative models leading to similar solutions.

Here, Sharpe is more than defending the restrictive assumptions of his theory. He is saying that since the existing theories of economics and finance assume equilibrium in markets and the CAPM conforms to those assumptions, you cannot question the reasonableness of his assumptions in building yet another equilibrium model, especially because there are no alternatives. He states that his purpose is not to investigate the accuracy of existing theories. Rather, he wants to build yet another model which would fit the existing mold. So, instead of starting from valid assumptions and letting the chips fall where they may, he turns the process on its head. He starts from an accepted premise – the equilibrium model – and works his way backwards to a theory that will conform to the existing falsities. In the process, he is forced to make quite a few assumptions, still fewer of which seem to correspond to reality. But he is following Friedman's guidelines on the role of assumptions. Thus, he is free to develop his model without regard to the restrictive realities of the real world.

Under the guise of abstracting, subordinating assumption to results has now become the accepted premise in finance. The freewheeling and arbitrary assumptions have gradually reached a point where they eliminate the very problem the theory must explain. This subversion of the scientific method of inquiry is not transparent to the "trained" eye of the scholar who is inculcated with the official doctrine, but the layman sees it. The punch line of the joke about two economists stranded on an island with a can of food and no can opener is one of them saying to the other: "Assume a can opener!"

Real-life problems, though, cannot be wished away; they tend to slyly intrude at every opportunity. If a model is to capture the essence of a phenomenon – and that is the purpose of every model – its assumptions must be based on, and derived from, the observed behavior of the subject under study.

What role do the assumptions play in a model?

The role of assumptions in a theory

A theory is an ideal, mental model of a real-world phenomenon. Its purpose is to better understand the properties of the subject under study, with an eye toward predicting its behavior. But real-world phenomena, whether the workings of the universe or of the financial markets, are often too complex for exact replication. That is why theorists make simplifying assumptions. Through trials, they disregard factors they determine to be unimportant to studying the properties of the object under study.

"Making simplifying assumptions," however, is not the arbitrary elimination of inconvenient facts.

The simplifying assumptions eliminate the "clutter" and enable researchers to focus only on those characteristics of the subject which are relevant to the investigation.

"Making simplifying assumptions," however, is not the arbitrary elimination of inconvenient facts. It is, rather, setting aside those aspects of the subject that are not *logically* required for the analysis.[18] And because every theory only pertains to conditions specified by its assumptions, in testing a theory, we test not only the logic of its construction, but also the accuracy of its assumptions. If the predictions of a theory do not correspond to its test results, we must examine both the logic of the theory and the validity of its assumptions, regardless of how self-evident the assumptions might seem.[19]

In finance, this fact is partly ignored, mostly not understood. After listing the assumptions of a model which include unlimited lending and borrowing, Elton and Gruber (1981, p. 276) write: "It is clear that these assumptions do not hold in the real world just as it is clear that the physicist's frictionless environment does not really exist. The relevant questions are: How much is reality distorted by making these assumptions?" The authors are mistaken in their identification of the *relevant* question. The relevant question is not how much is reality distorted because of assumptions. That question cannot be answered without knowing the reality. The question, rather, is: why are these assumptions necessary in the first place? The assumption of a friction-

The assumption of infinite borrowing and lending is a grotesque distortion.

less universe does away with the influence of the earth's atmosphere in order to capture a more fundamental aspect of the law of gravity. The assumption of infinite borrowing and lending is a grotesque distortion, made solely to do away with the problem of liquidity that the theory cannot capture.

Or, take the problem of gravity in physics. In the past 2000 years, our

---

[18] In constructing the model of stock price dynamics in Chapter 2, Vol. 2, we will see how assumptions are logically determined.

[19] The best example in this regard comes from quantum mechanics. If we shine a light on a wall with two holes, A and B, we would certainly expect the number of light photons on the other side of the wall to be equal to the number of photons that passed through hole A *plus* the number that passed through hole B. It turns out that is not the case. The mystery is under investigation.

understanding of the nature of gravity has gone through fundamental changes. Various theories corresponding to this change of knowledge have been advanced and then, having been found inadequate, discarded.[20] The theories have gone from assuming that the earth was the natural resting place of objects to assuming that space is curved.[21] The latest theories postulate that gravity is a wave. These theories progressed because each explained more of the observed phenomena than its predecessors did. To that end, they all proceeded from the assumptions that were derived from the observed phenomena. That is central to the construction of a theory. A theory attempting to explain the motion of falling objects cannot begin by assuming that objects do *not* fall. Yet, that is precisely the end result of assumptions in theories of modern finance, which is why to understand the real-world developments in finance, we must discard them. These theories more than fail to explain. They form an overgrown theoretical prism which stands in the way of evidence, deflecting their path and concealing their source.

A critical examination of the assumptions underlying derivatives valuation

The way arbitrary assumptions eliminate the problem under investigation and stand in the way of our comprehending finance can best be shown through their examination. Let us examine the set of assumptions made in the valuation of derivatives and, specifically, the Black–Scholes model. Here, we focus only on the functional aspects of assumptions. The full extent of their harm – and their absurdity – will gradually become clear throughout this book, as we introduce speculative capital and take on the subject of the valuation of derivatives.

---

[20] Newtonian mechanics has not been discarded. Its laws apply to everyday life. It is that Newton's laws are a special case of the even more fundamental laws postulated by Einstein.

[21] The counterintuitive notion of a "curved space" in physics is also deduced from the observed phenomena. See in general, Feynman (1997).

The Black–Scholes model is derived using the following assumptions:[22]

1 There are no transaction costs, no taxes, no bid/ask spreads, etc.
2 No single market participant can influence the prices.
3 There is no counterparty default risk.
4 There are no arbitrage opportunities.
5 Market participants prefer more to less.
6 Trading is continuous.

Of these assumptions, only the first is rational in the sense that it simplifies the problem but does not impact the outcome. Taxes, transaction costs, margin requirements and bid/ask spreads are institutional factors. They can change from time to time and from one jurisdiction to another. They should have no bearing on the *logic* of valuing derivatives.

The banal assumption that no single market participant can influence the prices is redundant because it is implied in the very definition of the market. The situation where a single buyer or seller could influence the market is the exception that demands an investigation. After World War II,

> *Of these assumptions, only the first is rational.*

such exceptional cases consumed many research dollars until the breakup of AT&T – the pet example of a "natural monopoly" – put an end to the subject. In any event, the assumption of "no arbitrage opportunities" – where great many buyers and sellers constantly interact – precludes a monopolistic market.

Next is the assumption of no counterparty default. This assumption is quite interesting. We will spend no time on it here because Chapters 2 and 3 in Volume 2 are devoted to this subject. Suffice it to say that option valuation is *nothing but* counterparty default valuation! Yet, the Black–Scholes model is derived from the assumption that it does not exist!

Let us now turn to the assumption of "no arbitrage opportunity" to see what it entails.

---

[22] See, in general, Jarrow and Turnbull (1996), p. 214.

What is arbitrage?

To understand what is meant by "no arbitrage opportunities," we must first know what arbitrage is. For that, it is difficult to find a more promising source than a book titled *Arbitrage*. After stirring our curiosity by a rhetorical question, its author, Rudi Weisweiller, defines arbitrage in this way (1986, p. 9):

> What is Arbitrage? It is the professional search for and pursuit of rate differences already known and usable, or reasonably expected to occur in the near future, with limited risk and on a relatively moderate scale, so as to achieve a steady profit.

This sleet and hail of verbal imprecisions raises many more questions that it answers. Phrases such as "professional search," "known and usable [!] rate differences," "reasonably expected to occur," "near future," "limited risk," "relatively moderate scale [!]" and "steady profit" themselves need definition. What is "reasonably expected to occur" for one person could be an implausibly rare event for another. Weisweiller fails to define arbitrage because instead of understanding the concept first – which is the prerequisite for explaining it – he attempts to define it by generalizing one of its specific functional forms. Arbitrage, per Rudi Weisweiller, is what would appear on the promotional brochure of a hypothetical society of fixed income arbitrageurs.

Defining arbitrage has tormented the proclaimed authorities of economics and finance for a long time.

Defining arbitrage has tormented the proclaimed authorities of economics and finance for a long time. As a matter of fact, Weisweiller stands out for offering a definition which avoided what he must have realized were the pitfalls of the standard definition. John Hull (1997, p. 12) cursorily provides the standard definition of arbitrage as "locking in a riskless profit by entering simultaneously into transactions in two or more markets." In this very misleading definition, simultaneous positions locked in a profitable spread are assumed to be riskless: Hull thus *a priori* eliminates the possibility of the basis risk, a crucial subject he is forced to visit several pages later.[23]

Arbitrage means buy low, sell high.[24] Its history is as old as the history of commerce itself. The Ricardian concept of comparative advantage and Keynes's interest rate parity in foreign exchange, for example, are based on the arbitrage argument.

The reason that such a simple concept has presented an insurmountable difficulty to economists and scholars of finance is that arbitrage is the designation of "buy low, sell high" *only in conjunction with the operation of speculative capital.* That is, "buy low, sell high" becomes arbitrage only when the dual transactions of buying low and selling high are executed by speculative capital. If we do not know what speculative capital is, we cannot define arbitrage. More accurately, we cannot differentiate it from the old dictum of commerce known to the ancient traders. Therein lies the difficulty of defining arbitrage which also manifests itself as the problem of the defining *speculation* in a way that differentiates it from *commerce*. After we discover speculative capital, these notions will assume a definiteness that is all but impossible in the context of the existing theories. It will then become clear that Black–Scholes's remaining two assumptions – that market participants prefer more to less and that trading is continuous – are the implications of arbitrage and need not be assumed independently.

Arbitrage and equilibrium

Authors often work their way out of the theoretical jam of defining arbitrage by resorting to an example. They *illustrate* arbitrage instead of defining it. Their pet example is the price of a stock such as IBM in two different places; say, the New York and Pacific Stock Exchanges. "A typical example of an arbitrage profit opportunity is that in which the

---

[23] The basis risk and its generalized form, the systemic risk, are the main sources of threat to financial markets. But we cannot as yet define basis risk because we do not know what speculative capital is.

[24] That is the functional meaning of the word in the context of our discussions. Analyzing its French root does not shed any light on the subject.

same asset is traded on two different exchanges at two different prices" (Chriss, 1997, p. 39). In this example, if the IBM shares are trading on the NYSE at $150 and on the PSE at $150¼, an investor can buy the stock in New York and sell it in San Francisco for a net profit of 25 cents a share before commissions. This simultaneous buying and selling continues until the pressure of buying lifts the NYSE price and the pressure of selling lowers it in the PSE. Both prices then find an equilibrium level at, say, 150⅛, after which the arbitrage activity, having equalized the prices and neutralized the difference, ceases.

So, if an arbitrage opportunity arises, investors would rapidly exploit it and, in doing so, would eliminate that opportunity by raising the price of the lower, and lowering the price of the higher, commodity. By the same token, if there is no arbitrage opportunity, risk-free profits are impossible to realize. That, in turn, would imply that capital markets are efficient. As a matter of fact, the definition of an efficient market in modern finance is one in which risk-free profits are impossible because prices are at equilibrium level. "Arbitrage ... helps make the markets more efficient because by ... increasing demand for 'cheap' securities relative to 'rich' ones, [it] acts to bring them in equilibrium" (Wong, 1993, p. 14). Economists use the euphemism of "no free lunch" to sum up these conditions.

The notion of equilibrium in financial markets is borrowed from physics. In physics, a system is said to be in equilibrium if it meets two conditions: the sum total of forces acting on the system must be zero; and the system must be such that, if it is disturbed, the disturbance would generate a counteracting force that would push the system back towards its equilibrium position. A balanced scale is a classic example of a physical system in equilibrium.

The counteracting force in finance that must restore equilibrium to a price-disturbed system is arbitrage. But arbitrage is an *act*. Unlike in nature, where the counteracting force of gravity is "just there," arbitrage in markets does not take place by itself. For arbitrage to happen, traders must buy and sell. A permanent presence of willing and able buyers and sellers is a necessary condition for arbitrage. That amounts to assuming that buyers and sellers can always find willing and able counterparties to take the other sides of trades at prevailing market prices. In other words, it amounts to assuming that every buyer brings his own seller to the market, and vice versa.

If that assumption were true, it would correspond to an economy unrecognizably different from the one we know. In this imaginary world, economic growth would be unbounded and would go on uninterrupted by recession because anything produced could be sold. There would be no need for inventory, marketing, advertising, or general cost of sales. And there would be no liquidity risk. The assumption of infinite buyers and sellers leaves no room for illiquidity.

The "fair value" of many financial products is derived from such grotesquely distorting assumptions. But when presented to the market, the product must come down to earth. It must incorporate the actual conditions of the market into its price structure. It must pay for the sins of the imperfect theory from which it is born by shedding its value. Thus, its theoretical and idealized *value* is turned into market *price*. The more severely the assumption of perfect liquidity is violated, i.e., the more illiquid a financial product is, the more pronounced is its pricing risk.

This point, the difference between the theoretical value and market price, has received scant attention because its importance is either not recognized or recognized too well. In their *Options Markets*, for example, Cox and Rubinstein (1985, p. 183) write: "To remain hedged, the number of calls we would need to buy back depends on their value, not their price. Therefore, since we are uncertain about their price, we then become uncertain about the return from the hedge." Nowhere prior to this passage does the book define either the "price" or the "value." But it is clear that, by price, the authors refer to what the option is actually trading for in the market and, by value, they mean what the formula shows. That is quite an interesting admission. Their entire book is based on the premise that if the value and the market price of an option are different, we can arbitrage the difference and, in doing so, close the gap and realize a risk-free profit. That is *how* options are valued. Suddenly, we learn that if the price and value of an option are different, the hedged portfolio that replicates the value of the option cannot have a certain return, which means that the value of the option would not be what the formula predicted!

One would have expected this observation to trigger extensive research in finance. Instead, it is passed over without any comment. The "official" finance has no interest in opening a theoretical can of worms. Its main theme and preoccupation remain the efficient markets where

> *A system in equilibrium is a dead system. It can neither generate nor explain a change.*

ever-present buyers and sellers continuously buy and sell and, by doing so, establish the equilibrium prices. But a system in equilibrium is a dead system. It can neither generate nor explain a change. Any change to a system in equilibrium must come from the outside, meaning that the explanation for the change must also be sought on the outside. The arbitrage argument, likewise, explains nothing.

Price and value

The discrepancy between values and prices and the forced transformation of one to another has claimed many victims in the course of history. In the eighteenth century, the victims were British countryside farmers whose saga George Eliot so movingly captured in her novels.

More recently, the victims are fund managers who, though armed with the latest advances technology can offer, are as helpless as the eighteenth-century British peasants in understanding the causes and effects of the "mysterious fluctuations of trade." The bond market debacle of 1994 and more recent events in Southeast Asia conclusively demonstrated that. In reporting the story of an investment firm that suffered losses from investing in derivatives, the *Wall Street Journal* quoted a managing director of the firm as saying: "the investment aim of the fund ... was that 'under normal market conditions' there would be low volatility of principal "while obtaining higher-than-market returns.'"[25] The managing director did not explain how the fund was expected to behave under *abnormal* market conditions, but the subject of the news story – that the fund was going to compensate the investors for the losses – had already answered that question.

Another victim in the bond market debacle of 1994 was the Askin

---

[25] "Robert W. Baird Sets Contributions to Fund Because of Derivatives," *New York Times*, December 27, 1994, p. 65.

Fund, which collapsed and lost its \$600 million capital. The fund manager, David Askin, had used the firm's internal pricing method to calculate the "fair market value" of his portfolio of mortgage-backed securities and reported little change to the investors.

Askin's reliance on mathematical models caught the attention of many commentators, who chastised him for being a fool. A Columbia professor remarked: "This is a guy who is not a crook, but who believed that mathematics could solve all valuation problems and eliminate the need for a market. One morning he woke up and found that was not the case."[26]

Askin did in fact rely on mathematical models for portfolio valuation, but in doing that, he was following a very common market practice. In an unrelated article many months earlier, the *Wall Street Journal* had reported:

> In times of turmoil, pricing theory runs amok of market reality ... Even plain-vanilla municipal bonds have been difficult to price ... James Perry, vice president of Capital Markets at Interactive Data ... is careful to say that his company offers to "evaluate," rather than "price," ... securities. "We're producing a fair valuation," says Mr Perry. "But it doesn't necessarily reflect where a trade will occur" ... In other words, there are two prices: one for figuring paper gains and losses, and another for transactions that involve real money.[27]

"In other words, there are two prices: one for figuring paper gains and losses." That is the ideal *value* calculated from the theory of finance. The other is for transactions that involve "real money." That is the *price*. The difference between the two is the main source of loss in markets. Finance, however, refuses to deal with that difference. In fact, it *cannot*, because its theories have assumed it away.

It is ironic that while the pioneers of modern finance adopted the functional aspects of physics, they ignored the normative elements in the approach of great men of physics. Many discoveries in physics were the result of attempts to explain minute differences of observed phenomena

---

[26] "Founder of Askin Capital Agrees to Settlement of SEC Charges," *New York Times*, May 24, 1995, p. D8.

[27] "Assessing Bond Market Gets Harder," *Wall Street Journal*, June 13, 1994, p. C1.

with the predictions of theory. In finance and economics not only subtle clues, but also quite forceful evidence from markets that cries out for attention, are ignored if they cannot be "explained" by the equilibrium models. So the *Wall Street Journal* details how business and academia clash over concepts that academia hold to be true but business people know from experience not to be true: "Business and Academia Clash Over a Concept: 'Natural' Jobless Rate."[28]

Finance, in brief, has become a self-contained discipline, firmly resisting any evidence from the markets that might contradict its theories.[29] More bizarre, the theorists at times disagree on the meaning of what they have jointly developed. Writing about the lawsuits brought by the savings and loans industry against the US government, the *New York Times* reported:

> Two Nobel Prize winning collaborators have disagreed on whether their shared work applies to the litigation. Merton H. Miller testified for the Government that the Modigliani-Miller Theorem, or M&M Propositions, which are the foundation of modern corporate finance demonstrated that the industry's claims were wildly overstated ... The industry responded with its own ... expert: Franco Modigliani, the other "M" in the propositions: "I have decided to testify ... because my name is associated with the M&M Propositions, and in my view, they are being misused ... in a way that I regard as damaging to the credibility of the theorem."[30]

---

[28] January 24, 1995, p. A1. The article described how businessmen disagree with the notions of a "natural" rate of unemployment – proposed by Milton Friedman – which must be preserved if inflation is to remain in check. Speculative capital relegated this "theory" to the dustbin of history of finance.

[29] In his presidential address to the American Economic Association, Paul Samuelson said: "My own scholarship has covered a great variety of fields ... like welfare economics and factor-price equalization; turnpike theorems and osculating envelopes; nonsubstitutability relations in Minkowski-Ricardo-Leontief-Metzler matrices of Mosak-Hicks type ... My friends warn me that such topics are suitable merely for captive audiences in search of a degree – and even then not after dark." Stiglitz (1966, p. 1499). These comments were too purposefully humorous, but as Freud said, there are no jokes. Samuelson's cynicism about his profession and its irrelevance to real life is quite telling.

[30] "The Debacle that Buried Washington," *New York Times*, November 22, 1998, Section 3, p. 1.

The theories are defended on the ground that they explain *most* of the workings of markets. But, using Ptolemy's principles, we could also explain most of the planetary movements. It is precisely in the exceptional and extreme cases, when the existing theory fails to explain the observed facts, that its shortcomings are revealed.[31] After all, if buyers and sellers can buy and sell any amount of securities at market price then financial crises cannot happen, stock markets cannot crash and mortgage-backed securities cannot suffer huge losses.

There is no hiding in the markets.

Modern finance is not cognizant of the crucial characteristics of financial products and markets. In fact, its theories frequently work to shield it from outside events. But there is no hiding in the markets. At the first hint of the trouble, the cover of the theory falls off and the reality reveals itself in the only way it can: by expressing itself as a drop in the value of a product, which is always "surprising" and "greater than expected."

In nature, when a body is disturbed from its equilibrium position, it produces a harmonic motion. Harmonic motion is the response of nature to a disturbance from equilibrium. Disturbance from the equilibrium models in finance and economics produces quite a different sound. That sound is not a harmonic oscillation but the screams of investors who have been betrayed by the theories. That is the ultimate proof of the social nature of finance and its fundamental difference with natural science.

Uncertainty in securities law: the manifestation of theoretical flaws in finance?

Where do the social aspects of finance "go" after they are driven away from the discipline? The answer is that they go to that quintessential social discipline, the law. They reach there raw and unexplored, becoming the source of uncertainty in securities law.

The relation between the law and finance has never been explored. A

---

[31] In the expression "the exception proves the rule," the verb *prove* is used in its archaic meaning, *test*. Exception *tests* the rule, which is indeed how it is.

few legal writers who have ventured into economics have gone no further than their starting point precisely because the mathematical finance does not lend itself to the analysis of social law. We will examine the relation between finance, law and politics in detail in Chapter 5.

The practitioners and scholars of the law, furthermore, have mistakenly lumped together the uncertainty in securities law with the confusion surrounding the law of derivatives. The two have very little in common. The source of confusion in securities law is the inability of law to coherently define the term "security." The source of confusion in the law of derivatives is the struggle between commerce and speculation and the attempt of the legislature to reconcile them. We will examine these issues in Volume 2, Chapter 4.

In the next chapter, as part of our investigation into the nature of speculative capital, we develop a coherent definition of security which dispels the theoretical uncertainties of the law. The word *define* is somewhat misleading as it connotes, however faintly, a measure of arbitrariness. The proper definition of a security is neither arbitrary nor idealized. Rather, it logically arises from the fundamental concept of capital in finance. Such a definition can be arrived at only when the existing theoretical problems of finance are also resolved. So it is not the magic of a clever definition but the correct formulation of the problem that solves the riddle. That is analogous to understanding the interaction of gravitational forces. It then becomes clear that the same force that makes the apple fall also keeps the moon in its orbit. There is no puzzle, inconsistency or contradiction.

References

Bernstein, Peter L. (1992) *Capital Ideas: The Improbable Origins of Modern Wall Street*, New York: Free Press.

Chriss, Neil A. (1997) *Black–Scholes and Beyond*, Burr Ridge, Illinois: Irwin Professional.

Cox, John C. and Rubinstein, Mark (1985) *Options Markets*, Englewood Cliffs, NJ: Prentice-Hall.

Dos Passos, John (1996) *U.S.A., 1919*, New York: Library of America.

Elton, Edwin J. and Gruber, Martin J. (1981) *Modern Portfolio Theory and Investment Analysis*, New York: John Wiley.

Feynman, Richard P. (1997), *Six Not-so-easy Pieces*, Reading, Mass.:Addison-Wesley.

Friedman, Milton (1953a) *Essays in Positive Economics*, Chicago: Chicago University Press.

Friedman, Milton (1953b) "The Methodology of Positive Economics," in Friedman (1953a).

Haavelmo, Trygve (1960) *A Study in the Theory of Investment*, Chicago: University of Chicago Press.

Hirschleifer, J. (1970) *Investment, Interest and Capital*, Englewood Cliffs, NJ: Prentice-Hall.

Hull, John C. (1997) *Options, Futures and Other Derivatives*, Englewood Cliffs, NJ: Prentice-Hall.

Jarrow, Robert and Turnbull, Stuart (1996) *Derivative Securities*, Cincinnati, Ohio: South-Western College Publishing.

Knight, Frank H. (1921) *Risk, Uncertainty and Profit*, Boston and New York: Houghton Mifflin.

Lewin, Leonard C. (1996) *Report from Iron Mountain*, New York: Free Press.

Markowitz, Harry M. (1991) *Portfolio Selection: Efficient Diversification of Investments*, Cambridge MA: Blackwell.

Roberds, William (1994) "Changes in Payments Technology and the Welfare Cost of Inflation," *Economic Review, Federal Reserve Bank of Atlanta*, Vol. 79, No. 33, (May/June), pp. 1–12

Roll, Richard (1977) "A Critique of the Asset Pricing Theory's Tests, Part I: On Past and Potential Testability of the Theory," *Journal of Financial Economics*, Vol. 4, No. 2 (March), pp. 129–76.

Roll, Richard (1980) "Is Beta Dead?," *Institutional Investor* (April), pp. 23–9.

Ross, Stephen A. (1978) "The Current Status of the Capital Asset Pricing Model (CAPM)," *Journal of Finance*, Vol. 33, No, 3 (June), pp. 885–901.

Saber, Nasser (1996) "Superficial?," *The Barron's*, January 8, 1996, p. 37.

Sears, Stephen and Trennepohl, Gary (1993) *Investment Management*, Forth Worth: Dryden Press.

Sharpe, William F. (1964) "Capital Asset Prices: A Theory of Market Equilibrium Under Conditions of Risk," *Journal of Finance*, Vol. 9, No. 3, pp. 425–42.

Sharpe, William F., Alexander, Gordon J. and Bailey, Jeffery V., (1995) *Investments*, Englewood Cliffs, NJ: Prentice-Hall.

Stiglitz, J. E. (1966) *The Collected Scientific Papers of Paul A. Samuelson*, Vol. 2, Cambridge, Mass.: MIT Press.

Tuckman, Bruce (1995) *Fixed Income Securities*, New York: John Wiley.

Weisweiller, Rudi (1986) *Arbitrage: Opportunities and Techniques in the Financial and Commodity Markets*, New York: John Wiley.

Wong, Anthony M. (1993) *Fixed Income Arbitrage*, New York: John Wiley.

THE THEORY OF SPECULATIVE CAPITAL

Concept of capital • Definition of a security • Manufacturing and industrial capital • The heart of finance • Finance capital • The puzzle of "market return" in capital asset pricing model • Commercial capital • Credit capital • Speculation • Speculative capital and the logical condition of its rise • Arbitrage • Opposition to the rise of speculative capital

Introduction

Speculative capital is a dialectical concept. It rises from within the already existing forms of capital and immediately confronts them. The confrontation is over appropriating a larger share of profits that, because the total amount of profit is fixed, can come only through a reduction in the share of others. In the inter-family, for-profit fight of various forms of capital, the guiding principle is: every man for himself and the devil take the hindmost.

But if speculative capital is destined to confront the other forms of capital from which it is born, the question arises as to why it is permitted to "rise" in the first place. Why, in other words, does not the confrontation take place in the early stages of development of speculative capital when it can easily be suppressed?

Part of the answer to this question is that speculative capital was indeed suppressed for a long time. Its rise is a recent phenomenon dating back to the early 1970s. That is why there is no reference to it in the classical works of economics. (And the contemporary theorists on economics and finance have been completely oblivious to it.)

> **Speculative capital is a dialectical concept.**

But more importantly, speculative capital is able to rise thanks to its dialectical nature: while it confronts the other forms of capital, at the same time it facilitates their attainment of profits. That is why they encourage its development. That is true of all forms of capital: while they constantly compete with one another, each one's presence contributes to the overall efficiency of production and circulation.

Our task in this chapter is to show how speculative capital is both encouraged and resisted by other forms of capital and under what conditions it gradually comes to rise into full bloom. But we do not as yet know what capital is. The first step towards understanding speculative capital is to understand the concept of capital.

The concept of capital

Let us follow an entrepreneur who plans to build a factory that will produce, as economists are fond of saying, a "widget." He prepares a detailed plan and concludes that he needs $10 million to build the plant, buy the equipment and raw materials, hire workers and start production.

Either because, like so many men of ideas, he has no money of his own, or because he is more comfortable using other people's money, he decides to raise the $10 million from people who might be interested in the venture. So, like the dedicated entrepreneur he is, he incorporates the widget company and offers 1,000,000 shares of the company at $10 each through the internet. The offering is a success and the shares are all sold. Our entrepreneur has $10 million. The investors have stock certificates totaling $10 million.

With $10 million in hand, the entrepreneur builds the plant, purchases the equipment, hires the workers and begins producing widgets. By the time the first widget is produced, the $10 million is spent. (A portion of that sum might still be available in the form of working capital, but such capital is tied to the production process and in that regard, must also be considered "spent.") The stockholders, meanwhile, are in possession of certificates totaling $10 million.

What exactly are these stock certificates? Currently, they are merely receipts. A person who bought 1000 shares of the company parted with $10,000 of his money and, in return, received a receipt in the form of a stock certificate evidencing the ownership of 1000 shares. If that person suddenly gets cold feet and decides that he wants his money back, he cannot go to the entrepreneur and demand the $10,000. His $10,000, together with money from others who purchased the shares, is incorporated in the widget production apparatus – it is spent. It is impossible, furthermore, to determine which $10,000 part of the widget factory – including the raw material and workers' wages – corresponds to his $10,000: it is dissolved into the production apparatus. The receipt he has in his hand is for something that he cannot physically claim.

Fortunately, he has no intention of making any such claim. He did not give $10,000 to the entrepreneur to claim something physical. He did so because he expected to receive something in return for his money. The return he expects is a payment in cash, over and above his initial $10,000.

Where would – where *could* – that return come from?[1] The answer is that it would come from the operation of the widget factory. After the entrepreneur pays for the raw materials and labor, including the cost of making widgets, he hopes to sell each unit of widget above its production cost and, hence, realize a profit. Our investor and all the other investors who paid money to buy the stock certificates share that hope. The profits would then be allocated, on a *pro rata* basis, to those who have in their hands the receipts that prove their contribution to the construction of the widget factory. Such receipts entitle their owners to the profits of the widget enterprise.

That the profits are generated from the operation of the enterprise is self-evident. If the factory stops for the lack of raw materials or because of a labor strike, the production of widgets and, with that, the generation of profits will cease. For profits to be generated, the production process must go on. That is what accountants mean by the expression a "going concern." An enterprise is a going concern not because it has a perpetual life, but because perpetual operation is the condition for its economic existence.

> *An enterprise is a going concern not because it has a perpetual life, but because perpetual operation is the condition for its economic existence.*

We called our product a "widget" purposefully, so as to draw attention to the fact that the physical apparatus of the factory and the particular use to which its product is put are irrelevant to the generation of profit. The entrepreneur could have started a high-tech venture, a restaurant franchise, an amusement park or a furniture factory. What lies behind the generation of profits is a concept. That concept is capital.

---

[1] We see that the theoretical problem of the source of the productivity of capital is never dead. It is only hastily dumped into a very shallow grave. It rises to confront us upon the slightest scratching of the surface.

What is a security?

Capital is not money. Money – cash – is in itself not capital. It becomes capital only when thrown into the process of production. The cash stashed inside a mattress or in a safe deposit box is money, not capital, because it would forever remain quantitatively unchanged. Only when cash is thrown

Capital is not money. Money – cash – is in itself not capital.

into production or circulation does it become capital and acquire the ability to expand. Participation in the perpetual profit-generating operation of capital turns the money into capital. The exchange of money with the receipt becomes investment. The receipts become securities.

We assumed our entrepreneur raised the money by selling stock in the widget company. But he could have also borrowed the money from investors. Then he would have to issue bonds. Or he could have raised it by a combination of bond and stock offerings. Such variations in financing strategies would not change anything in principle.[2] In the end, the entrepreneur would still have his $10 million, but now there would be bond – as well as stock – holders. The legal standing of bond – and stock – holders with regard to the proceeds of the enterprise is different, but of no concern to us. Bondholders, like stockholders, are owners of a security. Ownership entitles them to a *pro rata* share of the profit of the enterprise. For the bondholders, however, the amount of return and the length of time over which it will be paid are generally fixed in advance.

A security is a receipt for the exchange of a money that is spent and

A security is evidence of ownership of notional capital.

turned into capital. But it is impossible to determine which part of the physical capital belongs to any particular investor. The investors hold the evidence of ownership of a capital that can neither conceptually nor physically be divided. The definition of a

---

[2] This statement must not be interpreted to mean, as the Modigliani–Miller theories postulate, that a corporation should be indifferent between issuing stocks and bonds. Rather, it simply shows that stocks and bonds are both securities. This point will become clear as we examine various types of capital later in the chapter.

security follows from this observation: *a security is evidence of owner-ship of notional capital*. Those who paid $10,000 to purchase 1000 shares in the widget factory and were given a receipt are now investors whose capital of $10,000 is invested in 1000 shares or securities.

Now suppose an investor would like to get back his original investment. What are his options?

We know that the money he gave to the entrepreneur has been spent on plant and equipment. Furthermore, he cannot establish a correspon-dence between the value of his securities and a given $10,000 part of the widget producing apparatus. Fortunately, his situation is not hopeless. If he wants his original investment back, the investor can go to a securities market and offer his shares for sale. By selling his shares, the investor terminates his participation in the production process. In that case, the opposite of the first metamorphosis would occur. The investor relin-quishes his claim to the fruits of production and in return receives a sum of *money*.

After this sale, the ownership of shares, but nothing else, changes. The new owner would now have the right to claim a proportionate share of profits from the sale of widgets. If the new owner also wants to con-vert his stock to money, he would have to return to the securities mar-kets where similar claims on various enterprises are bought and sold. Outside this market, he can no more convert his shares to cash than the original owner could.

In the securities market, the owner of 1000 shares of the widget fac-tory might sell his securities for less than $10,000, more than $10,000 or exactly the original $10,000. The behavior of securities prices has its own laws. These laws are studied in finance. Finance is a specialized branch of economics precisely because the movement of securities prices is sep-arate from (albeit not unrelated to) the dynamics of the physical capital.

The heart of finance

Capital is formed by the coming together of many components, includ-ing plant, equipment, raw material and workers. The "coming together" is not an arithmetic addition. Indeed, these components are not arith-metically additive. Capital, rather, is formed from the unity of various components in the context of a social relation. Precisely for that reason, it is impossible to capture it mathematically.

As a practical man who must deal with real-world events, the accountant is forced to recognize the nature of capital. He does not ponder how those diverse items on the left side of the balance sheet – the individual assets – can be added together, but he adds them nevertheless because that is the only way for him to record the generation of profit. "Asset" is the accountant's parlance for a component of capital.

The theorist of finance does not face that real-world demand. He is in the world of pure theory. But the theory is mathematical, having banished the non-mathematical aspects of finance to some conceptual purgatory. Pity then a theorist who must "capture" this non-mathematical capital by means of a mathematical relation.

> *"Asset" is the accountant's parlance for a component of capital.*

That is precisely the root of the failure of the Capital Asset Pricing Model which we discussed in the previous chapter.

If the authors of the CAPM had understood the domain of application of their model, they would have gained considerable insight into the nature of capital. The CAPM is a theory in *finance*. But capital and its return are also legitimate topics in economics. What is the difference between the two? What is the definition, or the heart, of finance?

Professors of finance, always unsure about matters of definition and theory, use the expedience of indefiniteness to get round the problem: "In its broadest and, perhaps, simplest context, finance may be thought of as study of cash flows" (Beidleman, 1991, p. 3). Despite "broadest," "simplest," "perhaps" and "may be" in a single sentence, all further hedged with "thought of," the definition is uselessly narrow. The view of finance as the study of cash flows is the view of a deal maker. It is finance as understood by one Donald Trump. The purchaser of a business or property will indeed "think of" the cash flows of the deal, but that focus alone does not define the discipline of finance.

Finance is the study of finance capital, from the time it is advanced until its profit is realized and returned to its owner.

The realization of profits requires converting the products or commodities to money. That point is crucial. Just because the widgets are produced does not mean that they can be sold. For that, the entrepreneur needs buyers. If there are no buyers, the widgets will sit in boxes in the warehouse. Without sales, all his efforts and the hope of his investors for realizing a profit would come to naught. The theorist of finance who assumes infinite buyers and sellers in the market thus assumes away the very discipline of finance! The definition of finance as the "study of cash flows" conceals the error. But there is no escaping its consequences. They come back in the form of contradictions, inconsistencies and the most important of all, real losses, to haunt both the discipline and the theorist.

The importance of conversion of a product to money becomes clear if we recognize that the entrepreneur has no authority over sales in the sense that he cannot make them happen. His authority over the production process, which came about because he had paid for its components and therefore owned them, came to an end with the completion of the production. Now, he is at the mercy of buyers. Only when he sells the widgets will he be able to realize a profit and return it proportionately to stock – and bondholders. In that case, a circuit of capital for these securities owners will come to an end. The heart of finance is studying the dynamics of capital from the time it is advanced until it is returned to its owners, in our example the stock – and bondholders. The actual production of widgets, which is the primary source of the generation of the profit, is a subject in economics and will not concern us in this book.

The various forms of capital

Capital's *raison d'être* is earning profits. The sole concern of capital is increasing its rate of return. Over time, the rate of return can be increased and sustained only if capital's efficiency is improved. An incessant search for efficiency is thus the hallmark of capital. The search results in the development of new forms of capital. These forms develop in the context of social and historical relations. An existent social relation can retard or accelerate the development of one particular form of capital relative to, or at the expense of, other forms. The conditions for the rise of speculative capital, for example, did not appear until the mid-1970s.

Historically, capital has had three main forms, namely, industrial capital, commercial capital and credit capital. Combined together, they form finance capital. Before studying speculative capital, we briefly explain these forms and show how each contributes to improving the efficiency of capital proper.

An important point which we must keep in mind is that while various forms of capital developed to improve efficiency, their relation with one another is inherently antagonistic. That is because the profit generated in the production of products or commodities is a fixed value. No set rules govern its division among the various forms of capital. The final arbiter of profits is the power of the claimants in a struggle which changes with circumstances. It is this nature of the relation between the various forms of capital, at once beneficial and contentious, that drives finance. That is "the portentous force of negative," as Hegel described the driving force of dialectics, to which we alluded in the Foreword.

Industrial capital

Industrial capital is the capital invested in manufacturing and industrial enterprises. The development of industrial capital signals the dawn of capitalism.

In following the entrepreneur in our widget example, we described the circuit of industrial capital. Note that while in that example both stockholders and bondholders were considered the owners of securities, only the capital of stockholders qualifies as industrial capital. The capital of the bondholders is credit capital. We will see shortly that credit capital interacts with other forms of capital to increase their rate of return.

Commercial capital

Commercial capital is the capital of wholesalers, merchants, retailers and the like. In short, it is the capital earmarked for the sale of products. Commercial capital does not generate profits. Rather, it appropriates a portion of the profit of manufacturing capital.

To elaborate, let us return to our widget factory and pause at the point where the widgets are produced, placed in boxes and are ready for shipment upon receiving orders from customers.

The entrepreneur knows that selling a product is a different skill from producing it. Selling is sufficiently specialized to give rise to such "industries" as advertising, public relations and marketing. (These aspects of selling widgets are closely related to finance but fall outside of it.) Analyzing the historical data, he knows that, after widgets are produced, it will take three months on average for them to be sold. This pivotal point, where the production of products (or commodities) ends and focus shifts to their sale, is shown in Figure 2.1.

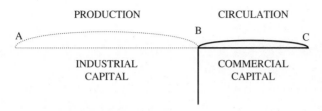

Figure 2.1 The two phases of the capital cycle

The entrepreneur would like to concentrate on what he knows best, which is producing widgets. So when a wholesaler approaches him with the idea of buying the widgets (at point B in Figure 2.1), he gladly listens. The negotiation immediately moves to the price.

The entrepreneur knows that a certain unit of widgets costs $100, takes nine months to produce and, on average, three months to sell. The data supporting these numbers were carefully analyzed and submitted to investors as part of the "pitch." He has thus set the price of widgets at $112. That selling price would translate to a return of 12 percent, which everyone agreed was enticing and better than the 4 percent offered in the bond market. He asks the same $112 from the wholesaler.

The wholesaler will have none of it. He is surprised at the entrepreneur's naiveté and gives him a lecture on the finer points of finance:

"Look! I know the common perception is that wholesalers add a 'markup' to the price of the products they buy. I understand that is also what economics and finance professors teach in the classroom. Frankly,

I am amazed at how long this nonsense has persisted despite the overwhelming evidence that points to the actual state of things. The actual state of things is as follows:

"The 12 percent rate of return that corresponds to your suggested price of $112 incorporates *all* the profits generated in the production of the widgets. But you know that mere production is not enough. To *realize* the profits, you must sell the widgets. Without sales, your capital is still 'tied up' in widgets; you can neither withdraw it nor realize any profit on it. So, although it is production alone that generates profit, in calculating the rate of return of the capital, you must also include the time that it takes to sell the widgets.[3]

"That is why you calculated the rate of return of the capital with reference to *one year*, comprised of nine months for production plus three months for sale. In that calculation, you assumed that you would produce the widgets and would also carry them until they were sold. Now, you have decided to sell the widgets to me right after production. If I pay $112 for the widgets, I would be paying all the profit incorporated in the widgets to you. I would be left with nothing to show by way of profit.

"Contrary to the misconception of the economics professor, I cannot add an arbitrary markup on top of $112. If that were the case, accumulated markups by successive middlemen would push the price of products above what the final users could afford. It would make the price haphazard and random. It would make economics and finance impossible disciplines to study. It would also mean that the more middlemen and brokers that came between the original producer of a product and its final consumers, the higher its price would

> **Contrary to the misconception of the economics professor, I cannot add an arbitrary markup on top of $112.**

---

[3] In general, if T_0 is the time it takes for the production of a product and T the time it takes for its sale and if the unit production cost and the selling price of the product are P and S, respectively, the rate of return of the manufacturing capital, r, would be given by the following relation:

$$r = (\frac{S-P}{T_0+T})/S$$

have to be. A socio-economic system which is based on competition and efficiency would not tolerate such gross and persistent violation of the principle of equality of exchange values.

"The best measure of inappropriateness and unacceptability of your asking price of $112 is its illogicality. Consider what would happen if I actually *pay* that price. In that case, your rate of return would increase from 12 to 16 percent. That is because the $12 return would then be realized in nine months instead of one full year, as the following relation shows:

$$ r = (\frac{112-100}{0.75+0}) /100 = 16\% $$

"In other words, if your sell the widgets to me at $112 at the completion of production, not only would you solve your sales problem but you would also increase the rate of return of your capital. That would surely come as a pleasant surprise to you. But, my friend, that would not happen in real life because I would not pay $112 for the widgets.

"The fair price of your widgets at point B, right after production, is $109. The math which enables us to arrive at that number is fairly simple: your initial 12 percent rate was realized over a 12-month period. Over a nine-month period, you must realize $12\% \times \frac{9}{12} = 9\%$. With the production cost of your widgets remaining constant at $100, that rate of return translates into a sale price of $109.

"If you still have any problem comprehending this calculation, ask your bond trader friends. They will readily confirm my calculation. Suppose, as in the bad old days, a bond pays a 12 percent coupon. If you buy and hold the bond for nine months, your share of accrued interest will be the face value of the bond times $12\% \times \frac{9}{12}$. That is exactly identical to your share of 'accrued' profit after holding the widget for nine months.[4] (Be warned that a bond trader will not be able to explain the reason for this calculation the way I did.)

"Now, I know what your have on your mind. You are worried about disappointing your investors because if you sell the widgets for $109

---

[4] Calculation of accrued interest in Treasury notes and bonds is slightly different. The difference, due to accounting for semi-annual payment, does not affect our argument.

instead of $112, your rate of return will drop from 12 to 9 percent. But thanks to the magic of commercial capital, you can sell your widgets for $109 and still realize a return of 12 percent over time. I have prepared a diagram which shows the secret of this magic [see Figure 2.2].

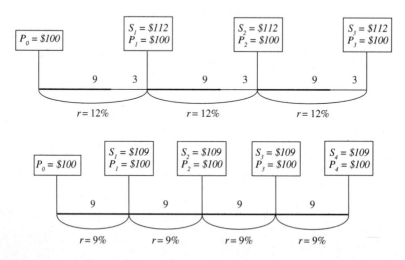

Figure 2.2 Comparison of production cycle of capital with and without the intervention of commercial capital

"The diagram shows a three-year time frame. Without me, if you produce and sell the widgets yourself, your capital will be turned over three times – once every year – with the rate of return of 12 percent. That is a total return of 3 × 12% = 36%. After my intervention, your nominal return drops to 9 percent, but the number of turnovers rises to four. So your total return over the three-year period remains the same at 4 × 9% = 36%. In the latter case, however, as you yourself had noticed, the production and circulation become more efficient, because each party concentrates on what it knows best. Furthermore, in shortening the cycle of the return of profit to the manufacturer, my commercial capital reduces the amount of capital necessary for manufacturing. In that regard, it makes the use of capital more efficient. And that is why a system based on efficiency and competition supports it, nay, *necessitates* it."

The entrepreneur is convinced. He sells the widgets at $109 and happily returns to give the investors their *pro rata* share of profits and start a new production cycle. The wholesaler, meanwhile, parts with $109 in return for the widgets which he hopes will sell for $112. Thus, one cycle of industrial capital ends and a new cycle of commercial capital begins.

Credit capital

A detailed analysis of credit and its role in economic development is beyond the scope of this book. Credit capital in the form of money provided by usurers and money-changers has a constant presence on the early economic scene. The money-changers whom Jesus drove away from the temple come back in the Middle Ages as usurers. Their demand for high interest rates played an important role in driving the landed aristocracy to bankruptcy and paving the way for the rise of capitalism.

With the dawn of the Industrial Revolution, credit capital came of age. While it was also lent as money – a practice which continues today[5] – it was in its capacity as capital that it interacted with the other forms of capital and, by boosting their return, advanced industrialization and commerce.

Like commercial capital, credit capital generates profit by appropriating a share of the profit of industrial capital. If credit capital is interacting with industrial capital, the appropriation is direct. If it is interacting with commercial capital, the appropriation is indirect, through appropriation of a share of the profit of the commercial capital

> *With the dawn of the Industrial Revolution, credit capital came of age.*

which is itself taken from the industrial capital. In all events, unlike commercial capital, whose mechanics of appropriation are camouflaged by appearances, the appropriation of credit capital is accomplished in plain view and is evident to everyone except perhaps the economist.

Credit capital acts as a leverage to other forms of capital. It provides

---

[5] A borrower might borrow a certain sum as money, i.e., for spending. But for the lender who lends it at interest, the money becomes capital. The point that every borrowing must also be a lending seems sufficiently simple. Yet it has created a genuine bafflement in securities law when judges and legal scholars ponder the definition of a "note" in order to decide whether or not it is a security. We will return to this issue in Chapter 4, Volume 2, when we examine the uncertainty in securities law.

them with the means of boosting their returns beyond what they could do on their own. When the wholesaler paid for the widgets entirely with his capital, his rate of return was 11.01 percent (calculated as $\frac{112 - 109}{112}$ $\times$ $\frac{12}{3}$). Now suppose that he divides his capital in half and advances only $54.50 for the widgets. He borrows the rest from the owners of credit capital – the local bank, a wealthy relative or a credit union – at an annual rate of 6 percent. In that case, his profit increases to 16.02 percent, as shown in the following calculations:

$54.50 \times 0.06 \times 3/12 = \$0.8175$ Interest accrued on borrowed capital

$3 - 0.8175 = \$2.1825$ Net profit of wholesaler

$\dfrac{2.1825}{54.50} \times 12/3 = 16.02\%$ Rate of return on wholesaler's capital

The reason for the increase is obvious. It is brought about because the wholesaler borrows at 6 percent for a venture which yielded 11.01 percent. The difference between the two is the additional yield which accrues to him. The wholesaler borrowing relatively cheap capital to buy and carry a product for delivery is something that the modern repo trader would readily recognize, except that in the repo market the fixed income securities have replaced the widgets.

The entrepreneur of the widget factory, too, could have borrowed some portion of the needed capital instead of raising it in equity form. In that case, he would have to pay the interest to the lenders prior to calculating the rate of return of equity investors.

The interest rate that credit capital commands is negotiated between the borrower and the lender. The gain of each side is made at the expense of the other. That is why the level of interest rates is the subject of unending discussion and analysis. The influence of the Federal Reserve follows in part from its power to affect the share of profits available to credit capital and its users.

It is easy to see that as long as the interest rate on credit capital remains below the rate of return on commercial or industrial capital, the use of credit capital boosts the rate of return. If the interest rate on credit capital exceeds the rate of return on commercial capital, its use would diminish the rate of return on commercial capital. In our example, if the interest rate is 12 percent, the rate of return of the wholesaler will drop from 16.02 to 10.02 percent:

$54.50 \times 0.12 \times 3/12 = \$1.635$ Interest accrued on borrowed capital

$3 - 1.635 = \$1.365$ Net profit of wholesaler

$\dfrac{1.365}{54.50} \times 12/3 = 10.02\%$ Rate of return on his advanced capital

Thus, the rate of return of industrial and commercial capital determines the ceiling of interest on credit capital. Beyond that ceiling, the use of credit capital would not be profitable.

The impetus for the rise of speculative capital

Speculation can develop within the sphere of operation of all forms of capital. Historically, commerce has been its most fertile ground. For our conceptual development of speculation, we thus turn to commercial capital.

After purchasing the widgets, the wholesaler has his commercial capital thrown into circulation. To extract his desired profit, he must be able to sell the widgets at $112 within three months. Here, the finance professor assumes infinite buyers in his theories. Our wholesaler is a man of the real world and knows that he cannot run his business on such foolish assumptions. Of course, in three months the widgets *could* sell for $112, or even more. But there is also the very real possibility that their price could drop below $112, or even below $109. In fact, they could sit in inventory without attracting any buyers. Under these conditions, the wholesaler would see his profits decline and eventually turn into a loss.

Such exposures to risk seem unavoidable and an inherent part of the business. Being a shrewd businessman, our wholesaler is not easily dissuaded. He looks around to see if he can find a way to at least mitigate this risk.

The sources of the risk, as he sees them, are twofold: the selling price of the widgets and the time it takes to sell them. If he had a guaranteed buyer willing to pay $112 for the widgets in three months, his problems would be solved. The assumptions of modern finance notwithstanding, he knows that only a legal contract would bring about such a guarantee. That was the reason for the birth of agricultural futures markets. For the time being, the idea remains wishful thinking. The chances of finding a customer who will agree to buy the widgets three months from now are no better than those of finding a buyer at the end of the three months.

The wholesaler then turns his attention to time, which he knows plays a role in shaping his rate of return. His normal rate of return, if he could sell the widgets every three months at $112, is 11.01 percent:

$$\frac{112-109}{109} \times \frac{12}{3} = 0.1101 = 11.01\%$$

Eq. (2.1)

If the "market is slow" and the inventory is turned over only twice a year, the rate of return drops to 5.5 percent:

$$\frac{112-109}{109} \times \frac{12}{6} = 0.0550 = 5.5\%$$

Eq. (2.2)

So when he senses that this merchandise does not sell, he reduces the price to $111.50. If this "sale" markdown could increases the speed of sale of the widgets from six months to four months, he could improve the rate of return to 6.88 percent:

$$\frac{111.5-109}{109} \times \frac{12}{4} = 0.0688 = 6.88\%$$

Eq. (2.3)

In Eqs. (2.1) and (2.2), the first term on the left hand side is constant. That is the fixed profit embedded in the widgets and available to the wholesaler. The second term is the constant number of months in a year divided by the time it takes to sell the widgets. (The unit could also be days or years.) As the denominator gets smaller, the second term, and with it the rate of return of commercial capital, increases. For example, if the wholesaler can increase the turnover rate to six times a year, his rate of return will climb to 16.51 percent:

$$\frac{112-109}{109} \times \frac{12}{2} = 0.1651 = 16.51\%$$

If, on the other hand, the widgets take longer to sell, the denominator in the second term increases. That leads to a decrease in the rate of return. Thus, the owner of commercial capital is constantly at work, trying to increase its turnover. It is precisely toward reduction of this average holding period that our wholesaler spends a sizable amount in advertising, marketing, public relations and the like.

Increasing the turnover rate shortens the holding period of the widgets and seems to be the best of both worlds. It disposes of the widgets at the same time that it boosts the rate of return of the capital. But a more rapid turnover of commercial capital increases its rate of return but does nothing to alleviate the problem of *finding* the buyer. In fact, it worsens it. When the turnover is three months, the wholesaler has to grapple with the problem of finding buyers four times a year. To reduce the turnover time to two months, the same problem has to be faced every other month. An additional 5.5 percent (16.51 – 11.01) improvement in the rate of return is obtained at the cost of a 50 percent increase in the "finding-a-buyer" risk. It is this relation between risk and return, looked upon from the narrow view of a wholesaler, that to Knight and his followers appeared to be the *source* of profit.

To alleviate the problem, commercial capital actively encourages new entrants into the market. If more people buy and sell, the chances of finding trading partners increase. These new entrants can be neither end users nor wholesalers. An increase in the number of end users is an increase in demand. That would alert the factory to produce more widgets. It might lead to a higher or lower price for the widgets. But it would have no effect on the problem at hand.

An increase in the number of wholesalers would probably lead to a lower profit margin for all, because they would tend to bid up the purchase price of the widgets. But again, the wholesaler's problem would be left unsolved.

The type of new entrants the wholesaler has in mind must have no impact on the production and use of the widgets. They must come solely to serve as the solution to his problem of "finding a buyer." That is, they must conveniently appear in the market at various points and be ready to buy if the wholesaler decides to sell. That is their function. These entrants are speculators.

Speculation

Why would speculators be interested in coming into the market? To use street jargon, what is "in it" for them? The obvious answer is that they hope to make a profit. But we said that the fixed amount of profit was divided between the industrial capital, the commercial capital and, if there was any borrowing, the credit capital. Whence does a speculator's profit materialize?

Suppose two months after the wholesaler has purchased the widgets a speculator appears in the market and is ready to buy them. The point is shown by D in Figure 2.3

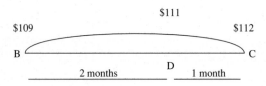

Figure 2.3 Earlier-than-expected sale of widgets

At that point, the value of the widgets should be $111, as only 2/3 of the $3 profit is apportioned to the wholesaler:

$$109 + (112 - 109) \times \frac{2}{3} = \$111 \qquad \text{Eq. (2.4)}$$

From there, one is obliged to assume that the speculator will carry the widgets for one month and then sell them at $112 for a profit of $1.

But that is not how speculators trade. Buying the widgets at a time-proportioned discount and selling them is wholesaling, not speculation. We might as well have assumed that the wholesaler carried the widgets for the entire three months and then sold them at $112. The introduction of a speculator who holds the product until it is bought by the user would take us back to our starting point.

The difficulty of differentiating speculators from wholesalers must not be taken lightly. Even *Economics*, the legendary book (in terms of sales) by the Nobel Laureate Paul Samuelson, is of no help in clarifying the difference. In its 15th edition, written in collaboration with Nordhaus, Samuelson defines the function of the speculator in the following way (Samuelson and Nordhaus, 1995, p. 181):

> We begin by considering the role of speculative markets, which serve society by moving goods from abundant times or places to those of scarcity. The activity is **speculation** [boldface in original], which involves buying a commodity with an eye to selling it later ... Speculators are not interested in using the product or making something with it ... The last thing they want is to see the egg truck roll up to their door!

Buying a commodity with an eye to selling it later is also *commerce*. It need not be speculation. This imprecision is more than a pardonable oversight. While Professor Samuelson goes on to differentiate speculators from wholesalers and retailers by saying that speculators are not interested in products or production, he creates a new puzzle with that elaboration: if speculators are unwilling to take possession of the products, how *can* they *move* products from abundant times or places to those of scarcity? *Economics* spends no time on that question.

The key to understanding the source of potential profit of the speculator lies in the difference between the individual random events and their mass characteristics. In discussing the risks of commercial capital, we saw that neither the price of the widgets nor the time it takes to sell them is fixed. They both fluctuate. These fluctuations are the result of numerous factors. Economists conveniently call them supply and demand and think that they determine the value. In reality, supply and demand determine the variation *around* a value and not its magnitude. In our example, the fluctuations are *around* two fixed values. One of them, the $3 profit, is established in the process of production. The other, the number of days it takes to sell the widgets, is established from experience and historical data.

In running his trade, our wholesaler ignored the short term fluctuations and trusted his capital to the operation of statistical laws. Statistics is the discipline of studying the mass characteristics of random phenomena. It is known and can be mathematically shown that when looked upon *en masse*, many random phenomena give rise to clear-cut patterns.[6] The wholesaler sets his time horizon in the three-month period and beyond. He knows that if one year the widgets take an unusually long time to sell, the next year (or the year after) they would have to sell in less than three months. That follows from the definition of average. Likewise, if two months after purchasing the widgets their price falls to $110.50 from $111, by the end of the third month the price can be expected to return to its "correct" level. If that does not happen in this cycle, then it must happen in the next

Speculators bet on the odds of individual random events.

cycle or the one after. *On average*, the wholesaler expects to realize $3 profit in three months.[7]

Speculators, by contrast, bet on the odds of individual random events. Unlike the industrialist, the wholesaler and the banker who commit their capital for a definite period as a way of insulating themselves against random fluctuations, speculators enter the market precisely to take advantage of those fluctuations. Their investment horizon, by definition, is short. That is what separates them from the rest of the pack. Otherwise, they all act on the principle of "buy low, sell high." No one has yet found another way of consistently making money. On the basis of that description alone, it is impossible to differentiate speculators from industrialists, bankers and merchants.

The early speculators were gamblers. They entered the markets to bet on the odds of short-term movements.

> No one hedged eggs or butter in the Merc's early days. The main concern of those who traded futures was to ensure the fulfillment of the contracts; the hedging interest simply wasn't there. Instead, dealers merely looked for speculative profits in accumulating butter and eggs, hoping that profitable years would more than offset the losing ones. (Tamarkin, 1993, p. 47)

---

[6] We briefly review the concept of randomness and the tools of statistics in the Appendix to Volume 2.

[7] Of course, prices can drop and remain low for sufficiently long to force our wholesaler into bankruptcy. That is a recession (or a depression) and does not concern us. Our focus is on differentiating the activities of speclators from those of wholesalers.

That is where the disciplines of modern finance found them and left them. Witness Professor Samuelson's reference to the "egg truck" in the earlier quote. The Butter and Eggs Exchange was established in 1895 to facilitate the speculative trading of the two products. Both contracts have long ceased to exist. In 1919, the Butter and Eggs Exchange became the Chicago Mercantile Exchange.

At one level, the presence of egg futures in *Economics* points to an urgent need for a revision of this *magnum opus*. More to the point, the out-of-date reference shows that time has stood still with regard to understanding speculation. The understanding of speculation by the scholars of economics and modern finance does not go beyond repeating what their mostly illiterate crowd in the Butter and Eggs Exchange aired many decades ago by way of promoting their business.[8]

Illiteracy, of course, does not imply a lack of insight or intelligence, especially in the hectic business of speculation. No fool can last long as a speculator. In fact, a high degree of shrewdness and constant learning are required for this business. What happens if speculators learn to improve the odds of their winning or reduce their risk? The answer is that they create arbitrage.

Arbitrage: the risk-free profit

The speculator earns his livelihood by constantly confronting randomness. If there is a trend or a "big picture" in the events, the random events he faces are as likely to move counter to it as they are according to it. So there is no use in being scholarly. The fancy theories spawned in academia are worthless to him. How many times has he seen the most

---

[8] The nonsense about the "service" of speculators is constantly repeated in the press. Here is the *New York Times* informing its readers: "If banks, pension funds and other investors could not easily use bond futures to manage their risks, the government would have to pay much higher interest to convince them to buy bonds. The result would be battles over Government spending and taxing that would make the conflict currently paralyzing Congress seem tame." ("Futures Exchanges Search for New Commodities," March 15, 1996, p. D1.) So in addition to increasing society's "welfare," the pit traders in Chicago exchanges also hold the Republic together.

unschooled traders make fortunes and refined MBAs ruined! A good trader would "feel" the market and react to it instinctively. If there is a secret to speculation, it can be summarized in two words: supply, demand. At any given time, if there are more buyers than sellers, the price goes up. If there are more sellers than buyers, the price goes down.

Leo Melamed, the chairman emeritus of the Chicago Mercantile Exchange, explains the reason he introduced currency futures in the aftermath of the collapse of the Bretton Woods system (1996, p. 176):

> I wanted to organize a futures exchange that would deal in monetary instruments. The first instrument was to be the real thing – money [!]. Instinctively, I knew there was a tremendous opportunity in the new contract – and something else: no one could squeeze and corner a currency market. Economics was going to dictate the market. Supply and demand was going to determine its value, nothing else.

After any purchase, the speculator faces the risk that what he has just bought will fall in price. That can only happen with the passage of time. It is through time that the price of widgets drops, and it is through time that the speculator fails to find a buyer. Time is the medium through which the risk – and everything else – materializes. To the uncritical, yet practical, mind of the speculator, time appears as the *source* of the risk. He concludes that if the time between his purchase and sale is shortened, the risks of the transaction must proportionally diminish. In the extreme case, when the time between the two is zero, the risk would completely disappear. In that case, he could earn a risk-free profit.

To the uncritical, yet practical, mind of the speculator, time appears as the **source** *of the risk.*

On the surface, the logic seems counter-intuitive. In examining commercial capital, we concluded that as the number of times it turns over increases, the problem of finding buyers is exacerbated. But if the time between the purchase and sale is so shortened that the two are simultaneous, the problem of finding a buyer is eliminated. That is because no purchase is made *unless a sale is already in hand.* When the time between purchase and sale is reduced to zero, the two acts become *simultaneous.* A simultaneous "buy-low, sell-high" results in a risk-free profit. That is arbitrage. The speculator has found the Holy Grail of finance: making money without risking money.[9]

Speculation and the theory of finance

The theorist of finance hears of arbitrage. He has no theory of his own and cannot evaluate the method. He only knows that arbitrage generates risk-less profit through simultaneous buying and selling. He reasons that the risk-free profits would naturally attract a large number of fortune-seekers. The condition in the market becomes as follows: many speculators – now arbitrageurs – taking simultaneous long and short positions which generate profits without exposing them to the risk of loss. Because it is good to earn riskless profits, and because there are many speculators, it is natural that trading in this world will go on incessantly, continuously.

That is certainly unprecedented. It calls for the construction of an equally uncommon theory, maybe even creating a large division within "modern finance." The theorist knows the mathematical tool that deals with instantaneous and continuous changes in time. It is differential calculus. If the time between purchase and sale tends to zero – that is the mathematical way of saying the two become simultaneous – the relations could be expressed in terms of infinitesimally small changes in time intervals, or in *continuous time*.[10] So the theory of modern finance becomes continuous-time finance where arbitrage-induced continuous buying and selling create an efficient market in which no risk-free profit is possible.

Deducing continuous-time trading from the concept of arbitrage is a quantum leap for the sake of convenience. It is made to make use of differential calculus. But the premise has become so central in modern finance that some believe it to describe the real world. Dixit and Pindyck (1994, p. 26), two Princeton academics, write: "Firms make, implement,

---

[9] We are developing the concept of arbitrage from the viewpoint of a speculator. The "riskless" profit should be understood in that context. As we proceed, we will see how the "risk" enters into a speculator's arbitrage trading.

[10] For an explanation of this concept, see the Appendix to Volume 2 under Differential Calculus.

and sometimes review their investment decisions continuously through time. Hence much of this book is devoted to analysis of investment decisions as continuous-time problems." Robert Merton, the author of *Continuous-Time Finance*, knows better (1994, p. 58): "Of course continuous trading, like any other continuous revision process, is an abstraction from physical reality." This assertion is not completely accurate either. Abstraction is simplification; it is the act of setting aside what is not directly related to the subject of study. Continuous-time is not simplified discrete-time. It is the other way round.

That real-life securities trading is not continuous-time hardly needs proving. In real life, Nobel Laureate Merton Miller resolves the conflict between being one of the architects of continuous-time finance and a consultant to Nasdaq in a price-fixing dispute in a pragmatic way and in favor of reality: "Mr. Miller concedes that the Big Board's pricing pattern is noticeably different. 'I've argued that the New York Stock Exchange is the anomaly – [its] price patterns are much too continuous,' the professor said."[11]

The arbitrage argument, however, remains the *animus mundi* of modern finance. It propels all the actions and sustains all relations, including the value of derivatives. As a matter of fact, derivatives cannot be valued *but* through the arbitrage valuation.[12] The stage is now set for the rise of speculative capital.

Speculative capital

We arrived at arbitrage by following the speculators who learned to improve their trading strategy. To that end, our attention was focused on speculators, their viewpoint in the market and their mode of operation. However, it is not the speculators but their capital which is the subject

---

[11] "Nasdaq Fights Back on Pricing Allegations," *Wall Street Journal*, April 6, 1995, p. C1.

[12] The alternative methods of valuing options are constructed with "hindsight." Without prior knowledge of the answer provided by the arbitrage argument in the Black–Scholes model, these methods could not produce the correct value. We will return to this point in detail in Volume 2, Chapters 2 and 3, when we analyze options.

of finance. What are the characteristics of capital that engages in the act of arbitrage?

Such capital is, by definition, "opportunistic." It is constantly on the lookout for "inefficiencies" across markets which it can exploit. The opportunities arise suddenly and at random points in time, so the capital that hopes to exploit them must always be available; it cannot afford to be locked into long-term commitments and investments. The requirement to be opportunistic translates into the need to be mobile, to be nomadic and interested in short-term ventures. Capital that has such characteristics is *speculative capital*. Indeed, speculation is defined precisely in terms of short-term engagement of capital in arbitrage trades.

Because these attributes *define* speculative capital, the manager of speculative capital must employ it in activities that are consistent with these attributes. True, the manager can decide the specific occasions of the capital's employment, but that selection must be made from a menu of choices predefined by the attributes of speculative capital. He cannot commit the speculative capital to long-term mortgage lending. Thus, in the absence of any real option, the manager of speculative capital turns into its agent, someone who nominally "runs" the speculative capital but must in fact follow its "agenda." Speculative capital becomes the grammatical subject of the sentence as if it were alive: speculative capital seeks arbitrage opportunities. Of course, it does so through its agent, the fund manager, but it is the speculative capital which determines the nature of its own employment and calls the strategic shots.

> *In the absence of any real option, the manager of speculative capital turns into its agent.*

There is no better example of this subjugation of person to the dynamics of speculative capital than the Black–Scholes option valuation model. There, the owner of the portfolio must not think. He is there only as an agent: to buy when the market is rising; to sell when the market is falling. It is only under these conditions that an option can be valued.

It is now easy to see why the definition of arbitrage bedeviled academia. The reason is that the concept of arbitrage can only be understood in conjunction with speculation and speculative capital. It is impossible to define arbitrage "on its own" or explain how it is different from the ordinary "buy low, sell high" practice. Arbitrage is refined, mature speculation. It is also speculation pushed to its limit, where the already short interval between purchase and sale is reduced to zero and the two acts have become simultaneous.

> *Arbitrage can only be understood in conjunction with speculation and speculative capital.*

Speculative capital is a worthy object of philosophical pondering. Its *raison d'être* is generating profit for itself and reducing risk for commercial capital. Yet it does so through arbitrage, an act which eliminates the differences that give rise to it. Speculative capital is also the antithesis of the forces which give rise to it: it reduces the spreads and eliminates their profit opportunities.

This antithetical function of arbitrage is displayed in the contrasting way it works to reduce risk. While all other forms of capital weed out risk by *increasing* the time between purchase and sale to some average period, arbitrage does it by *reducing* that time to zero. The mathematics of finance captures this paradox of speculative capital, but no one is there to interpret what is plainly in view.

We explain.

In continuous-time finance, the interest rate is compounded continuously.[13] A finance professor who thinks that interest is an inherent property of money would think nothing of that absurdity.[14] In reality, interest is ultimately a deduction from the profit of industrial capital.[15] The frequency of the compounding of interest corresponds to the frequency of

---

[13] For a explanation of continuous compounding, see the Appendix to Volume 2.

[14] The mechanical view of interest rates as an inherent property of money and detached from economic activity is pervasive. Advertising brochures for retirement accounts frequently show the exponential growth of an initial $2000 investment with a 15% annual return after 30 years. Few stop to question how that 15% will be generated each year over the next 30 years. One could presumably offer an even better investment plan that would reach $1 billion in a month. It only requires daily doubling of an initial investment of $1! In this example, it is easier to see that what is promoted is not an investment plan but the power of geometric progression.

[15] Commercial capital also pays interest but ultimately that interest is a deduction from the profit of industrial capital as well.

the turnover of industrial capital. The turnover of capital invested in manufacturing a product that takes nine months to produce and three months to sell is yearly. If the same product is produced in five months and sold in one, the capital's turnover is twice a year. In the first case, the borrowed credit capital is returned to the lender after one year, in the second case after six months.

Continuous compounding of interest corresponds to the *continuous turnover* of capital, a notion so utterly absurd as to be insane. Continuous

> ***Continuous compounding is the vision of a Shylock gone mad.***

compounding is the vision of a Shylock gone mad. That such absurdity logically follows from the concept of arbitrage is evidence of speculative capital's paradoxical nature.

Opposition to the rise of speculative capital

Speculative capital is encouraged to enter into market to reduce the risk for the wholesaler. Afterwards, it begins to eat into the wholesaler's profits. The competition for a larger share of the profits is a fact of life in the fraternity of capitals. Each form establishes its share through a constant battle of give and take. But speculative capital is a particularly unkind kin. It does not merely take a given portion. It rises to graze on the differences until nothing is left for sustenance. In that regard, it acts as an instrument of a financial entropy. Little wonder that its rise is strongly resisted.

We will return to the opposition of the various forms of capital to the expansion of speculative capital in detail in Chapter 5. But even though we have not yet shown how speculative capital develops historically, it is important to give a real-life example of this struggle. The example highlights the theoretical points that we developed here, namely, the method of operation of speculative capital, the consequences of its operation and the subsequent and inevitable resistance to it.

The "SOES bandits" and the principle of arbitrage: theory meets practice

It is said that if the principles of geometry ran into conflict with people's interests, they would be disproved. The controversy over Nasdaq's

Small Order Execution System (SOES, pronounced SoS) came close to confirming that maxim.

The background of the controversy is as follows: in the market crash of 1987, Nasdaq market makers refused to take trade orders; in fact, they refused to answer their phones. Legions of small investors who could not reach their brokers suffered heavy losses. Three years later, their complaints led to the creation of SOES. Using SOES, retail investors could trade up to 1000 shares of stock directly with market makers without having to call them.

The SOES had the blessing of the market makers. Some of them expressed concerns about its potential harms, but in general the system was deemed harmless. So much was certain: the system was going to bring more customers into the Nasdaq market and thus, more commissions. That alone would neutralize any negative impact.

The SOES is a so-called "level III" machine. Unlike regular quote machines that only show the best *bid* and *asked* prices for a stock, a level III machine displays the prices of all market makers. It can also *execute* trades. The user of a level III machine can directly sell stocks at the best bid price to, and buy at the best offered price from, the market makers almost instantly and without intervention of a broker. Figure 2.4 shows a level III-type display with four market makers MM1 to MM4 in ABCD stock.

ABCD 20¼ × 20½	
Bid	**Ask**
MM1 20¼	MM3 20½
MM2 20¼	MM1 20¾
MM4 19⅞	MM2 20¾
MM3 19¾	MM4 20⅞

Figure 2.4 SOES display of market makers and their prices

On top of the screen, the stock symbol ABCD is followed by the best bid/asked price for the stock, 20¼ × 20½. It shows the highest price at which a market maker is willing to buy the stock (market maker MM1 for 20¼) and the lowest price at which a market maker is willing to sell it (market maker MM3 at 20½). A SOES trader can submit a sell order at 20¼ or a buy order for 20½ for up to 1000 shares of ABCD. Because market makers MM1 and MM3 have posted these prices, they must accept such order.

Virtually from the time the SOES was introduced, its sometimes creative users were branded "bandits," implying that they "stole" money that justly belonged to market makers. The scenario that allowed this theft, market makers said, was as follows: Suppose there is positive news on a stock which cause its price to move higher. All market makers change their prices, except market maker MM4 who keeps his bid/asked at the previous 19⅞ × 20⅞. Figure 2.5 shows the new prices, with those of MM4 unchanged.

ABCD 21¼ × 20⅞	
Bid	**Ask**
MM1 21¼	MM3 21½
MM2 21¼	MM1 21¾
MM4 21¾	MM2 21⅞
MM3 19⅞	MM4 20⅞

Figure 2.5 Changed prices in a level III machine

Market maker MM4 is now selling the stock at 20⅞. A SOES trader can buy ABCD for 20⅞ from him and immediately sell it to the highest bidder, MM1, who is paying 21¼ for the stock. The SOES trader realizes a profit of $375 (minus commissions) on 1000 shares of ABCD. For Nasdaq market makers accustomed to easy profits this eventuality proved unacceptable. The financial press reflected their views:

> SOES has a provision that the SOES bandits – who are hardly the typical small investor–have been able to exploit very profitably. Basically,

the system requires that brokers exercise constant vigilance in keeping current the prices ... A few-second delay by a broker in updating the price of a volatile stock is all a SOES trader needs to hammer the broker with repeated automatic orders to buy or sell. The hapless broker has to execute the orders regardless of whether they will be profitable [sic]. Nasdaq ... argues that [SOES firms] distort prices. [!][16]

So the SOES traders were "hardly the typical small investor." They were "bandits" – thieves, really – who abused a minor oversight by a "hapless" broker to "hammer" him with buy and sell orders. Market makers vehemently object to bandits not because of money matters – that was not really the point – but because the bandits' actions distorted prices.

This complaint was aired for six years. Market makers repeatedly urged the regulatory agencies to stop the SOES trading, and complained that not much was being done to that end:

[The] president of the STA [Security Traders Association], along with other traders, complained that the SEC has failed to address alleged problems in the Small Order Execution System ... Some market-makers claim that SOES traders abuse the system to "pick off" big dealers who don't update their price quotations fast enough.[17]

As it became clear that the regulators were not about to stop the "abuse," market makers took matters into their own hands. When they found themselves "robbed" in this way, they simply refused to honor their trades. This illegal conduct continued without Nasdaq officials moving to stop it. Only much later, in the midst of the investigation of the "spread scandal," were they finally forced to slap the wrists of a few market makers who had "backed away" from their trades. A *Wall Street Journal* report tells the story, not forgetting to mention the "unsympathetic victims":

---

[16] "Nasdaq's 'SOES Bandits' Seek Recruits," *Wall Street Journal*, June 1, 1995, p. C1.
[17] "SEC Official Chides Nasdaq Traders for Complaining About Regulations," *Wall Street Journal*, October 24, 1995, p. B9.

Major backing-away sanctions have been rare partly because so many of the backing-away complaints have come from … "SOES bandits," whom dealers accuse of bombarding the market … with orders at dealers' expense. The 12 backing-away incidents in the Morgan Stanley case all involved orders from SOES bandits, and the Lehman matter is understood to derive from bandits' complaints, as well … yet despite unsympathetic victims, backing away from quotation is forbidden in the markets.[18]

Perhaps in the early days of SOES, some market makers failed to update their prices and were "SOESed." But this possibility was hardly the reason for their attack on SOES traders.
Market makers quickly learned to be more "vigilant" and updated their prices, *as required by law*. As shown in Figure 2.5, a price quote in the form of 21¼ × 20⅞ – in which the bid is

> *The real problem of SOES trading was that it pressured bid/asked spreads.*

less than the asked price – would immediately alert the market makers to the presence of an out-of-line price. In any case, the amount of money involved in SOES "robbery" was a pittance. It hardly explained the ferocious attack of Nasdaq on the bandits. The real problem of SOES trading was that it pressured bid/asked spreads. The bandits could narrow the spread between the bid and asked prices and, in doing so, throw a monkey wrench into the wheels of the money machine.

Let us return to Figure 2.4. At the top, ABCD is quoted at 20¼ × 20½. The bid/asked spread for the stock is ¼ of a point or 25 cents. This is what the public sees. But this best bid and asked for the stock come from two *different* market makers. In our example, market maker MM1 provides the best bid at 20¼. Market maker MM3 provides the best asked, at 20½. The bid/asked spread for each individual market maker is considerably larger. In the case of market marker MM1, the spread is 20¼ × 20¾, or 50 cents. In buying and selling a share of ABCD, market maker MM1 makes a profit not of 25 cents but of 50 cents, twice as large as the already high spread of ¼ point.

If a SOES trader submitted a bid of 20⅜ for ABCD, market makers

---

[18] "NASD is Expected to Penalize Lehman for Failing to Honor Stock-Price Quotes," *Wall Street Journal*, September 26, 1995, p. A4.

ignored his bid, even though it was higher than the existing best bid of 20¼. Market makers who accepted better bids from the outside traders and posted them on the system were censured by their colleagues.

For years, the complaints of investors about the artificially high bid/asked spreads in Nasdaq stocks went unheeded. In 1994, the publication of a paper by two professors who claimed "collusion" among market makers finally drew the attention of the Justice Department which began an investigation. That forced the Securities and Exchange Commission (SEC) to act. In 1996, after two years of investigation, the Commission issued a scathing report about the conduct of Nasdaq market makers and demanded a series of changes to the system. One of the more significant of these changes was requiring market makers to post outside prices that improved the current best bid and asked.

In fighting that plan, the market makers showed what the real issue had been all along:

> Three of the biggest Nasdaq Stock Market Dealers are mounting a behind-the-scenes campaign on Capitol Hill to block the Securities and Exchange Commission from imposing new rules on their market. [A lobbyist hired by some Nasdaq firms] has drafted a proposed amendment to a securities bill that ... would obstruct the SEC's plan to enact rules requiring more open display of prices on the Nasdaq over-the-counter market. The amendment would require the SEC to study, at great length, the rules' effect on "the competitiveness and liquidity" of the market.[19]

So now the open display of prices had the potential to adversely affect the competitiveness and liquidity of the market.

The fight of Nasdaq market makers to preserve their golden goose at the expense of the investing public does not concern us here. We would like to merely show how the rise of speculative capital is resisted by those whose interests it threatens. SOES trading is as close to arbitrage as one can get in the equities market. It involves buying low and selling high in a very short interval; SOES traders sometimes close their positions in a matter of minutes. But of the legion of free market advocates, no one stepped for-

---

[19] "Nasdaq Dealers Launch Campaign In Congress to Block SEC Rules," *Wall Street Journal*, July 29, 1996, p. A14.

ward to defend SOES trading as "the mechanism for price discovery," "the invisible hand at work," "an action increasing the overall utility of society," etc.

That was bad enough. Then came the preposterous. Two academics, Meeta Kothare and Paul Laux, picked up the market makers' fiction about liquidity and prices and in a complete reversal of tables argued that arbitrage – the same arbitrage that sustains the entire theories of modern finance – is actually bad when done by SOES traders. SOES trading, they argued by favorably quoting "critics," increases the bid/asked spread in the

> *That was bad enough. Then came the preposterous.*

markets and decreases the liquidity! They wrote (1995, p. 42):

> Extensive short term trading activities on the [SOES] system have adversely affected volatility and spreads, according to critics. If this activity causes significant losses to market makers, they will attempt to reduce and recoup these losses. To reduce the losses, market makers may spend more resources monitoring their participation in SOES, which would result in fewer deals per issue and a reduction in the depth of the market. To recoup losses, market makers may widen bid-ask spreads for all investors in stocks that are heavily traded in short-term trading tactics and possibly in other stocks as well.

In January 1997, in a compromise, the SEC approved the market makers' demand that the maximum number of shares traded in SOES for major stocks be reduced to 100 from 1000. The *Wall Street Journal* reported "Nasdaq officials have asked the SEC to permanently lower the 'minimum quote rule' to 100 for all Nasdaq stocks, saying it would help the market accommodate the SEC's new sweeping order-handling rules."[20] Note that the name of the rule, the so-called "minimum quote rule," is quite misleading because it is in fact the *maximum* quote rule: the maximum number of shares eligible for SOES trading was reduced from 1000 to 100.

The SEC approved the request, beginning with a test program for

---

[20] "SEC Clears Pilot Program that Slashes Nasdaq Market's 'Minimum Quote Rule'," *Wall Street Journal*, January 13, 1997, p. A13.

some of the most actively traded stocks. The change naturally cut the profits of SOES traders:

> [SOES] traders also hotly complain about Nasdaq's 90-day test program that lets market makers trade only 100 shares of certain stocks at a time with SOES traders. The difference is vast; a quarter-point profit on 1,000 shares is $250; on 100 shares it's only $25. And the pilot program includes the top-10 Nasdaq-traded stocks like Microsoft, Intel and Cisco Systems.[21]

The Nasdaq market makers were not alone in trying to protect their interests. The pit traders in the Chicago exchanges also showed that when it came to defending their easy profits, they could advance arguments every bit as creative as their Nasdaq brethren. The *Wall Street Journal* reported the opposition of the Board of Trade's "locals" – the pit traders – to broadcasting trading information to outsiders and the reason for their opposition:

> Locals feel that broadcasting the information over the headset to an order desk gives the off-the-floor customer an unfair advantage in the market … They claim that headset users have been broadcasting where locals were buying and selling, who the big players were and who was in the pit.[22]

So the news from Chicago, the bastion of free-market principles and the home of "Chicago School of Thought," is that broadcasting trading information to off-the-floor customers – telling them what insiders are buying and selling – gives these customers an "unfair advantage." For a long time, bond traders have also been resisting the pressure of the SEC to report their trades and prices at which they were transacted.

> *Ultimately, under the onslaught of speculative capital, such resistance is doomed.*

Ultimately, under the onslaught of speculative capital, such resistance

---

[21] "'Bandit' Life Gets Tougher for Nasdaq's SOES Traders," *Wall Street Journal*, March 31, 1997, p. C1.

[22] "Headsets Get Toehold in Futures Pits, but Debate Over Their Use Continues," *Wall Street Journal*, August 5, 1996, p. A15B.

is doomed. Futures pit traders, Nasdaq market makers and New York Stock Exchange specialists are merely "inefficiencies" which speculative capital will relentlessly arbitrage away. The pressure might come in the form of high-volume buying and selling or legal action. But regardless of its form, it will be persistent and relentless. The Nasdaq bid/asked controversy, for example, came to a conclusion as a result of legal pressure; the market makers settled a lawsuit by agreeing to pay almost $1 billion in fines:

> A federal judge … granted preliminary approval to 30 securities firms' $910 million settlement of a class-action suit alleging that the firms fixed prices in the past on Nasdaq Stock Market trades … The investors' lawsuit alleged that more than three dozen Nasdaq dealers conspired to widen spreads on trades involving 1,659 stocks.[23]

Under the pressure of speculative capital, even the 1/8 spread in stocks is being eroded. There is no doubt that in coming years, the spreads will be quoted in decimals, thus paving the way for a further decrease in the bid/asked spreads.

> After more than centuries of using a system descended from Spanish pieces of eight, American stock markets now appear to be moving toward having stocks priced … in dollars and cents … If Wall Street does move, it is widely expected that it would lead to better … prices for investors. That gain would come at the expense of brokers, who have resisted the move in the past … A change in pricing could shrink their profit margins.[24]

For a light ending to this topic, let us return to Rudi Weisweiller's *Arbitrage* and listen to him telling us why arbitrage is attractive (1986, p. 8):

> Where then lies the attraction of arbitrage? Surely in this: that the conscientious dealer will seek to be not luckier nor even cleverer than his peers, but consistently harder-working and more vigilant.

Indeed.

---

[23] "Securities Concerns' Settlement of Suit by Investors Wins Backing from Judge," *Wall Street Journal*, December 30, 1997, p. C13.

[24] "Fractions Edge Closer to Wall St Extinction," *Wall Street Times*, June 4, 1998, p. C1.

References

Beidleman, Carl R. (1991) *Interest Rate Swaps*, Homewood, Illinois: Richard D. Irwin.

Dixit, Avinash K. and Pindyck, Robert S. (1994) *Investment Under Uncertainty*, Princeton, NJ: Princeton University Press.

Kothare, Meeta and Laux, Paul A. (1995) "Trading Costs and the Trading Systems for Nasdaq Stocks," *Financial Analysts Journal*, Vol. 51, No. 2, (March/April) pp. 42–53.

Melamed, Leo (1996) *Escape to the Futures*, New York: John Wiley.

Merton, Robert (1994) *Continuous-Time Finance*, Cambridge, Mass.: Blackwell.

Samuelson, Paul and Nordhaus' William (1995) *Economics*, 15th edn, New York: McGraw-Hill.

Tamarkin, Bob (1993) *The Merc: The Emergence of a Global Financial Powerhouse*, New York: Harper Collins.

Weisweiller, Rudi (1986) *Arbitrage: Opportunities and Techniques in Financial and Commodity Markets*, Cambridge, MA: John Wiley.

3

THE RISE OF
SPECULATIVE CAPITAL

**Historical formation of finance capital •
Fundamental problem of international finance •
Bretton Woods system • Rise of finance capital •
Historical formation of speculative capital • Collapse
of Bretton Woods system • Transformation of
hedging to arbitrage • Rise of speculative capital**

Introduction

In the previous chapter we developed various forms of finance capital logically. We must now show that the logical developments have also come to pass historically. That is, the forms of finance capital we developed theoretically *do* exist.

There is little need to prove the existence of credit capital by pointing to 1.5 million bonds in a multi-trillion-dollar market. In that regard, proof belittles the obvious. So is the case with commercial capital, which is the capital of all wholesalers, retailers, importers and exporters. In short, it is any capital that interjects itself between the original producer and final user.

But speculative capital needs pointing out. This most recent form of finance capital is no less a potent force than either credit or commercial capital. Its rise has profoundly affected the financial markets, national economies, politics and the course of the future development of societies. Yet, despite its manifestations being widely felt, the force itself has remained unknown. In this chapter, we will show how speculative capital developed in practice and how it came to rise so rapidly in the past quarter of a century. We begin our investigation from the rise of finance capital proper, as it is from within finance capital that speculative capital was born.

It is from within finance capital that speculative capital was born.

The words "develop" and "rise" will present certain ambiguities. What exactly do these terms mean when applied to the various forms of capital? How could, and why would, finance capital "rise?" If so, what would it rise against and what would such a rise entail?

The answers to these questions will be become clear as we proceed in this chapter. Briefly and by way of introduction, we state that the rise and development, as the social content of these terms implies, refer to social conditions where one or more specific forms of capital are able to appropriate a relatively large share of profits at the expense of other forms.

How could, and why would, finance capital "rise?"

Recall that the amount of profit created in the production is a fixed quantity. At one level, the share of profits from that fixed portion going to each form is decided through bargaining, with the dual weapons of negotiation and confrontation. In our example of the widgets, the greater the price concession the wholesaler is able to extract from the industrialist, the more he will be able to increase his rate of return at the expense of shareholders in the widget factory. Likewise, if the lender is able to demand and get a higher interest rate, he will increase the rate of return of his capital at the expense of commercial and industrial capital.

These negotiations, while taking place in the "market" and between private parties, are conducted in the context of much larger social and economic conditions. When the relations favor one or more specific forms of capital over the other forms, that form is universally able to appropriate a bigger share of profits. Naturally the winner develops a high stake in maintaining the status quo while the "underdog" forms agitate for change. That is politics, whose seamless fusion with finance will become all too clear as we proceed. We begin our investigation from the rise of finance capital proper and its attempt to dethrone industrial capital.

The historical formation of finance capital

In Chapter 2, we reached commercial capital after the cycle of manufacturing capital had come to an end. That sequence is liable to create the false conclusion that commercial capital is somehow "secondary" to manufacturing capital, or subordinate to it. If there were no widgets, there would be no need for commercial capital.

Historically, commercial capital appears long before the rise of industrial production and parallel to production of commodities and simple hand-crafted products. The Silk Road, passing through ancient Persia to China, the caravan routes of the Middle East and the prominence of Venice as a trading center, all attest to this development. The prevailing form of commercial capital in these periods was the merchants' capital. What the merchant appropriated then was a portion of the profit of the producers embedded in the commodities or the products.

When a set of definite social conditions develops, commercial capital has the capacity to operate "independently," with little or no connection to the production of commodities. At times, its dynamics can even influence the production tempo. The examination of these conditions is beyond our subject. We only note briefly that a necessary condition in that regard is the ability of the credit-capital also to operate freely. In the Islamic societies, the strict prohibition against usury crippled credit capital. That is why despite a prosperous merchant class, joining forces of various forms of capital in these societies did not come to full bloom.

> *When a set of definite social conditions develops, commercial capital has the capacity to operate" independently," with little or no connection to the production of commodities.*

In Europe, the primitive form of credit capital – in the person of the usurer – operated relatively freely. Every Anthony had his Shylock. The presence of usurers, together with the mode of transportation of goods – ships instead of camels – paved the way for the rise of finance capital. Bills of ships' cargoes could travel by land and reach the destination faster than the cargo itself. There, the bills, evidence of the ownership of the cargo, were sold at a discount to usurers and money-changers. That is how and why the first banks were established in Venice and financial markets developed in Denmark and England. The discounting of bills of exchange is nothing but finance capital purchasing the widgets priced at $112 for $109. To date, US Treasury bills are traded at a "discount to par."

The early instances of commercial capital dominating the production of commodities appear in the early seventeenth-century maritime centers, where cargoes were shipped from colonies solely for the purpose of trading their bills. It was from there that, along with the rise in trading and commerce, occasional speculative "bubbles" developed in the European trading centers. There is no record of such bubbles in the Middle East despite active trading markets there.

After the industrial revolution, joining of various forms of capital accelerated. By the early twentieth century the trend had resulted in the formation of powerful trusts which were the organization forms of finance capital. J. P. Morgan and John D. Rockefeller represented the two sides of this powerful alliance.

The Allied victory in the war, led by the US, brought about a fundamental shift in the economic relations between nations. It also paved the way for complete dominance of finance capital of production. The instrument of the shift was the Bretton Woods system and the way it tackled the fundamental problem of international finance.

The fundamental problem of international finance

The fundamental problem of international finance is that of the balance of payments.

In international trade, a country's imports and exports are rarely balanced. When there is an imbalance in trade, the value of imports exceeding or falling below exports, the difference must be settled.[1] Unlike in domestic transactions, where this settlement is a matter of simple exchange of the local currency, in international transactions the local currencies would not do. The balance of payments must be settled by the exchange of something of value acceptable to both countries. Until the end of World War II, that something had historically and traditionally been gold, which was accepted as the universal store and measure of value. A country experiencing a deficit with its trading partner would deliver gold to that partner. The physical delivery of gold would zero out the deficit and the partners would begin a new trading cycle.

The fundamental problem of international finance is that of the balance of payments.

The factors that shape the magnitude and direction (whether positive or negative) of a country's balance of payments are many and varied. Their study is outside the scope of this book. This much must be said: when a country experiences a persistent disequilibrium in its balance of payments – when its inflows and outflows show a considerable discrepancy over an extended period of time – it must take measures to remedy

---

[1] This is the definition of balance of trade, which is narrower than balance of payments. Balance of payments is the measure of the difference between annual inflows and outflows from all sources including trade. The distinction is immaterial to us.

the situation. A persistently large deficit means that expenditures out-strip income. This situation cannot continue indefinitely. (In the gold standard, it would require constant shipment of gold, which no country could afford. Even in gold-producing countries, the annual production is limited.)

There are two basic policies for correcting a balance of payments problem: reduce foreign exchange-based expenditures, or manipulate the exchange rate by devaluing the currency. The former curtails the domestic consumption of foreign goods. The latter aims to shift the pain of erasing the deficit to the trading partners. Each of these policies has considerable social, political (and obviously economic) implications not only for the country implementing them but also for its trading partners. The impact is greater if the country in question is a link in the trading chain that connects a group of countries, such as Japan in East Asia or Germany in Europe.

Despite being in the realm of "international finance" and the subject of learned papers, both policies are readily discernible to any financially strapped home maker. They boil down to reducing expenses or paying less by declaring a partial bankruptcy through devaluation. In the latter case, the hope is that the creditors will have to accept, say, 80 percent of what is due to them. Naturally, the devaluing country's trading partners resist the scheme. They might even institute a devaluation of their own to put relations on an equal footing.

It was the competitive devaluation and counter-devaluation, the erec-tion of trade barriers by the European countries and the neglect of these issues by signatories of the World War I armistice, which first set the stage for, and then led to, World War II.

In July 1940, with a confidence which proved premature, Robert Funk, the president of the Reichsbank, offered his plans for the "New Order" – the reconstruction and development of Europe after the war. He said, in part (Van Dormael, 1978, p. 3):

> We will use the same methods of economic policy that have given such remarkable results, both before and during the war, and we will not allow the unregulated play of economic power, which caused such grave difficulties to the German economy, to become active again …
> Money is of secondary importance; the management of the economy

comes first. When the economy is not healthy, the currency cannot be healthy.

Great Britain became concerned about the appeal of Funk's speech to the European masses suffering from recession and unemployment. It commissioned John Maynard Keynes to develop a counter-plan to the German "New Order." It was clear in 1940, and it became clearer still with the passage of the time, that for a British agenda to be taken seriously, the US had to be brought on board. Exchanging views and negotiating technical points between the two powers in the midst of a war proved time consuming. By the time the issues were sufficiently clear to warrant a presentation, World War II was coming to an end, with the US having emerged as the undisputed superpower. In 1944, delegates from 44 countries gathered in the resort town of Bretton Woods, New Hampshire, to hear the Anglo-American plans for the postwar world. The agreement which came out of the conference became known as the Bretton Woods system.

The Bretton Woods system

The Bretton Woods system was a regime of fixed exchange rates built on the twin pillars of gold and the US dollar. It fixed the price of gold at $35 per troy ounce. The US pledged to buy and sell gold to other central banks at that price. Other major currencies were pegged to the dollar and, through the dollar, to gold. Governments were obliged to maintain the parity of their currencies against the dollar within a narrow 1 percent margin in either direction by buying and selling dollars as the need arose.

An enduring myth about the Bretton Woods conference is that it was successful.

An enduring myth about the Bretton Woods conference is that it was successful. Even now, the system is nostalgically held up as the prime example of what can be achieved if nations cooperate or, at least, if the meeting is well planned!

> Bretton Woods was probably the most successful economic conference ever held. One of the main reasons for its success was the years of plan-

ning that went into it. By January 1944, three years of intensive draft-
ing and redrafting by U.S. and U.K. officials had taken place and these
officials had met often to exchange ideas and drafts and to negotiate
their positions. (Kirshner, 1996, p. 3)

This fanciful story has it roots in the high-powered campaign of the US
Treasury Department to portray the conference and the resulting agreement as an achievement that Congress could not but approve. The real
story is considerably more complex.

At the time of the conference and in the years leading up to it, it was
universally recognized that only through cooperation among nations
could prosperity be ensured for all. Cooperation entailed balancing
employment, production, investment and consumption; in short,
planned economic development. These are the factors of concern to
industrial capital, the capital earmarked for production. Funk's speech
that we quoted earlier was constructed on that theme.

In the Bretton Woods conference, the delegates started out by seeking
a plan for coordinated economic development and ended up with a monetary agreement. Edward Bernstein of the US delegation expressed the
US view which had led to the changes:

> We cannot expect to see a balanced expansion of international trade or
> adequate international investment, if countries maintain fluctuating
> exchange rates, if they depreciate their exchanges to secure temporary
> competitive advantages, if they restrict exchange transactions for cur-
> rent trade, and if they block the proceeds of international investment.
> Given orderly, stable and free exchanges, other measures can be taken
> to assure a balanced expansion of trade and investment. (Commercial
> and Financial Chronicles, 1944, p. 2134)

We see that Bernstein is solely concerned with "fluctuating exchange
rates," depreciation of currency, "restricting [foreign] exchange transactions" and "block[ing] the proceeds of international investment." He
starts from "orderly, stable and free exchanges" to arrive at "other measures" to balance expansion of trade and investment. But in fact the
Bretton Woods conference went as far as *barring* the participating governments from adjusting their balance of payments through controlling
their imports and exports and, by extension, production: "the denial of

the right of external balance adjustment by direct controls was central to Bretton Woods System" (Scammell, 1975, p. 114).

How the focus and the outcome of the Bretton Woods conference changed so drastically is best left to a book on one-upmanship. This much must be said: that Harry Dexter White of the Treasury Department was instrumental in engineering the changes. He also managed to put the US dollar on a par with gold without the knowledge of the other delegates. Armand Van Dormael's informative book on Bretton Woods sheds a glaring light on this little-known episode:

> On 28 June [1944 at the pre-Bretton Woods Conference in Atlantic City], Keynes's recommendation that the words "gold and gold-convertible exchange," which appeared in several provisions of the Statement of Principles, be replaced by the words "monetary reserves" was discussed at some length. When asked whether "gold and dollars" would be satisfactory, Keynes said *no* [italics added]. Other currencies would be convertible some time in the future, and the dollar should not be given a special position. White did not take up the matter. (p. 164)

> Then [in the Bretton Woods conference] came Alternative A, p. 16. This alternative, submitted by the American delegate, provided that "The par value of the currency of each member shall be expressed in terms of gold, *as a common denominator, or in terms of gold-convertible currency unit of the weight and fineness in effect on July 1, 1944'* [italics in original]." This alternative was later presented in the official record of the conference (p. 1651) as an American and British proposal, which is not accurate. It was, in fact, one of the numerous alternatives worked out by White and his group. Keynes obviously would never have agreed to the proposal, and he was not aware of it. (p. 202)

> The change from "gold" to "gold and US dollars" was lost in the ninety-six page document the chairman of the delegation would sign a few days later. Whether or not any of them noticed it, or understood its implications, it seems that none of them expressed any reservations about it. Keynes would not find out until later, when he studied the Final Act. (p. 203)

So unbeknown to other delegates, and especially the British delegate,

Harry White inserted "US dollars" into the agreement. In doing so, he could not have been acting on the instruction of his boss, Treasury Secretary Henry Morgenthau. Morgenthau was notoriously uninterested in international affairs and had put White in charge specifically to "make life easier" for himself: "'To make life easier for me,' Morgenthau said to his advisers the day after Pearl Harbor, he intended to put Harry White 'in charge of all foreign affairs for me … I want it in one brain and I want it in Harry White's brain'" (Chace, 1998, p. 98).

The other members of the US delegation had little knowledge of, or interest in, the daily technical meetings, which were sufficiently prolonged and exhausting to give Keynes a mild heart attack. Prior to leaving for Bretton Woods, Dean Acheson, who was representing the State Department at the conference, wrote to his son: "I have to go to the Monetary Conference on July 1 [1944] … Neither I nor the other delegates know what the hell we are doing and we can't get the Treasury to take time off to work it out with us" (ibid., p. 97).

Just on whose behalf White steered the direction of the Bretton Woods agreement away from economic planning and towards a monetary system, and then blatantly tampered with the Articles of Agreement to put the dollar on a par with gold, must be a fascinating story. For all we know, the idea could have been his; one can only speculate as to his motives. What is certain is that his actions influenced the course of history of finance and politics for decades to come.[2]

> *Just on whose behalf White steered the direction of the Bretton Woods agreement away from economic planning and towards a monetary system, must be a fascinating story.*

Acheson might not have been interested in the fine points of international finance but the man who went on to become Truman's Secretary of State was no fool. He read White's strategy, if not his hand. According to Van Dormael (1978, p. 220), when Acheson pointed out to White

---

[2] In the McCarthy era, Harry White was accused of being a communist sympathizer. He was extensively investigated, but no evidence was found against him. He died shortly after.

that the procedures of the conference were – he thought, deliberately – confusing, White disagreed, saying that the "commission on the Fund was 'running as smooth as silk, and I don't know where you get your idea. There is no confusion as far as the Fund is concerned. All the important problems have been settled. They have either gone then –' 'I am sure they have been settled,' snapped Acheson, 'but I don't think the delegates know that.'"

The rise of finance capital in the shadow of the Bretton Woods system

At the time of the Bretton Woods conference, approximately 75 percent of the world stock of gold was in the US. That left little for the rest of the world. In particular, the European countries and Japan did not have nearly sufficient amounts of gold to use in the settlement of their balance of payments. This enhanced the role of the US dollar, which, thanks to the intervention of Harry White, emerged as the "key currency" in the Bretton Woods system. The central banks could now issue notes covered not only by gold but also by their holdings of dollars. For the first time, a national currency had become the means of settling the international balance of payments.

For the first time, a national currency had become the means of settling the international balance of payments.

Although the central banks could convert their dollar reserves to gold, in the years immediately following World War II they had no reason for doing so. The gold stock of the US was more than sufficient to cover its dollar liabilities. Furthermore, the dollars could be put to work by investing in Treasuries in the US which paid interest. That is how the dollar became as good as gold, and, in fact, at times it seemed to surpass the advantages of holding the metal itself.

The Bretton Woods system put the US at a tremendous advantage in the world economic scene. After a balance of payments deficit all other countries had either to spend gold to cover the deficit or reduce their expenditures. The US did not need to do anything because its currency was the means of settling the balance. In fact, a balance of payments deficit which required infusion of dollars could stimulate its economy. Nothing could overcome or match this advantage, which, as the 1950s began, had reached its zenith. The locomotive that was to become finance capital was set in motion.

It was against this background that in 1952 Markowitz published *Portfolio Selection*. This work ostensibly "began" modern finance. But thanks to Harry White, modern finance had already begun in the real world. And on the evidence of his work, Markowitz was not consciously affected by it. He went about merrily comparing standard deviation and stock returns.

An infinitely more perceptive book, published the same year as *Portfolio Selection*, is Cameron Hawley's *Executive Suite*, which was made into a Hollywood movie of the same name a couple of years later. The novel centers on the contest for the office of chief executive between a company's two vice presidents – one of production, the other of finance. Hawley keenly detected the onslaught of a rising tide that was to be finance capital on the established position of industrial capital. The year being 1952, ultimately the VP of production wins the race by a rousing speech about the importance of improving products. But even there, his victory is achieved by appealing to emotions, something that Hollywood captured by casting comely William Holden as the production VP opposite a mean-looking rival in finance. Otherwise, the VP of finance is a more competent and decisive officer. And Hawley gives the most compelling lines to him. He argues, for example, that a tax maneuver of his had saved more money for the stockholders than was possible through any product improvement. These lines foretold what, around the end of the twentieth century, were to become the official recommendations of international panels:

> Companies around the world should adopt American concepts of corporate management, ... an international panel has concluded. The advisory group agreed ... that the chief corporate objective should be to maximize shareholder value.[3]

---

[3] "Firms World-Wide Should Adopt Ideas of US Management, Panel Tells OECD," *Wall Street Journal*, April 2, 1998, p. B17.

In Oliver Stone's 1988 movie, *Wall Street*, there is also a brief speech exalting the virtues of production – the "real work" – and sneering at playing with stocks and bonds. But it is telling that the speech is given by an airline mechanic, a blue-collar worker decidedly not in line for the executive suite. The two movies provide anecdotal evidence of the shift in the balance of power in favor of finance capital in the intervening years.

An avalanche of hard evidence is also there and grows day by day. The wealth of material is such that it is impossible to even list it in the limited pages of this book. J. P. Morgan replacing US Steel as a component of the Dow Jones *Industrial* Average; industrial corporations such as GM and GE establishing financial subsidiaries, a purely industrial corporation (American Can Co.) reinventing itself into a purely financial company (Primerica), banks and bank holding companies being allowed to own industrial corporations, these are all evidence of the various aspects of the rise of finance capital.

The theory of finance is silent on these developments. In fact, it is not even cognizant of them. It happily notes that the business cycles of boom and bust, which had plagued the economy of industrial countries since the eighteenth century, have become less frequent and even seem to be fading. That is a matter of simple measurement at which modern finance excels. But it cannot relate that observation to the decline of manufacturing under the pressure of finance capital. Business cycles are the by-product of an manufacturing and industrial production. As finance capital gains the upper hand, it subjugates manufacturing and industrial production to its own dynamics, hence the fading of business cycles. But as a result of the rise of finance capital, a hitherto non-existent risk – the systemic risk – comes into existence whose dynamics are understood far less than business cycles.

In the US, the far right of the Republican Party reflects the voice of the manufacturers who have been forced to follow the agenda set by finance capital. Patrick Buchanan is the champion of their cause. He laments (Buchanan, 1998) sacrificing people to the "gods of global economy" and advocates a "nationalist" view of production where factories will not move to cheap-labor locations and the American economy will be protected against the flood of foreign goods.

He is advocating a lost cause. His Norman Rockwellian ideal of the economy no longer exists. Neither can it be brought back. In the latter years of the millennium, finance capital has the economies of many countries under its firm grip. What is more, its hold only gets stronger. Here is Deputy Treasury Secretary Lawrence Summers speaking of the benefits of the financial crisis in Southeast Asia before he understood the magnitude of the problem: "'There has been more progress in scaling back the industrial policy programs in these countries in the last several months than there has been in a decade or more of negotiations,' Mr. Summer said".[4]

An examination of these issues falls beyond the subject of our book. Such a study must await another occasion. But before turning to speculative capital, let us return to the terms "rise" and "dominance." In light of what has been covered since then, they should now be easier to understand.

By finance capital rising and dominating industrial production, we mean a state where products are produced (and by extension, industrial capital is employed) in order to serve as a catalyst for the employment of other forms of finance capital.

This disorder in the logical direction of the production–circulation circuit has various forms and degrees. In its simplest form, it assumes the guise of "consumer finance." In this stage, a physical product is used as a "lure" in a transaction whose real aim is extracting interest from the borrowers, who think of themselves as buyers. Witness a news story in the *Wall Street Journal* describing the practice of the consumer finance industry dealing in satellite-TV dishes:

> *Products are produced in order to serve as a catalyst for the employment of other forms of finance capital.*

> That industry aggressively markets loans to lower and middle-income consumers, mostly at double digit interest rates. It is accustomed to the tough end of the credit business: riding herd on loan salesmen so they

---

4 "US Presses Japan to Stimulate Economy," *Wall Street Journal*, February 13, 1998, p. A2.

don't sign up too many deadbeats or trample disclosure laws, and then efficiently collecting the payments.[5]

When conditions are ripe, "consumer finance" becomes sufficiently profitable to discard its original industrial incubator. One such example is General Electric's finance capital arm, which now operates but as an independent unit. It is the most profitable unit of General Electric. The *Wall Street Journal* reports:

> GE Capital isn't a bank [!]. Founded in the 1930s to help customers purchase General Electric products, GE Capital began to diversify in the 1980s. Today, well under 5% of GE Capital's business has to do with its parent ... It has a healthy presence in insurance, equipment financing for middle market companies, consumer insurance, and rein- surance. It contributes 40% of the profit of General Electric.[6]

This is not an exception but a trend that is becoming the norm: "As profit margins on its merchandise shrink under pressure from more efficient rivals such as Wal-Mart, Sears has come to rely heavily on its credit card business for profit."[7]

Consumer finance, no matter how large its size and the diversity of its operation, is still the relatively early stage of the development of finance capital, where it is content to co-exist side by side with industrial capi- tal. Gradually, though, as it grows, it assumes a predatory posture and attacks industrial capital. The junk bond phenomenon of the 1980s and the "reengineering" of corporations which followed were scenes from this battle.

Of course, manufacturers can also fight back. Recall that Drexel's junk bond machinery was effectively crippled. But predatory finance capital is not dependent on one individual or institution; it appears in other forms and under various guises. The *New York Times* describes

---

[5] "Lenders Probably Wish They Had Never Heard of Big Satellite Dishes," *Wall Street Journal*, October 15, 1997, p. A1.

[6] "Low-Key GE Capital Expands in Europe,"*Wall Street Journal*, September 17, 1998, p. A18.

[7] "Sears Agrees to Sell to Citigroup Unit 81% Stake in Furniture-Store Chain," *Wall Street Journal*, November 20, 1998, p. A6.

how "two guys in a hurry" can build a hotel empire without actually building hotels:[8]

> J. Willard Marriott built his ... empire from a root beer stand ... Conrad Hilton turned a $5,000 investment ... into one of the world's best-known hotel empires ... So much for humble beginnings. Today ... the hotel moguls ... need ... control of ... a paired-share real estate investment trust. Most people don't have a clue what that is, of course, and that is where two improbable magnates – ... a financial whiz from Connecticut who is the son of a Holocaust survivor ... and a lawyer from Brooklyn ... have a great advantage: They do.[9]

The most recent example of the onslaught of finance capital on a traditionally independent segment of the economy is the development in the US pertaining to the so-called healthcare industry – the much heralded "1/7th of the nation's economy." Finance capital, in the form of health maintenance organizations, targets the practice of medicine with the aim of appropriating a share of the profit that went to physicians. The development has nothing to do with either quality or

> *Finance capital, in the form of health maintenance organizations, targets the practice of medicine with the aim of appropriating a share of the profit that went to physicians.*

---

[8] "Hiltons They Aren't: 2 Guys In a Hurry," *New York Times*, September 7, 1997, Section 3, p. 1.

[9] Building hotel empires through paired-share real estate investment trusts has its perils. The empire becomes vulnerable to notoriously frequent changes in Congressional tax policy: "The Clinton administration and congressional leaders have agreed to curb an increasingly popular corporate-tax loophole involving manipulation of real-estate investment trusts. The unusual bipartisan move effectively blocks an 'abusive transaction that threatens the corporate tax base,' said ... the Treasury Department's top tax official." "Clinton, Congressional Leaders Agree to Curb Tax Loophole Involving REITs," *Wall Street Journal*, May 26, 1998, p. A4.

More importantly, this business becomes dependent not on the real estate market but on the stock market: "An odd thing is happening in the commercial real-estate market: Rents are rising, but the prices of office towers, apartment buildings and hotels are beginning to come down for the first time in six years. The decline reflects the recent tumult in global capital markets." "Commercial-Property Market Cools Off," *Wall Street Journal*, September 21, 1998, p. A2.

quantity of care: "Managed care has so far served as a different way to pay for medical care, not a better way to provide it."[10]

Having sensed the threat, physicians have begun to join unions to resist the pressure of health management companies. The battle, however, is an uphill one. Barring an intervention by the government, there is little doubt that they will eventually succumb to finance capital and become generally prosperous workers rather than the always prosperous small business owners that they are now. The writing is on the wall:

> Over the last five years, as managed care has transformed American medicine, the independence of doctors has often been the first thing to go. Last year [1997], 92 percent of the nation's physicians had some type of managed-care contract ... "Capitated" contracts, which pay a set fee for each patient, accounted for one-third of the average doctor's salary. Five years earlier, capitation was ... so negligible that [the American Medical Association] did not bother keeping tabs on it.[11]

Finance capital operates without any regard to industrial capital.

The most extreme form of "independence" of finance capital – its break, really – from the production circuit comes about when its speculative capital component develops. At that stage, finance capital operates without any regard to industrial capital.

The historical formation of speculative capital

We saw that in the course of his speculation, the speculator discovered arbitrage. He could earn a risk-free profit by buying widgets low and simultaneously selling them high. But arbitrage under the condition of our example cannot take place. The speculator could not buy widgets low and, _at the same time_, sell them high. Arbitraging in this way presupposes the existence of a legion of utterly ignorant and foolish play-

---

[10] "Reality of the H.M.O. System Doesn't Live Up to the Dream," _New York Times_, Octoer 5, 1998, p. A1.

[11] "As Doctors Trade Shingle for Marquee, Cries of Woe," _New York Times_, August 3, 1998, p. A1.

ers in the market who would be handing over their money to the specu-lators. The wholesaler could buy low and sell high in the context of his commercial activities, when there is a time lag between his purchase and sale. But the speculator could not do so *simultaneously*. So while the urge to earn riskless profit always lived in the bosom of finance capital, in the primitive markets of the eighteenth and nineteenth centuries the practice could not take place. The rise of speculative capital had to wait for historically ripe conditions.

The first sign of arbitrage in the current meaning of the word appeared early in the twentieth century. The expansion of trade which followed the rapid pace of industrialization created a strong base for finance cap-ital. Modes of transportation also improved, so prices could rapidly be communicated from one place to another. These factors allowed for establishing exchanges in the major European cities where stocks, options and currencies were traded. The requirements for arbitrage were now in place. Upon discovering a price discrepancy for the same com-modity or currency in two different countries, speculators could arbi-trage the difference and generate a riskless profit.

Early in the century, a book on arbitrage taught the tricks of the busi-ness to its readers:

> When one of the prices is expressed in foreign money ... the working out of the difference is more complicated ... thorough knowledge of all usage, and quickness at figures in order to work out rapidly the differ-ence in the prices are therefore essential qualifications for a capable Arbitrageur. (Deutsch, 1910, pp. xiv–xv)

"Quickness at figures" is now a "qualification for a capable Arbitrageur" because the source of profitability of arbitrage is hidden in the relation between the two rates and requires some calculation to be determined.

Still, in the primitive markets of the early twentieth century, the opportunities for arbitrage were limited. Until 1945, the gold standard, currency controls, competitive devaluation of currencies and erection of trade barriers prevented speculative trading in currency markets – the cradle of speculative capital – from forming. After World War II, finance capital came of age but, again, the fixed exchange rates left no room for arbitrage.

In 1971, the Bretton Woods system began to unravel. The environment of free-floating currencies which followed provided the fertile ground for the rise of speculative capital.

The collapse of the Bretton Woods system

Within the framework of the Bretton Woods system, the US took full advantage of its privileged position: it ran large and persistent balance of payments deficits. The deficits were covered by dollars which then found their way into foreign central banks. Successive US administrations claimed that the large deficits were necessary for providing liquidity that was needed to facilitate the economic recovery in Europe. Europeans countered that the US got a free ride at their expense by purchasing goods and paying for them with paper. Whatever the merits of claims and counterclaims, the fact remains that the quantitity of dollars on the balance sheets of central banks snowballed.

These dollars, while assets for foreign central banks, were the liability of the US. They had to be exchanged for gold on demand by the holders. As the amount of dollars increased, foreign central bankers became concerned that the US did not have sufficient gold to cover its liabilities; it could not exchange the existing dollars at the rate of $35 per ounce of gold.

The details of the events which led to the breakdown of the Bretton Woods system are outside our concern. These events are discussed in myriad books and articles written since 1971, some with more clarity and competence than others.[12] Even a cursory glance at the index of the

---

[12] A popular textbook on international economics explained the concept of "key currency" and the reasons for its existence: "Instead of gold ... the central reserve assets could consist of a national currency ... The most obvious reason for preferring a national currency over a commodity is that the former may be more easily managed in regard to its supply and valuation[!]" (Walter and Areskoug, 1987, p. 463.)

It is interesting that not one book discusses the relation between the "oil price shocks" and the increase in dollar reserves. Even an informed observer such as Paul Volker treats the quadrupling of the oil price in 1974 as an arbitrary decision by the OPEC members without linking it in any way to the collapse of the Bretton Woods system. The following equation, expresses the relation between dollar and oil before "price shocks:" 1 barrel of oil = $2. If the left hand side of the equation increases, the result is an "oil glut:" the oil price decreases. If, on the other hand, the right hand side

New York Times or *Wall Street Journal* for the 1960s points to a rapid deterioration of the Bretton Woods system, which began with concern about the flight of dollars from the US as the Kennedy administration took office and became a full-blown crisis by the end of the decade.

By 1968, dollars were being dumped wholesale in the expectation of devaluation. The flight to quality from the dollar to more stable currencies transferred the pressure to foreign central banks, as they were forced to preserve the exchange rate of their currency with the dollar. The dollar reserves, which had hitherto been assets, turned into liabilities.[13]

The editorial pages in the US were filled with articles attacking the Bretton Woods system. The exchange of gold for dollars was criticized as insupportable and unsound. Gold was denounced as a "barbaric relic." The opinions of Milton Friedman, a proponent of floating exchange rates, became more vocal and were given prominence.

Cut the relation of gold and dollar, let the currencies fall where they may, the arguments went, and everything else would be fine. In fact, one of the most "persuasive" arguments in favor of floating exchange rates was that setting exchange rates at the market-determined "equilibrium" level would automatically eliminate the balance of payments deficit!

President Nixon is much maligned for destroying the Bretton Woods system. But the relation between the man and the event is accidental. The crisis in the Bretton Woods system happened to reach breaking point on his watch. He was left with no options, as there was simply not enough gold to cover the mass of dollars in circulation, whether at $42.50 per ounce or even $50. In a televised speech on August 15, 1971, he announced his plans for combating inflation that included a wage

---

increases, it is a "dollar glut:" the price of dollars expressed in oil decreases, meaning that the price of oil will *increase*. The latter case, however, is not a "dollar glut." It is called an "oil crisis."

[13] This conversion of asset to liability is an exquisite example of how a category in dialectics turns into its opposite. US lawmakers prove themselves dialecticians of the first order when the need arises to put this abstract concept to work: "In ... 1989 legislation ... [gave] the savings and loans permission to use an unusual accounting rule that had the effect of letting many institutions satisfy their capital requirements by booking huge liabilities as assets." "The Debacle that Buried Washington," *New York Times*, November 22, Section 3, p. 1.

freeze. Almost in passing, he also mentioned that he was suspending the convertibility of the dollar to gold. That was the beginning of the end of the Bretton Woods system. The central banks that were holding dollar reserves thus found themselves in possession of the proverbial paper without the possibility of its conversion to gold.

For the next two years, the US Federal Reserve, working with the central banks in Western Europe and Japan, tried to prevent a complete collapse of the system. At the Smithsonian conference in late 1971, they agreed to raise the price of gold to $38.50, thus devaluing it by 10 percent. The margin for exchange fluctuations was also raised to 2.25 percent at the insistence of the US. But the system was doomed. At the time of the Smithsonian conference, foreign central banks held $50 billion in dollar reserves. The gold stock of the US stood at only $10 billion.

In June 1972, Great Britain was forced to float the pound sterling. Other currencies soon followed. By the end of 1973, the last remnants of the system had disintegrated. The currencies were thrown into the market to find their equilibrium level. The markets, and not the governments, were to be the arbiters of exchange rates.

The transformation of hedging to arbitrage: the rise of speculative capital

There had been other times when currencies had been volatile, but the environment of the 1970s was drastically different. Now, there were large multinational corporations whose activities spanned the four corners of the world. These corporations operated from plans put together after careful analysis. In the post-Bretton Woods chaos, it became impossible to plan with any degree of confidence. An adverse exchange-rate movement could wipe out the hard-earned profits of a full quarter or even a year. There had to be a regulating mechanism. In the absence of government authority, the only remaining source of discipline was private finance – finance capital – which stepped in and assumed the role of regulator.

The transfer of responsibility was neither planned nor conscious. Finance capital is a concept. It can no more assume responsibility than it can walk or eat. That is why many, including the financier George Soros, deride those who attribute a "will" to the market and speak of it as though it were a live entity. But perhaps the intuition of the masses should not be dismissed too hastily! It turns out that the markets do have a will, and finance capital *can* regulate markets if both the will and the regulation are understood in the context of Adam Smith's invisible hand. As Smith is hardly ever read – much less understood – no one ever asks how exactly the invisible hand works and what the consequences of its working are.

Governments achieve stabilization through decree; finance capital does it through arbitrage. Arbitrage is the act of buying low and selling high. If for whatever reason a currency is deemed undervalued against, say, the dollar, the currency speculators sell dollars and buy the undervalued currency. In doing so, they drive up the undervalued currency and restore equilibrium to the market. In the absence of government regulation, arbitrage-induced equilibrium is the regulator of markets.

The working of the invisible hand in the form of arbitrage began sufficiently innocently, when, in the post-Bretton Woods era, corporations set out to insulate themselves against currency fluctuations through hedging.

> *Governments achieve stabilization through decree; finance capital does it through arbitrage.*

That was the logical thing to do. An international company such as IBM which knew it would need a billion Japanese yen in six months could not risk a sharp rise in the yen. So it would call its traditional banker – till then it had always been J. P. Morgan – and buy six-month forward yen at the prevailing price. In the intervening months, if the yen rose, IBM was insulated, as J. P. Morgan would compensate it for the difference between the market rate and the forward price of yen.

J. P. Morgan, in turn, had to hedge itself; it could not afford to leave its yen position open to a rise in the yen. That meant that it had to find a counterparty needing or willing to sell a billion yen, six months forward. Of course, the new forward had to be struck at a slightly more favorable rate to the bank. Otherwise, it would be left with nothing to show by way of profit in two forwards. If such a counterparty could be found, J. P. Morgan would be locked in a profitable hedge position. It would be insulated against the yen fluctuations and, at the same time, it could pocket the spread between the two trades. What would happen to the last counterparty if yen rose was strictly the counterparty's problem, as long as it made good on its obligation to deliver.

It did not matter to J. P. Morgan where the counterparties to its two trades were physically located. The request for the initial forward could come from IBM Japan and the second, hedge forward could be struck in Germany. The bank, furthermore, knew the exchange rate of the yen in Tokyo and Germany. The global network of banks had put them in a unique situation where they could see the rates for a given currency in different parts of the globe. If a rate difference existed between two locations, they could arbitrage the difference. They would buy the currency in the cheaper location and *simultaneously* sell it in the expensive one. This was a dream come true for arbitrageurs. The practice seemed to have no risk. In arbitraging the same currency with the same due dates, the banks' assets and liabilities were matched. The bank was left with a profitable spread. The golden era of riskless profits had begun.

The most important aspect of arbitrage trading is that the practice develops logically from hedging and, on paper, is indistinguishable from it. A brief technical description of the transformation helps with understanding this crucial point.

> *The most important aspect of arbitrage trading is that the practice develops logically from hedging and, on paper, is indistinguishable from it.*

The purpose of hedging is to insulate the owners' equity against the adverse changes in the markets. The owners' equity is the difference between a firm's assets and liabilities. (The same difference in the case of individuals is called "net worth.") We can express this fundamental accounting relation by the following equation:

$$\text{Owners' Equity} = \text{Assets} - \text{Liabilities} \qquad \text{Eq. (3.1)}$$

The requirement and condition of hedging that the owners' equity remain constant is the same as saying that it should not change. Or, its change must be zero.

$$\textit{change}\ (\text{Owners' Equity}) = 0 \qquad \text{Hedge condition}$$

For that condition to hold, the change in the right hand side of the accounting relation, Eq. (3.1), must also be zero. That is:

$$change \text{ (Assets)} - change \text{ (Liabilities)} = 0$$

or

$$change \text{ (Assets)} = change \text{ (Liabilities)} \qquad \text{Eq. (3.2)}$$

Eq. (3.2) shows the requirement for a hedge: the change in the value of assets must be equal to the change in the value of liabilities. That is called "matching" assets and liabilities.

The purpose of hedging is preserving the owners' equity. The hedger begins with an existing asset (liability) and seeks to find a liability (asset) which will offset its adverse price changes.

The purpose of arbitrage, by contrast, is profit. The arbitrageur has neither an asset nor a liability. To that end, he uses the final relation of the hedge in Eq. (3.2) to search for *any two* positions which will enable him to "lock in" a spread. Hedging and arbitrage are *mathematically indistinguishable*. What *logically* separates them is the purpose of each act which translates itself to the *sequence* of execution of trades. When done sequentially, the act is defensive hedging. When done simultaneously, it is aggressive arbitrage. Otherwise, the transformation of one to the other is seamless.

For evidence that transformation from hedging to arbitrage did take place in real life, let us listen to a certain Mr Murray, reminiscing about his old institution, Citibank, in a context that does not at all seem to be related to our subject:

> Alan P. Murray ... remembers the 1970s at Citibank, "where the budget was build around the bank's own forecast." Today, Citibank ... has virtually abandoned in-house forecasting in favor of risk management. Rather than predicting interest rates and then borrowing and lending accordingly, for example, the bank matches liabilities against assets in way intended to protect the bottom line no matter what happens to interest rates.[14]

---

[14] "This Model Was Too Rough," *New York Times*, February 1, 1996, p. D1.

There are two issues in this story. One is matching assets and liabilities to protect the bottom line "no matter what happens to interest rates." We will return to this curious belief later, when we examine basis risk. For now, let us focus on the shift of trading strategy in Citibank. We learn from Murray that Citibank abandoned forecasting in favor of risk management. But forecasting and risk management are two very different things. How could one replace the other?

Forecasting is a tool for action. Its purpose is to provide a "most likely" scenario, and therefore a view, that can serve as the basis for investment decisions. The view might be derived from econometric forecast, fundamental analysis or reading tea leaves, but there must be a view that *precedes* the action. That precedence is a logical necessity, as even a decision of "no action" follows the view that markets will remain at their present level.

Citibank made its investment decisions on the basis of its own in-house forecasts. Then, it "virtually abandoned in-house forecasting in favor of risk management." But how can "risk management" – by which both Murray and Citibank understand asset-liability matching – become a substitute for forecasting?

The immediate answer is that it cannot. Asset-liability matching is an "after the fact" operation; it presumes prior existence of either assets or liabilities. But to have acquired either assets or liabilities, there must have been a view about the direction of the markets that preceded the acquisition. But the bank abandoned forecasting that was necessary for forming his view. We seem to be in a vicious circle with no logical way out.

Of course, there is one way to trade in financial markets without the need for forecasting *and* at the same time match assets and liabilities: match them first and *then* acquire them. That is precisely what Citibank does. Specifically, the bank first identifies two sets of targets whose difference, after accounting for all technical factors, allows it to "lock in" a profit. It then proceeds to trade the targets, acquiring them as assets and liabilities. If the execution of trades is successful, the bank would have a set of matched assets and liabilities and, at the same time, would have locked in a profitable spread between the two.

The fine line separating hedging and arbitrage, and why and how one is turned into the other, has completely escaped the attention of theorists. As a result, whenever a combination of long and short positions results in a loss, the defenders and critics of the strategy engage in exchanges that amount to deciding whether zebras are white animals with black stripes or black animals with white stripes. One such case was the controversy over the losses in the American subsidiary of the German trading firm Metallgesellschaft. The *New York Times* explains the case and the source of controversy:

> When Deutsche Bank whisked Metallgesellschaft ... from the brink of ruin, most observers accepted the bank's version of events: A bunch of financial cowboys ... were making hugely risky bets with oil futures. When an unexpected plunge in oil prices threatened staggering losses, Deutsche Bank, Metallgesellschaft's biggest shareholder ... fired the old management, brought in a SWAT team to liquidate the bets ... and lent the company money to cover the losses ... Now three American financial sleuths ... are saying that the Deutsche Bank is the culprit. It misunderstood a prudent, fully hedged ... strategy ... and in a blind panic, sold off the hedges with catastrophic consequences.[15]

Neither the supporters nor the critics of Metallgesellschaft's strategy understood why what was a risky bet to one side appeared as prudent hedging to the other.

The timing of the change in Citibank's trading strategy is familiar to us. In fact, we could have accurately guessed it without Murray's help. The change was triggered by the collapse of the Bretton Woods system, which released a tidal wave of uncertainty. The decision to change was obviously made by the bank's executives. But in so deciding, they we reacting to circumstances beyond their control and thus acting as the agents of the invisible hand. The logical hedging strategies that they had set up gradually turned into arbitrage trading from which speculative capital was born.

Needless to say, Citibank was not the only institution to embark upon "matching assets and liabilities." All the major banks and brokerage houses followed the same path. They established "proprietary trading"

---

[15] "The Oil-Futures Bloodbath: Is the Bank the Culprit?," *New York Times*, October 16, 1994, p. F5.

operations and ventured into arbitrage trading. To some bankers, it appeared that the nature of their business had changed:

> In 1992, [J. P. Morgan] had losses of between $200 and $300 million in arcane mortgage-backed securities ... The mistake prompted Morgan to rethink how it manages its risks, and in late 1992, it put together a new corporate risk committee that elevated market risk to the same level of importance as credit risk ... "These days, the business of banking *is* risk management," says Mr. Weatherstone [then chairman of J. P. Morgan].[16]

We see the familiar "risk management" strategy, which, the then chairman of J. P. Morgan declares, was now the "business" of banking. What he meant to say was that arbitrage trading by employing speculative capital is now the primary source of revenue of major banks such as J. P. Morgan. That is an accurate assessment of the business of an institution where approximately 70 percent of revenues were generated from trading.

Chase Manhattan Bank followed in the same footsteps: "Trading in ... foreign currencies, interest rate contracts and bonds, specially emerging-markets bonds – contributed $1.91 billion of the $2.59 billion in revenue that Chase's global-markets business brought in during the first three quarters of 1997."[17]

The new trading strategy was quickly adopted by the brokerage houses.[18] With their ready capital, trading facilities and resources, they were the logical next-in-lines. As just one example, we read about Salomon's "famed" fixed-income arbitrage group. The fame of the group came from the size of its bets and bonuses.

> Wall Street professionals are buzzing over the $23 million in salary and bonus paid to ... a bespectacled 31-year old "rocket scientist" or high-tech trader, in Salomon's bond-arbitrage group ... [that] makes its

---

[16] "Risk Management Has Become Crucial In a Year When Strategies Proved Wrong," *Wall Street Journal*, September 29, 1994, p. C1.

[17] "Chase's Global Pit Boss," *New York Times*, January 16, 1998, p. D1.

[18] Ken Auletta's *Greed and Glory on Wall Street* (1986) that chronicled the fall of Lehman Brothers is an early and readable account of the rise of speculative capital.

money by making huge bets – positions totalling billions of dollars – on tiny price discrepancies between different securities.[19]

This story precisely defines arbitrage and speculative capital. "Making huge bets – positions totaling billions of dollars – on tiny price discrepancies between different securities" is the essence of employing speculative capital. The increasing size of the bet is the necessary counteract to shrinking spreads. By its very operation, arbitrage tends to reduce and finally eliminate the differences which give rise to it.

> *Arbitrage tends to reduce and finally eliminate the differences which give rise to it.*

> Of late, Long Term Capital [a hedge fund] had been devoting much of its efforts to so-called convergence trades, betting that the difference between government-bond yields of weak and strong European economies would narrow ... "Everyone who played in these markets made a lot of money," says ... an analyst ... "But these bets have largely gone away as the differences in European interest rates have narrowed significantly."[20]

To compensate for the shrinkage of profit margins, the size of the capital must constantly increase. This paves the way for the emergence of an organization form to specifically accommodate speculative capital. Hence, the private partnership pools of capital known as "hedge funds" appear on the scene. The number of investors in these funds is limited to 499 – recently increased from 99 – and the investors must be "qualified," meaning that they must meet minimum net worth requirements. In return, the funds are exempt from various registration requirements of the SEC that mutual funds must comply with. And unlike mutual funds where the strategy of the fund is spelled out in detail, hedge fund managers have a virtual *carte blanche* for their investment decisions. The need for that freedom is dictated by the requirements of speculative

---

[19]"Roaring '90s? Here Comes Salomon's $23 Million Man," *Wall Street Journal*, January 7 1991, p. C1.

[20] "Hedge Fund to Shrink Capital of $6 Billion by Nearly Half," *Wall Street Journal*, September 22, 1997, p. C1.

capital, which must be nimble and capable of being readily employed as situations arise.

There has always been a mystery of sorts as to why hedge funds, whose investments are generally high risk, carry the adjective "hedge" in their name. In the early days of their appearance, hedge fund managers arbitraged various markets by taking simultaneous long and short positions.

The growth of hedge funds is testimony to the growth of speculative capital.

The strategy appeared, and for the sake of marketing was promoted, as hedging, hence the name hedge fund. Later, believing that a simultaneous long and short position was indeed riskless, the managers of some of the hedge funds borrowed a meaningless term from option valuation and promoted their investing strategy as "risk neutral."

The growth of hedge funds is testimony to the growth of speculative capital. Reporting on hedge funds in 1994, *Business Week* wrote: "Hedge funds are among the fastest-growing segments of Wall Street ... the total number of hedge funds, and their assets, is probably much higher than generally estimated: 3000 funds with assets exceeding $160 billion." The article then went on to add an important point:

> The trading of the large hedge funds is overshadowed by the trading of banks and brokerages, many of which also take leveraged bets in the market ... The only genuine difference between hedge funds and the proprietary trading operations of the big institutions is that hedge funds are much smaller.[21]

Indeed, the size of speculative capital in hedge funds is dwarfed by the capital that banks and financial institutions have earmarked for "proprietary trading."

Growth in size translates to growth in influence, as speculative capital gradually comes to impact the financial markets and, from there, national economies. The impact comes about in two ways. One is from the "unintentional," the incidental effects which follow from the operation of a large pool of capital in pursuit of arbitrage opportunities. The

---

[21] "Fall Guys, Business Week," *Business Week*, April 25, 1994, p. 116.

other is "by design," when speculative capital in the person of its bene-
ficiaries moves to change the rules and regulations to widen its profit-
making opportunities. The interaction of these multiple influences
creates a dynamic which, to those unaware of speculative capital, takes
the form of some mystifying, inexorable phenomenon: "In a speech full
of echoes of his long-ago association with free-market political philoso-
pher Ayn Rand, Mr. Greenspan celebrated 'a significant and seemingly
inexorable trend toward market capitalism and political systems that
stress the rule of law.'"[22]

But all is not well with the operation of speculative capital as it has a
self-destructive aspect as well. Over time, the interaction of its multiple
influences on markets, law, regulation and politics, puts the financial
markets on the path toward a system-wide collapse. That is the systemic
risk we will examine in the final chapter of this book. But first, we must
understand how speculative capital influences the markets.

References

Auletta, Ken (1986) *Greed and Glory on Wall Street*, New York: Random House.

Buchanan, Patrick J. (1998) *The Great Betrayal: How American Sovereignty and Social Justice Are Sacrificed to the God of Global Economy*, New York: Little Brown.

Chace, James (1998) *Acheson*, New York: Simon & Schuster.

Commercial and Financial Chronicles (1944) "Bernstein Commends Bretton Woods Plans," November 16, p. 2134.

Deutsch, Henry (1910) *Arbitrage in Bullions, Coins, Bills, Stocks, Shares and Options*, London: Effingham Wilson.

Hawley, Cameron (1952) *Executive Suite*, Boston: Houghton Mifflin.

Kirshner, Orin (1996) *The Bretton Woods–GATT System: Retrospect and Prospect After Fifty Years*, Armonk, NY:M. E. Sharpe.

Scammell, W. M. (1975) *International Monetary Policy*, London: Macmillan.

Van Dormael, Armand (1978) *Bretton Woods: Birth of a Monetary System*, New York: Holmes and Meier.

Walter, Ingo and Areskoug, Kaj (1981) *International Economics*, New York: John Wiley.

---

[22] "Greenspan Sees Asian Woes Aiding Free Markets," *Wall Street Journal*, April 3, 1998, p. A2.

4

SPECULATIVE CAPITAL'S IMPACT ON MARKETS

Increased volatility • Linkage of national and international markets • Impact beyond financial markets on: central banks, public institutions, corporations, farming and society

Introduction

U nlike the other forms of capital which are logically grown from, and are thus historically connected with, production, speculative capital is born from arbitrage trading. It has no connection to either the production or circulation process of commodities and products.

The word "connection" must not be understood to mean that speculative capital and the mainstream economic activities do not cross paths. They do. The point is that the driving force and lodestar of speculative capital are the arbitrage opportunities between markets, products, currencies, rates, etc. So it does not follow the tempo of, say, merchants' commercial capital or bankers' credit capital. Commercial activity might be slow and lending to business down to a trickle, but all the while speculative capital could be reaping handsome profits. The only condition is the existence of arbitrage opportunities. Precisely for that reason – because the speed and direction of movement of speculative capital are unlike those of mainstream economic activities – it can affect these activities the most. The randomness inherent in the movement of speculative capital cannot but be keenly felt by the cyclical economic activities.

Because the speed and direction of movement of speculative capital are unlike those of mainstream economic activities – they can affect these activities the most.

In this chapter, we examine those influences of speculative capital that materialize automatically from its operation. They naturally begin from financial markets but soon, as speculative capital grows, extend to all markets and then beyond, to society at large.

Increased volatility

We use the term "speculative capital" to refer to capital employed in arbitrage. Such capital is not a single entity. Nor does it have a command and control center. A large number of private fund managers and institutions control various pools of speculative capital. They all have access to the same information. When a profit opportunity opens up, they direct their capital towards it. If the British pound, for example, seems vulnerable, hundreds of funds would bet on its devaluation using swaps, forwards, options and futures.

The rush of fund managers to position themselves in a profitable arbitrage situation overshadows the mathematical exactness of the arbitrage, with the result that the target is overshot; the undervalued currency becomes relatively overvalued. So the process is repeated in reverse. As a result, we have the constant ebbs and flows of money directed from one market to another that seek to arbitrage the spreads and, in doing so, restore "equilibrium" to the markets:

> All week long, traders have been jumping from one currency to another. On Wednesday, they couldn't get enough sterling after Britain raised its key lending rate. Earlier in the week, market players were gobbling up marks amid concern over Europe's planned single currency. "There is a lot of switching out of hedge funds. We're seeing the speculative part of the cash flow which is creating this foreign-exchange volatility," said [the] ... vice president of foreign exchange at Wells Fargo Bank in San Francisco.[1]

But if the equilibrium is restored, there can be no arbitrage opportunities and speculative capital must sit idle. Idleness brings no profits and speculative capital cannot self-destruct in this way. So it looks for new "inefficiencies" and, in doing so, it disturbs the prevailing equilibrium and creates volatility. *Volatility is the result of the attempts of speculative capital to restore equilibrium to markets.*

For a real-life example of this phenomenon, we look at the case of the exchange rate between the dollar and the yen beginning in 1996 and continuing to 1997.

Idleness brings no profits and speculative capital cannot self-destruct.

By way of background, strengthening the dollar against the yen was the hallmark of the policy of US Treasury Secretary Robert Rubin. From his first days in the Clinton administration, Rubin, a former partner and currency

---

[1] "Swiss Franc Tumbles Amid Warnings From Officials That It Is Overvalued," *Wall Street Journal*, November 1, 1996, p. C24.

trader at Goldman Sachs, advocated a "strong dollar policy," tirelessly arguing that a strong dollar was in the "national interest." By September 1996, the dollar had begun to improve against the yen. The same month, the *New York Times* examined the secret of Rubin's success:

> Mr Rubin's first, tentative efforts to bolster the dollar ... failed; the intervention was washed away by investors who knew that the governments did not have the resources to outbid them. So he and his deputy ... retreated ... Then, when the dollar had fallen off the front pages and the market's attention was elsewhere, they ambushed the currency speculators, ordering the Treasury to buy dollars. The idea was to sow so much uncertainty about the Treasury's tactics that no big speculators or hedge funds would risk being caught with a huge position in yen.[2]

So the Treasury Secretary of the United States fixes the exchange rate of the dollar against the yen by sowing uncertainty about that exchange rate!

Intervention in the currency markets has always been a component of the policy of governments. In the Bretton Woods era, central banks repeatedly bought and sold currencies with the aim of influencing the exchange rates. But those interventions were always a part of an overall plan that had various economic and even legal dimensions. Intervention in currency markets was either a "last resort" step – it came after the political actions had failed to cure an exchange rate imbalance – or a complementary tactical move in conjunction with broad policies.

Now, intervention in the currency markets and "sowing uncertainty" about exchange rates are the policy. Exchange rate manipulation is both the strategy and the tactic, with the result that central banks and treasury departments gradually turn into large hedge funds and "join the game."

Let us now pick up the story in early 1997, when the dollar has surged against the yen and concerns are being voiced about the *strength* of the dollar. Rubin again hints at "sowing uncertainty," this time in the opposite direction:

---

[2] "An Old Wall Street Pro's Voice in the Campaign," *New York Times*, September 22, 1996, Section 3, p. 1.

Allies Welcoming US Hint At Pause In Dollar's Surge

Mr Rubin, the most seasoned market player among the finance ministers because of his long career at Goldman, Sachs & Company, was clearly trying on Friday to sow fear in the markets that a surprise intervention in the markets by the United States and its trading partners is possible. That fear alone could keep the dollar from rising further ... Independent analysts agree that the dollar's current value in relationship to the mark and yen is about right.[3]

(February 9, 1997)

But if the "dollar's current value in relationship to the mark and yen is about right," arbitrage trading between the two must theoretically come to an end. So the dollar's surge continues. Traders know that "sowing uncertainty" has its limits:

Dollar Continues Its Climb as Traders Defy G-7's Accord to Slow Its Advance

In congressional testimony, Treasury Secretary Robert Rubin said the dollar had "come back into a normal range" and "corrected itself" after earlier misalignment ... Traders said the dollar dipped following his remarks and then rallied when they realized it wasn't headed any lower.[4]

(February 12, 1997)

Continued Rise In the Dollar May Compel Officials to Act

Treasury Secretary Robert E. Rubin and his allies in the Group of Seven industrial nations are trying to rein in the dollar, which has jumped 14 percent against the German mark and 16 percent against the Japanese yen in the last year.[5]

(February 13, 1997)

Two months later, the dollar's surge continues. The Treasury Secretary voices "concern":

---

[3] *New York Times*, p. A1.
[4] *Wall Street Journal*, p. C22.
[5] *New York Times*, p. D1.

Rubin for First Time Shows "Concern" On Dollar's Sustained Rise Against Yen

In a cautiously worded statement, Mr. Rubin tried to make clear that the US government hasn't been encouraging a further rise by the dollar, which has soared nearly 50% against the yen in the past two years.[6]

(April 11, 1997)

One month later, the concern turns to warning:

Treasury Head Rubin Warns of Currencies Getting "Out of Sync"

Treasury Secretary Robert Rubin yesterday warned of currencies getting "out of sync" with economic fundamentals and said such a state could negatively affect the global trading system.[7]

(May 5, 1997)

Finally, after a surge of 50 percent, the dollar "stabilizes." By then, Rubin's warning about the strong dollar negatively affecting the global trading systems has come to pass. A crisis is looming in Southeast Asia and speculative capital turns there:

Speculators Press Attack On South Asian Countries

Currency speculation continued to take a toll on South and Southeast Asian economies yesterday, as the Indonesian rupiah tumbled as much as 7 percent.[8]

(July 22, 1997)

and:

Currency War Survivors Scan Battlefield

[Traders] are scrambling to figure out which currency is likely to be next on hit lists drawn up by hedge funds and then adopted by frightened local traders.[9]

(July 28, 1997)

---

[6] *Wall Street Journal*, p. A2.
[7] *Wall Street Journal*, p. A4.
[8] *New York Times*, p. D15.
[9] *Wall Street Journal*, p. C1.

The sudden rush of capital to buy or sell a currency or commodity is too obvious to go unnoticed. But the phenomenon is always misinterpreted as the manifestation of a "herd-like" mentality that "investors" possess because they somehow do not have the independence of judgment or analytical skills to draw their *own* conclusions. Financier George Soros reiterates this point, arguing "that the IMF is failing to address a more fundamental problem: that banks and other international lenders 'move in a herd-like fashion in both directions,' lavishing cheap money on nations deemed promising, then fleeing at bad news."[10]

At least George Soros has an "explanation." An American-bred, less well-read colleague looks at a similar phenomenon and sees absolutely nothing:

> Mr Steinhardt, then a fast-moving money manager and now retired, says, "The stock market is supposed to be an indicator of things to come, a discounting mechanism that is telling you of what the world is to be. All that context was shattered. In 1987, the stock-market crash was telling you nothing."[11]

The spreading of volatility from one market to another – from foreign exchange to stock market – is the logical consequence of the operation of speculative capital. Speculative capital is born in the currency market. This market is large, liquid, and lends itself easily to arbitraging: buying the stronger currency and selling the weaker one. But no market is constantly turbulent. So speculative capital probes other markets and, finding arbitrage opportunities in them, invades them. In the US, the intrusion of speculative capital into the equities and fixed income markets is a *fait accompli*, with the result that the volatility in these market has drastically increased. The *New York Times* reports on the increased volatility in mid-1997:

In the US, the intrusion of speculative capital into the equities and fixed income markets is a **fait accompli.**

---

[10] "With the Focus on South Korea, Thai and Indonesian Aid Falters," *New York Times*, January 7, 1998, p. A1.

[11] "After the Fall: Some Lessons Are Not So Obvious," *Wall Street Journal*, August 25, 1997. p. C1.

The [stock] market acts as if it is confronting storms blowing every which way. One day prices soar; the next day they sink just as fast. And then they lift off again ... So far this year [1997], 31 percent of trading days have seen 1 percent moves based on closing figures. If that continues, this could be the most volatile year since 1987.[12]

The *Wall Street Journal* picks up the same story early in 1998. By now matters had become worse:

last year [1997], there were 80 trading days during which the Dow rose or fell by more than 1%, up from 18 in 1995 and 43 in 1996. In January [of 1998] alone, 1% price swings were seen on eight trading days, or an average of two of every five trading days.[13]

The trend continues. The same paper reported about the rise in volatility in the last trading month of 1998:

Stock price volatility is getting downright scary ... "The sentiment swings in this market are making everybody's head spin," says [a technology stock trader]. "It is leading to exceptional volatility. Unprecedented volatility." ... James Stack of InvesTech Research ... says that by his calculations, intraday volatility is at its highest level in 65 years.[14]

Why has volatility increased?

While there is a sharp division of opinion on what volatility means for the market's direction, analysts largely agree on its causes. Topping the list: the quest for new investment ideas ... Quick dashes in and out of individual stocks and sectors as fickle investors try out, then discard, new investment ideas have fueled volatility.[15]

---

[12] "Wall Street Is Growing Crazier By the Day," *New York Times*, August 24, 1997. Section 3, p. 1.
[13] "Prudence Needed Amid Market's Mood Swings," *Wall Street Journal*, February 2, 1998. p. C1.
[14] "Market Analysts Ponder Meaning Of Head-Spinning Stock Swings," *Wall Street Journal*, December 7, 1998, p. C1.
[15] "Hair-Raising Turns for Stock and Bond Markets," *Wall Street Journal*, January 13, 1997, p. C1.

"Quick dashes in and out of individual stocks" are the signature activity of speculative capital. But the paper does not know that, so it attributes the problem to "fickle investors." The tone of the article, furthermore, suggests that the surge in volatility is a passing phenomenon, an anomaly perhaps fueled by a bull market. The issue is further muddled by the frequent nonsensical comments such articles elicit from experts. (In the same article, one fund manager dispenses wisdom about the cause of the volatility in the stock market: "Volatility is the price of admission [!] when you buy stocks offering good returns in this environment.")[16]

The issue is further muddled by the frequent nonsensical comments such articles elicit from experts.

In the absence of an understanding of why the volatility has increased, decision-making becomes increasingly difficult and even seems arbitrary:

> When stocks or sectors move in and out of favor in a matter of days, it becomes harder for professional money managers ... to cling to their convictions that a stock is a good long-term investment ... says ... [an] equity strategist: "The fundamentals are very, very hard to understand and analyze, so the market becomes more emotional, and emotion translates into volatility at the micro level."[17]

The strategist quoted in this story is correct when he observes that an incomprehensible market makes the participants uneasy and emotional, and thus, ultimately, exacerbates the volatility. But the emotional behavior is not the cause of the volatility. Voltaire observed that incantations could indeed kill a flock of sheep if administered with a dose of arsenic. Money managers becoming emotional is the consequence of the operation of speculative capital which creates volatility that money managers do not understand.

Then what about the Treasury Secretary strengthening the dollar by "sowing fear" in the hearts of speculators? Was that not an instance of emotions superseding the principles of finance? It turns out that that

---

[16] Ibid.

[17] "Market Is Diagnosed As Manic-Depressive," *Wall Street Journal*, February 23, 1998, p. C1.

episode, too, was driven by more tangible events. In 1996, the Secretary's loquacious deputy had let slip the truth:

> A senior United States Treasury Official defended their stewardship of the world economy yesterday, saying they had corrected exchange-rate misalignments, reduced currency volatility and promoted fiscal discipline, while strengthening the international monetary system against shocks. Deputy Secretary of the Treasury Lawrence H. Summers ... said that by seeking a consensus on prudent domestic policies rather than by direct intervention in the markets, the major economic nations had carried out an "orderly reversal" of exchange rate movements.[18]

Summers's statement shows that the dollar was already in an "orderly reversal." There was no need for "ambushing" the markets and adding to volatility.

The developments in the bond market were virtually identical:

> No longer are bond markets ruled by old-fashioned "real money" investors – the buy-and-hold pension funds and retail coupon-clippers. Taking their place: global spanning hedge funds and aggressive proprietary trading desks of global banks ... The volatility in the shape of the yield curve has nearly doubled in the '90s from ... 23 basis points to 41 basis points ... And despite an inflation rate that has barely budged from about 3 percent over the past four years, bond yields have been all over the map.[19]

The source of increased volatility in the bond market is arbitrage trading which increases the volatility through sudden ebbs and flows of capital, as shown in this *Wall Street Journal* story: "In late spring [1994], Mr Steinhardt [a hedge fund manager] sold a large part of the $11 billion in Canadian bonds ... Mr Steinhardt's wholesale dumping pushed Canadian bond prices so low, and yield so high, that the Canadian government was forced to amend its budget."[20]

In addition, there is the indirect effect of speculative capital on the

---

[18] "As Summit Talks Near, A Defense," *New York Times*, June 6, 1996, p. D4.

[19] "The Boy in the Bubble," *Institutional Investor*, July 1997, p. 51.

[20] "Steinhardt Moves to Avoid Anti-Trust Case," *Wall Street Journal*, September 9, 1994. P. C1.

bond market caused by dynamic hedging strategies which "link" stock prices to bonds. The linkage acts as the conduit through which the volatility in one market travels to others.

Linkage of markets

Speculative capital is not bound to any one market or place. Rather, it is constantly on the lookout for profitable opportunities wherever it can find them. Upon finding such opportunities, it enters into these markets and, through arbitrage, "links" them together.

Arbitrage is buying relatively undervalued A and selling relatively overvalued B. This buying and selling will tend to increase the price of A and decrease the price of B. If A and B happen to be in two different markets, and if the arbitrage is systematic, sustained and occurs on a large scale, the linkage goes beyond the individual products and encompasses the markets themselves. Movements in one market are then transferred to other markets.

The linkage knows no limits. It can be between the various markets in the same country or different markets in different countries.

Linkage of various segments of national markets

The most elementary form of arbitrage linkage of two markets within a country is the one we visited earlier: the price of a stock (such as IBM) being different in the New York and the Pacific Stock Exchanges. Such differences cried out for arbitrage. Consequently, they were the first to disappear. The assumption of the shares of IBM trading at different prices in two different exchanges in the US is an example of lazy teaching in the classroom; it has no correspondence to reality. For all practical purposes, the stock exchanges within the US act as one entity.

Derivatives are the functional form which speculative capital assumes in the markets.

The linkage of equities, fixed income and currency markets is less simple. Arbitrage between these markets requires mathematical calculation and is less direct. That is why, in conjunction with the rise of speculative capital, derivatives appear on the scene. Derivatives are the functional form which speculative capital assumes in the markets. Their flexible structure is designed precisely to "link" various markets. That is the reason for the tremendous growth in the volume and variety of derivatives, and indeed the very derivatives market itself.

The disposition of speculative capital to link various markets is also behind the growth in "correlation models." These models aim to establish a historical and statistical link between the prices in various markets, so speculative capital can then arbitrage them. We will briefly look at the correlation models and their shortcomings in the context of arbitrage in Chapter 6. Dynamic hedging strategies and derivatives will be discussed in detail in Volume 2. But for the evidence of the linkage of fixed income and equities markets in the US we need not venture into technical discussions. We can find such evidence in an innocuous organizational restructuring in a Wall Street brokerage house. The Wall Street trading houses are keenly attuned to changes in the market. Their organizational structure reflects the division and the interaction between the various segments with a good degree of accuracy. The following news story shows that the linkage between the equities and the fixed income markets has become sufficiently strong to make them indistinguishable:

> Morgan Stanley & Company, reflecting recent changes in financial markets ... reorganized itself yesterday ... Morgan Stanley executives said that the impetus for consolidating the securities business lay in blurring in recent years of the distinction between debt and equity departments on Wall Street, with the increasing use of derivatives and other hybrid instruments.[21]

The impetus for the change, we learn, was in "blurring ... the distinction between debt and equity departments on Wall Street." This blurring could not have involved the legal differences between bonds and stocks. The distinction between stocks and bonds in 1997 remained as clear as

---

[21] "Shadowing Industry Trends, Morgan Stanley Creates 2 Big Divisions," *New York Times*, January 17, 1997, p. D1.

it had ever been. The blurring, rather, is the result of the disappearance of the *functional* difference between the two; debt and equities both come to serve the same purpose the same way: lending themselves to arbitrage operations.[22] In the era of dominance of speculative capital, that is the primary function of markets; it supersedes other technical and legal differences. The bond market volatility is in part due to this blurring of the lines between the markets, so the

Debt and equities both come to serve the same purpose the same way: lending themselves to arbitrage operations.

volatility of the equities market is visited upon the traditionally stable bond market.

The coupling of the two markets is a relatively recent development, tied to speculative capital. As early as 1980, textbooks on finance described how the stock and bond markets acted asynchronously. Their reasoning was that when the bond market rose, the stock market declined and vice versa because the "investors" took their money from the falling market and invested it in the rising market. Such were the happy days of pre-speculative capital!

Commodities have also been drawn into the oscillations:

> While global stock markets plunge, a major index of commodity prices, on products from oil to cotton, fell to its lowest level in 21 years yesterday [August 27, 1998]. And that may be more worrisome for investors in the long run than yesterday's 4.19 percent decline in the Dow Jones industrial average.[23]

We saw in Chapter 1 that the Wall Street firms developed commodity funds as a hedge against the decline in stock prices. Thanks to the operation of speculative capital, that hedging refuge is no longer there, which is why the reporter characterizes it as "more worrisome … in the long run."

---

[22] Shortly after the *New York Times* story, in a sign of far more blurring of the lines between various markets, Morgan Stanley merged into retail insurer/broker Dean Witter.

[23] "No Refuge in Plunging Commodity Prices," *Wall Street Journal*, August 28, 1998, p. D1.

Linkage of international markets

After arbitrage opportunities in the home market have been grazed, speculative capital sets out to find virgin markets outside the original national boundaries. This excursion begins with more developed markets. That is partly because they can more easily accommodate the large size of speculative capital. Also, the primary tools of speculative capital – derivatives – are more likely to be found in these markets. Gradually, even in these markets, the profit opportunities are arbitraged away: "Once one of the raciest and most profitable areas of investment banking, the Eurobond market has become boring and, even worse, not very profitable".[24] So speculative capital sets out to seek even more virgin territories outside the developed markets and economies. When these markets are found, they become the "emerging markets."

> *After arbitrage opportunities in the home market have been grazed, speculative capital sets out to find virgin markets outside the original national boundaries.*

The specifics of how speculative capital links various international markets are, again, quite technical and vary from one case to another. For example, if interest rates in Japan are low, arbitrageurs borrow yen, convert the borrowing into US dollars, lend the money and hedge the strategy by a mix of long Eurodollar positions and dollar-yen swaps. In this way, speculative capital links the fixed income markets in the US and Japan with the global interest rate and currency derivatives markets. That mechanism has little in common with the bond arbitrage between various fixed income markets.

In all events, though, the end result of cross-border arbitrage is a replay of what takes place in national markets: the markets become coupled and their price movements synchronized. The evidence of this cross-border linkage is widely known and reported:

> Some of the savants who originated the global diversification theory are adding an ominous postscript: In times of shock, when volatility is

---

[24] "Eurobond Market No Longer Affords Investment Banks Big Profit Margins," *Wall Street Journal*, October 31, 1994, p. A9D.

greatest, global diversification may not be quite the safety net that some investors expect. "An unpleasant characteristic has appeared" in recent studies of world markets, says [the head of the] finance department ... at ... a leading French university. "The correlation among US and international markets seems to increase when these market are most volatile."[25]

The appearance of correlation between various markets as a result of the operation of speculative capital is a mere tendency, albeit a strong one. Only the most artless would interpret it as meaning that each day all the linked markets must go up or down synchronously. But the tendency exerts itself with sufficient frequency for a routine market report in the *Wall Street Journal* to take note of it:

Last week, Wall Street fell and much of the world followed. Monday, Wall Street rose and yesterday much of the world followed ... "I doubt the rest of the world can get a divorce from Wall Street," says [an investment officer]. "Investors nowadays are so international that it's the same money flowing all over the world. Markets are getting closer and it's becoming one big global market."[26]

Now, the linkage of various markets around the globe has become the norm. The following *Wall Street Journal* headlines during one business week in August 1998 tell the story:

Global Markets Dragged Down by US Plunge
(Wednesday, August 5, p. C16)

European Issues Get Hit by US Aftershocks
(Thursday, August 6, p. C16)

Stocks Fall on Currency Devaluation Worries in Asia
(Friday, August 7, p. C12)

Asian Stocks Continue to Slide With No End in Sight
(Monday, August 10, p. C14)

---

[25] "Global Diversification Has Its Down Side And May Not Be The Strongest Safety Net," *Wall Street Journal*, April 14, 1994, p. C1.

[26] "US Leads World Markets on Wild Ride," *Wall Street Journal*, August 20, 1997, p. C1.

Asian Currency Worries Send Stocks Reeling in Asian, European and Latin American Markets
(Tuesday, August 11, p. C16)

World Markets Fall on Fears of Global Downturn
(Wednesday, August 12, p. C14)

Global Stocks Rebound After Yen Regains a Bit On Dollar, Easing Fears of Asian Devaluation
(Thursday, August 13, p. C14)

Note that the smallest "unit" of the market the headlines describe is "European," "Asian," "Latin American." Generally it is "global." There is no mention of individual countries because no individual country can escape the gravity pull of speculative capital and "buck the trend." The sole exception in that regard is the US but that is because, ironically, it is at the very center of the gravity pull, as we will see in the next two chapters.

That was the equities market. The story in the bond market is similar:

> World bond yields now tend to track changes in the US economy surprisingly closely ... According to [a] global investment management firm, the two trends have been 79% "correlated" since 1993 ... By comparison, that relationship had been slightly negative over the past 25 years – meaning that yields around the world used to fall.[27]

The implication of such synchronization is clear, as the *Journal* explained to its readers: "For investors, it means there is little hope of escaping the crumbling US bond market by switching into bonds overseas."[28]

The markets that are linked by speculative capital form a distorted union. Parts of the union are very advanced and have developed financial markets. Other parts are relatively less developed, with the financial markets organized around equities and little by way of derivatives. In developed markets, the volatility brings about *price* fluctuations in financial markets. In less developed markets, it forces a *currency* devaluation. In all cases, it wipes out the relatively small capitals. For the individual firms, that means bankruptcy. When the bankruptcies res-

---

[27] "Bond Declines May Spread World-Wide," *Wall Street Journal*, April 9, 1996, p. C1.
[28] Ibid.

onate, they lead to systemic risk. The collapse of the currencies in Southeast Asian countries that began in mid-1997 is a classic case in this regard: "Their [Southeast Asian] countries were like 50-watt bulbs plugged into 250-watt sockets, and when the surge came from the electrical herd of global investors, they blew up" (Friedman, 1998, p. A17). Thus opines the *New York Times* columnist in explaining the causes of the crisis in Southeast Asia in 1998. The pundit has sensed that movement of capital has played a role in the crisis. He is even conscious of the speed of operation of speculative capital, to which he alludes with "the electrical herd of global investors." But like the economics and finance professors, that is all he sees. So he concludes with a crude and ultimately incorrect analogy.

The impact of speculative capital beyond the financial sector

As speculative capital expands, its impact extends beyond the financial markets and reaches to various parts of the economy and, indeed, society. That impact is especially pronounced in the case of the US. As we explain in the next chapter, the US is the birthplace of speculative capital, so it is in the US that the influences of speculative capital outside financial markets first surface. (The one exception is the case of central banks which, by virtue of their unique position, were exposed to currency markets and arbitrage trading from the early days. At times, some of them could not resist the temptation of easy profit through speculating in, or the manipulation of, currency markets.)

Even a cursory analysis of how speculative capital pervades various industries would demand a book on its own; we cannot examine the subject in detail. We merely provide "snapshots" of press reports, which, in light of the material we have already discussed, will explain more than they otherwise would.

Central banks

Even before Robert Rubin brought a trader's perspective to the US Treasury, some central banks were active in arbitrage trading. In 1992

Thailand's central bank reportedly speculated against the British pound and made in excess of $1 billion.

The exchange rate game is mostly played subtly by the central banks. But when need be, it can assume the crudeness of a shakedown:

> Disagreement over repayment arrangements for a $200 million bond issue has set off an angry dispute between three commercial banks and the Turkish government. The dispute centers on a one-day delay that the banks argue cheated them out of lot of money ... Bank officials said the ... decision to postpone by one day the date for fixing the dollar/Turkish lira rate at maturity lowered the amount repaid [by $16 million] ... because in the space of that one-day delay ... intervention by Turkey's Central Bank strengthened the Turkish lira by 7% ... Government officials charge that the banks themselves manipulated the market to drive the value of the dollar higher.[29]

Private banks manipulate the market to drive the value of the lira lower. The central bank manipulates the market to drive the value higher. As a result, the lira moves 7 percent in a single day and the "equilibrium" is restored to the markets. Such is the current status of international high finance under the influence of speculative capital.

Public institutions

In the 1990s, a variety of public institutions, from small community colleges in Texas to various counties, lost billions of dollars of their money in trading. Perhaps the most celebrated example in this category is the bankruptcy of Orange County in California. The case is an ideal teaching tool because it has the full cast of characters who made the bankruptcy possible.

The county

Dale Scott succinctly describes the root of the county's problems:

> "You can pin this [the bankruptcy] almost 100 percent on Proposition 13," said Dale Scott, a San Francisco financial adviser to local govern-

---

[29] "What a Difference a Day Makes, or So Say Banks Angry Over Turkish Bonds," *Wall Street Journal*, September 7, 1994, p. A10.

ments. "The only reason people are out there trying to turn two dimes into a quarter is they can't finance basic needs anywhere else," he added. "The Music Man comes in and says, 'I can get you 10 percent when everyone else gets 5 percent,' and he's a hero."[30]

Proposition 13 limited property taxes in California, a major source of income for the state's municipalities. In the early 1990s, the breakup of the Soviet Union led to a reduction in defense spending. The income of military industries in Southern California and, with that, the region's tax revenues, fell sharply. The role of savior was thrust upon the county's unassuming treasurer, who reached for the elixir of the financial markets to turn two dimes into a quarter.

The trading strategy

His trading strategy was arbitraging the long and the short end of the US Treasury yield curve. At the time his trading began, the yield curve had a positive slope, as shown in Figure 4.1

The treasurer borrowed in the short term repo market at the rate of B and used the proceeds to buy long-term bonds which paid a coupon rate of A. The difference between the two, A − B, was the profit.

An important feature of the repo trade is that the security which is being purchased is pledged as the collateral for the loan. That is, the long-

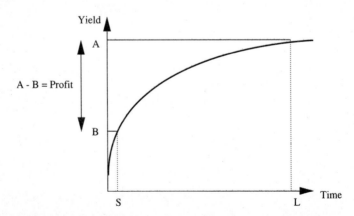

Figure 4.1 Profit of arbitraging the long and short end of the yield curve

---

[30] "A Bankruptcy Peculiar to California," *New York Times*, January 6, 1995, p. D1.

term bonds of the county which paid a coupon of A were the collateral for the short-term loan which had financed it. At its peak, the county had a portfolio worth $20 billion, of which $14 billion was borrowed.

The arrangement worked as long as the shape of the yield curve remained unchanged. Then, in early 1994, the Federal Reserve raised interest rates. As a result, the cost of short-term borrowing increased and the value of the long-term bonds pledged as collateral dropped. The brokerage firms demanded additional collateral, which the county could not provide. So they seized the collateral, which forced the county to file for bankruptcy.

The brokerage firm

Orange County traded with several brokerage firms. Among them, Merrill Lynch was by far the most active: "Merrill dominated the [Orange] county fund's business to an uncommon extent … Merrill also had access to an exceptional amount of information about the county fund."[31]

Almost two years before the bankruptcy, the risk managers in Merrill Lynch had apparently become concerned about their exposure to the county and warned their superiors. The *Wall Street Journal* wrote:

> Some at Merrill were concerned about those dealings [with Orange County]. The risk managers' primary concern was a simple one: losing money. Merrill was lending against illiquid, volatile securities as collateral, and could have been on the hook for millions. But the risk managers, depending on how you look at it, were either wrong about the exposure or did their job well, because Merrill didn't lose a dime in Orange County. In fact, it made tens of millions in commissions, fees and such.[32]

There is of course a third way of looking at the performance of the risk managers. In zero-sum trading, one can also lose money as a result of *very favorable* market movements, when these movements bring about the

---

[31] "Orange County's Suit Against Merrill Highlights Importance of Its Fees to Firm," *Wall Street Journal*, January 13, 1995, p. A10.
[32] "Merrill Lynch Officials Fought Over Curbing Orange County Fund," *Wall Street Journal*, April 5, 1995, p. A1.

ruin of a counterparty. While Merrill was increasing its positions with the county, it was at the same time increasing both its exposure to the county and the probability of the county's default in the event of adverse market moves. That is exactly what came to pass: Merrill did not lose a dime in trading *and* was subsequently sued by the county for $3 billion. In 1998, it settled the case for $400 million with the county but is still a defendant in suits brought by parties who refused to join the settlement.

In zero-sum trading, one can also lose money as a result of **very favorable** *market movements, when these movements bring about the ruin of a counterparty.*

The rating agencies

The rating agencies found themselves in an unprecedented predicament and could offer little by way of defense:

> An S&P spokesman, and high-ranking officials at S&P yesterday vehemently objected to the view that they were somehow responsible for closely monitoring the Orange County fund. That would include "responsibilities … that are way beyond what is reasonable," [the spokesman] said. "We're not regulators."[33]

The claim of S&P that "we are not regulators" was in part meant to be a defense against lawsuits charging the agency with negligence. But the confusion was nevertheless real. The rating agencies had traditionally evaluated the rating of corporations and municipalities by analyzing their balance sheets. A balance sheet is a snapshot of an entity's holdings. For industrial corporations, that picture changed only gradually and in accordance with their operating and production cycle, generally over many months and sometimes even years. An annual rating review was sufficient to capture these changes.

The operating horizon of speculative capital is weeks, even days.

The operating horizon of speculative capital is considerably shorter: weeks, and even days. The fortunes of an entity trading speculative

---

[33] "Orange County Fund Had Green Rating Light," *Wall Street Journal*, December 6, 1994, p. C1.

capital can drastically change long before the "regularly scheduled" reviews are due.

Several months later, the rating agencies showed that they had become aware of the role of trading when they reduced J. P. Morgan's rating on the basis of its trading exposure: "J. P. Morgan & Co.'s banking units ... have lost their prized triple-A ratings from Moody's ... [which] cited risky investment-banking activities for the downgrade."[34] A few days later, S&P followed suit, offering the same reason:

> "In explaining its move [to lower J. P. Morgan's rating], S&P said the volatile environment for many trading businesses during the past year "has highlighted the endemic risks of those businesses." ... the trading activities have rendered Morgan's overall performance "less stable than in the past," S&P said.[35]

Corporations

Banks learned arbitrage trading in the course of devising ways to respond to the hedging needs of their corporate clients. But the flow of knowledge works both ways. Corporate treasuries, specially those of large corporations, in turn learned arbitrage trading from their banks. In calmer days, merely knowing a trading strategy may not have sufficed for trying it. But in the era of speculative capital, the days of corporate treasurers were anything but calm.

The "reengineering," driven by the indirect influences of speculative capital, forced the organization of corporations along profit lines. Departments which were not traditionally expected to generate profits came under pressure to contribute to the bottom line. One such department was the treasury, which had been responsible for managing corporations' cash flows and, in more complex cases, its foreign exchange transactions. The pressure to generate profits, a relatively large pool of available money and frequent exposure to banks and matters of finance

---

[34] "Morgan Loses Triple-A Ratings From Moody's," *Wall Street Journal*, February 15, 1995, p. A4.

[35] "Morgan Debt No Longer Gets S&P's Triple-A," *Wall Street Journal*, February 28, 1995, p. B4.

which created an illusion of "sophistication," all came together to turn the treasury departments of many multinational corporations into small trading centers.

> Treasurers of many multinational companies ... made money for their companies off the dollar's plunge ... to make even more money from the dollar's descent, corporate treasurers of some of the nation's largest businesses have quietly been betting against the dollar in the futures market. While many treasurers fully hedge against currency fluctuations, the majority operate within a predetermined band of flexibility. A few months ago, with the dollar declining so deeply, more and more treasurers took advantage of their allowable flexibility to join Wall Street traders in betting that the dollar would keep falling.[36]

This "revenue enhancement" method had its downside. As the dollar gained strength, the easy streak turned into a corporate trail of tears. The losses hit corporations across the board:

> The British pharmaceuticals concern [Glaxo] invested as much as $1 billion of its cash in mortgage-backed securities and asset-backed bonds. As paper losses on these bonds ran as high as $100 million ... executives at the company decided to liquidate the entire portfolio. Selling has begun, and the losses could be much higher by the time the selling is completed ... The portfolio manager who designed Glaxo's strategy apparently tried to outperform short-term cash-equivalents with a heady cocktail of mercurial bonds that were *supposed to do well no matter how interest rates moved* [italics added].[37]

In the second fiscal quarter of 1995, Sony lost 32 billion yen because it "hedged against currency risks based on the assumption that the yen would remain at a high rate against the dollar. The gamble backfired when the yen weakened."[38] And there were European companies:

---

[36] "Treasurers of Many Multinational Firms Took Risks to Profit From Falling Dollar," *Wall Street Journal*, April 17, 1995, p. A2.

[37] "Glaxo Holdings Is Taking a Hit on Derivatives," *Wall Street Journal*, July 13, 1994, p. C1.

[38] "Sony Back to Profitability But Hurt by Hedge on Yen," *New York Times*, November 10, 1995, p. D2.

> The German airline Lufthansa AG says foreign-exchange fluctuations
> will cost it 200 million marks ... this year [1995]. Danone SA, the French
> food group, says currency movements cost it 1.63 billion francs ... of
> sales in the first half, and auto-parts group Valeo SA says first-half sales
> would have risen 16%, not 11%, without currency fluctuations.[39]

The much-publicized case of Procter & Gamble, which lost $150 million in various transactions with Bankers Trust, fell within this trend.

The extent of the involvement of corporate treasuries in trading could be seen from the announcement of a single bank, made in relation to its forgiving some derivatives-related losses:

> Bankers Trust ... indicated yesterday that it has had far more customers
> with problem deals involving derivatives than the handful of cases that
> have been made public so far. The bank said it had forgiven $72 million owed by those clients in such derivatives ... in addition, Bankers
> Trust said it had reclassified other derivatives deals valued at $351 million as non-performing loans.[40]

While in municipalities and other public institutions the use of trading for revenue enhancement has been at least temporarily curtailed, corporations remain active in the field.

Farming

The most devastating impact of speculative capital has been on farming. It created a fully fledged farm crisis by turning a rare opportunity for profits into ruinous losses for farmers who could afford it least. The story has received very little attention. Lawmakers partly acknowledged the problem when in the 1999 budget they allocated emergency funds for aiding farmers.

The most devastating impact of speculative capital has been on farming.

The story begins with the deregulation of farming by eliminating the price support which, for better or worse, had sustained the small and fam-

---

[39] "Monetary Chaos Precedes Europe's Single Market," *Wall Street Journal*, July 28, 1995, p. A10.

[40] "Derivative Losses Up for Bank," *New York Times*, January 20, 1995, p. D1.

ily farmers in business. (In the next chapter we will see that the force behind deregulation is speculative capital.) Faced with the prospect of perhaps even lower grain prices, the farmers followed the path of municipal and corporate treasurers to financial markets. At the same time that sophisticated urban players were being drawn to arbitrage trading, the technique was also being sold to farmers. It came in the guise of an instrument which the farmers had known for generations: a forward contract.

Farmers had traditionally sold forward contracts to grain elevators. The contracts called for the delivery of crops at a certain price after the harvest.[41] The new "hedge-to-arrive" forwards differed very little conceptually but they allowed farmers to contract for more than they could produce. A farmer who could produce only 50,000 bushels of corn sold contracts calling for the delivery of 80,000 bushels. He reasoned that, at the time of harvest, the prices would fall – that is what had happened as far back as anyone cared to remember – and he could gain an extra profit of 30,000 bushels times the difference between the contract price and the market price. The idea seemed perfectly logical.

Then, the price of grain soared. Corn, perennially at around $3 per bushel, reached $5. The farmer who had sold forwards calling for the delivery of 80,000 bushels at $3 found himself the subject of a "double whammy." Not only was he not able to benefit from the rise in prices, he also had a deficit of 30,000 bushels which he had to deliver at a cost of $5 per bushel. Family farms did not have that money.

Meanwhile, the grain elevators had hedged their position, selling grain futures calling for the delivery of 80,000 bushels in the Chicago futures exchanges. As the farmers failed to deliver, its price of grain further increased, squeezing farmers even more. Many went bankrupt. The *Wall Street Journal* wrote:

> Observers fear that as the debacle grows, it is likely to roil the already frothy grain markets. At the very least, the hedge-to-arrive problem will permanently alter the social fabric of many small communities. In these towns farmers and elevator managers often attend the same social gatherings. And now both are going to be fighting for their livelihood.[41]

---

[41] "Some Grain Accords Leave Farmers in Bushels of Debt," *Wall Street Journal*, May 20, 1996, p. C1.

As if to draw attention to itself, speculative capital left its footprint – increase in price volatility – on farm products. Without speculative capital, the price of agricultural products could increase or decrease but never "zigzag:"

> Wildly zigzagging prices are whipsawing investors and speculators. Indeed, the prices of grains and other commodities have become so volatile these days that it's not uncommon to see prices gyrate as much as 40% – in either direction – over 10 days.[42]

Society

It is impossible for a phenomenon that affects central banks, public and private institutions and farms, among others, not to have an impact on society at large. The influence of speculative capital goes beyond what is implied in this chapter. How familiar, for example, are President Clinton's "flip flops" in light of our subject?

> Clinton is at mid course. Will there be a mid course correction? A thing must first have a shape for the shape to be correctable. How does one "correct" a chaos? … Sam Smith, the editor of Progressive Review, wrote: "Clinton often seems a political Don Juan whose serial affairs with economic and social programs share only the transitory passion he exhibits on their behalf." Clinton is so temperamentally adjustable that his mind, dragged along on the emotional roller coaster ride, can veer into purest dither … The natural question that arises is: Does Clinton really believe in anything? (Wills, 1997, p.28)

The *Wall Street Journal* attributes this conduct to Clinton, but admits that the President's "hybrid political style" has thrived and now extends to the Republican politicians: "Even as the President's personal misconduct has exposed him to a congressional impeachment inquiry, the hybrid political style he has fostered is thriving – and in some of the most unlikely places."[43] The "hybrid style" went beyond politics, provoking the Pope to devote his encyclical in the twentieth anniversary of

---

[42] "This Bull in Futures Pit Wreaks Havoc," *Wall Street Journal*, May 6, 1996, p. C1.

[43] "Clinton's 'Third Way' Inspires Republicans To Forge Their Own," *Wall Street Journal*, October 14, 1998, p. A1.

his papacy to criticizing the moral "relativism." A theologian (Novak, 1998) elaborated the papal view: "a legitimate plurality of positions has yielded to an undifferentiated pluralism, based upon the assumption that all positions are equally valid."

An analysis of the way speculative capital influences society belongs to a book on the joint subject of finance and sociology. We must return to the more tangible influences of speculative capital, as they are our main concern in this book.

References

Deutsch, Henry (1910) *Arbitrage in Bullions, Coins, Bills, Stocks, Shares and Options*, London: Effingham Wilson.

Friedman, Thomas (1998) "Heal Thyself," *New York Times*, February 7, p. A17.

Novak, Michael (1998) "It Is Not All Relative," *New York Times*, September 16, p. A27.

Wills, Gary (1997) "The Clinton Principle," *New York Times Magazine*, January 19, p. 28.

5

LAW AND POLITICS

The anti-regulatory drive at home • Influence over the executive branch, the IMF and the Federal Reserve • The drive beyond home base • Penetration into emerging markets • Transparency • Southeast Asian monetary crisis of 1997 • Opposition to expansion of speculative capital • Finance capital and the Federal Reserve

"For all the talk about free markets and the spreading of American-style capitalism," said Jeffrey Garten, Dean of the Yale School of Management and a former Under Secretary of Commerce, "the fact is that global finance has become the quintessential interweaving of public and private institutions, mechanisms and interests." [1]

---

[1] "Fail-Safe Strategies in a Market Era," *New York Times*, January 4, 1998, Section 4, p. 1.

Introduction

Speculative capital abhors regulation. Regulations interfere with the cross market arbitrage that is its lifeline. If speculative capital cannot freely operate, it cannot generate profits and must cease to exist. The opposition of speculative capital to regulation is thus not a matter of some technical or tactical disagreement but a question of life and death.

The attack of speculative capital on regulation, of course, is not indiscriminate. Though generally suspicious of regulation, speculative capital singles out only those regulations which directly or indirectly hinder its free flow across the markets. The same speculative capital, meanwhile, supports and pushes for the passage of sweeping laws. In so opposing the regulation and supporting the law, speculative capital distinguishes between the two in ways few philosophers of law could.

Speculative capital abhors regulation.

Regulation is a subset of law. It deals only with a relatively small part of a group. As such, by definition, it is exclusionary. It separates the small part from a larger whole. Law applies to the majority and is thus, inclusive. Laws are passed to apply to "all." The difference between regulation and law is a quantitative one. Regulation turns into law if its minority subject grows or develops to become the majority. The perverseness of, say, apartheid is shown partly in the violation of this logic, where the interest of a minority is the *law*.

The purpose of both, law and regulation, is directing the actions of individuals or functions of enterprises towards a certain goal. But in societies comprised of groups with contrasting interests, the goals vary because the interests are conflicting and, at times, mutually exclusive. The attempts of groups to make *their* interest the purpose of the law translate themselves into a fight for regulation and the law and, because the rulemaking bodies are political, to politics. The political system represents interests.

In an autocracy, one group dominates to the exclusion of the others. In the kind of democracy that has developed in the West, opposing groups settle their differences through negotiation and compromise. The contentions over economics matters become legal, and from there political, fights within the democratic government. Law and regulation are the nomenclature under which the fight for advancement of special interests takes place. In following speculative capital, we learn of the link between group interests, law and politics in a most informative way.

The anti-regulatory drive of speculative capital's home turf

The home turf of speculative capital, the place where it was born and from which it operates, is the US. That fact is the result of historical conditions, as we saw in Chapter 3. After its formation and gaining a critical mass, the newly born expanding force of speculative capital encountered the regulatory walls and began to push against them. That is why it is in the US that we first hear the battle cry of deregulation. While in the public's mind Ronald Reagan's name is generally associated with deregulation, deregulation in finance, beginning with the passage of the Commodities Exchange Act (CEA) in 1974, was well under way by the time Reagan took office.

There is no inconsistency in citing the passage of an act as an example of *deregulation*. The CEA was a concession to speculative capital. It allowed for the development of an over-the-counter (OTC) derivatives market outside the regulatory reach of the Commodities Futures Trading Commission (CFTC) and, in doing so, disturbed the long-standing balance between trading and speculation in favor of speculation.[2] Through the OTC derivatives, speculative capital was able to increase its reach in the markets.

The home turf of speculative capital is the US.

The rise of an OTC market as a rival to the CFTC-supervised exchanges was a victory for speculative capital and facilitated its deregulatory push. In describing two bills in Congress that aimed to fix some

---

[2] We will examine the differences between exchange traded and OTC derivatives in Volume 2, Chapter 5.

of the "problems" of the futures industry, the *Wall Street Journal* pointed to the source of the need for deregulation:

> What needs to be fixed? For starters, it still takes months for an exchange to get regulatory approval if it wants to launch a new futures contract. This was annoying 20 years ago when virtually all trading took place on US exchanges. Today, exchanges say the provision puts them at a horrendous disadvantage … commodity traders contend that foreign exchanges' ability to introduce new contracts without regulatory oversight gives them an edge in a world where trading is becoming increasingly global.[3]

Parallel to this, regulation was discouraged:

> Federal Reserve Chairman Alan Greenspan argued that it would be a mistake to make derivatives a scapegoat for the last year's [1994] upheaval in financial markets. "Singling out derivative instruments for special regulatory treatment," he said, misses the point, because the swings in financial derivatives are only a "symptom" of volatilities throughout the financial markets.[4]

Another important front on speculative capital's assault on regulation was the Depression Era Glass–Steagall Act. The Act divides the financial industry into separate areas of banking, securities and insurance and, in doing so, hampers the expansion of speculative capital by preventing its concentration. In 1994, the *New York Times* reported:

> Alan Greenspan … called today for Congress to expand banks' business options by allowing them to sell insurance and stocks. Mr Greenspan also suggested that some limits could be placed on bank deposit insurance and seemed to imply that these limits might be imposed as part of a compromise that would allow banks into securities and insurance activities. Depository insurance makes it possible for

---

[3] "Two Futures Trading Bills Aim to Fix Problems," *Wall Street Journal*, September 23, 1996, p. C14.

[4] "Few Support Any New Rules on Derivatives," *Wall Street Journal*, June 6, 1995, p. A3. The Fed chairman was correct in saying that derivatives are only a symptom of, more accurately, a conduit for volatility. It is less clear if he knew the *cause* of the volatility.

banks to hold larger and riskier asset portfolios than otherwise, distorting the economy and exposing taxpayers to possible significant losses, Mr Greenspan suggested.[5]

The fighting between the banks, securities firms, and specially the opposition from the insurance companies has thus far prevented the repeal of the Act. In the interim, the Fed instituted its own mini-repeal: it raised the ceiling of percentage of revenues that bank holding companies could generate from brokerage business.

> The Federal Reserve ... [proposed] new regulations that would allow some of the largest banking companies to expand greatly the business they conduct on Wall Street ... The most important change would allow the securities subsidiaries of bank holding companies to generate as much as 25 percent of their revenue from underwriting and dealing stocks and many types of bonds, up from a limit of 10 percent.[6]

This deregulatory intervention had little to do with any philosophical conviction. The Fed was forced to change the rules under pressure from the banks because, as one analyst in the same article explained, the banks were "bumping up against the revenue limits."

In April 1998, the Travelers Insurance Company and Citicorp agreed to merge. The agreement, between an insurance and a bank holding company, showed that executives in the financial industry considered the Glass–Steagall Act all but dead. In fact, the only reason the Act has not yet been repealed is the jockeying of the banks, brokerage houses and insurance companies to secure the most advantageous position in the post-Act era. But the repeal of the Act is a foregone conclusion. It stands in the way of expansion of speculative capital and therefore must go.

> *The Glass–Steagall Act stands in the way of expansion of speculative capital and therefore must go.*

---

[5] "Greenspan Wants Laws To Let Banks Expand," *New York Times*, September 20, 1994, p. D2. The Fed chairman first calls for expanding the domain of banking activities and then, as a "compromise," suggests lowering the FDIC insurance limit on bank deposits. This is an example of deregulation from both ends!

[6] "Banks' Access To Wall Street May Widen," *New York Times*, August 1, 1996, p. D1.

Speculative capital and the executive branch

The chairman of the Federal Reserve and various industry groups carry substantial weight in shaping economic and financial policy in the US. But it is the executive branch which runs the government machinery. As speculative capital expands, it reaches beyond the regulatory walls and comes face to face with the legal structure. Now it is no longer a local regulation about derivatives but a national law about transfer of capital which stands in its way. One important way of eliminating such legal impediments is through influencing the executive branch.

The executive branch is of course separate in the technical meaning of the words from the legislative and judicial branches, but few laws can pass without its support or consent. Contacts and negotiations with foreign governments and international institutions are through the executive branch. Speculative capital cannot meaningfully claim to have its desired influence over laws and regulations without bringing this part of the government machinery on board. Or, rather, without itself climbing on board the executive machinery.

In the US, the attempt of speculative capital to enter the executive branch began immediately after the collapse of Bretton Woods and continues uninterrupted. The resulting developments are very gradual and very subtle. They certainly are not linear. That is, the influence of speculative capital does not visibly increase from one administration to another, or with each new cabinet change. But over time, the trend is unambiguously there. Just how speculative capital has come to influence the executive branch can be seen if we compare the background and the style of the present Treasury Secretary, Robert Rubin,[7] with those of John Connally, who held the same job at the time of the collapse of the Bretton Woods system. Paul Volker describes Connally's background and the circumstances of his appointment (Volker and Gyohten, 1992, pp. 71–2):

[7] As this book was going to press, Rubin resigned and his deputy, Lawrence Summers, was nominated to replace him. Assuming that Summers's nomination clears the Senate (see "Opposition to the expansion of speculative capital" later in this chapter), his policies will be indistinguishable from those of Rubin as the underlying policies remain unchanged. In that regard, the present tense we use in this book with regard to Secretary Rubin remains in full force and need not change.

David Kennedy resigned ... and John Connally from Texas was appointed secretary of the Treasury. None of us in the Treasury knew Connally ... A protégé of Johnson's, he had been secretary of the navy under John Kennedy, returned home to be elected governor of Texas ... He was a man who knew his way around government and had greatly impressed Nixon with some work he had done on a commission to reorganize the government ... One thing he was not: He was not a great figure of international, or even domestic, finance.

It is clear from this that the job of Treasury Secretary was political. It had very little, or nothing, to do with any background in finance. Compare that with Rubin's background.

Robert Rubin is a former foreign exchange trader. Unlike Connally, "who knew his way around government," Rubin had no experience in government prior to his appointment. His "style" of operation, described in the *New York Times*, is as far from Connally's as one could imagine:

> Mr. Rubin's style – working the inside, minding the office – stands in sharp contrast to the approach taken by his predecessors ... [who] viewed the Treasury as a place for high diplomacy and savored the constant world travel and the pomp and ceremony ... Mr. Rubin dislikes all that. His aides know that 24 hours before most foreign trips, he will question whether he could accomplish the same results on the phone. As Treasury Secretary, he has yet to visit Tokyo, the world's next biggest financial center.[8]

Earlier, we noted that governments restore equilibrium to markets by decree; private capital does it by arbitrage. Prior to the collapse of the Bretton Woods system, the issue of foreign exchange relations was a political question. Even in the 1980s, the topic of exchange rates was considered sufficiently political to require what the *Times* calls "high diplomacy," "constant world travel" and "pomp and ceremony." James Baker was the last of this breed, whose transition from the Treasury Department under the Reagan administration to the State Department in

---

[8] "An Old Wall Street Pro's Voice in the Campaign," *New York Times*, September 22, 1996, Section 3, p. 1.

the Bush administration constituted a promotion and, thus, underscored the dominance of politics over finance.

Rubin is the first of a new breed. He is an arbitrageur. He sees no reason for diplomacy. Indeed, there is no room left for diplomacy when actions in foreign exchange markets can speak for themselves. Like any good trader, he does his work on the phone. And we saw in the previous chapter, his plan for restoring the correct exchange rate between the dollar and the yen involved not a trip to Tokyo but ambushing the markets with buys and sells and sowing uncertainty and fear in the hearts of currency traders.

> *Rubin is an arbitrageur. He sees no reason for diplomacy.*

It would be naive to think of Rubin as the sole "representative" of speculative capital. The changes brought about in the government under the steady onslaught of speculative capital go beyond individuals and reach into political processes. Witness a recent use of the White House Situation Room, as described in the *New York Times*:

> While the "Sit[uation] Room" is still where the nation's leaders go to discuss loose nukes in Russia or Iraq's latest act of defiance, it has repeatedly been used lately to hash out America's next moves to contain the financial crisis in Asia. On that Friday in mid-December [1997], the Secretary of State, Defense Secretary and national security adviser all took part in a debate over whether American taxpayer dollars should be committed to a redoubled effort to keep South Korea's private banks afloat – and over the consequences if the banks were simply allowed to go under. "You could tell this was New Age foreign policy," one participant recalled later, "because the assessment didn't come from the CIA. It came from J. P. Morgan."[9]

Dean Garten of Yale's School of Management, whom we quoted at the start of this chapter, must have read similar passages to conclude that "global finance has become the quintessential interweaving of public and private institutions, mechanisms and interests." But speculative capital – "global finance," in his words – is more than an "interweaving"

---

[9] "Fail-Safe Strategies in a Market Era," *New York Times*, January 4, 1998, Section 4, p. 1.

element, a mere glue connecting public and private interests. It is, rather, the private force that rises to *command* the public institutions with the aim of furthering its goals. Incorporating these goals into US foreign policy is formally acknowledged:

> Secretary of State Madeleine K. Albright described for the first time her vision of the role of international economic issues in American foreign policy. She argued today that leadership in opening markets ... was critical in bolstering American influence. "The best course for our nation is not to curse globalization, but to shape it, to make it work for America," she said.[10]

The "New Age" foreign policy is conducted by the Treasury Department, a logical transfer of responsibility in the era where assessments come from J. P. Morgan rather than the CIA. In fact, the technical nature of the subject *demands* that Treasury be put in the driver's seat. And the country is better for it.[11]

> *In matters related to international finance, the Treasury Secretary is the Administration.*

So after acknowledging the role of opening up the markets, the Secretary of State returns to the standard foreign policy and the Treasury Department takes charge of guiding the relations between the nations as defined by the needs of speculative capital. In a news article about Rubin's efforts to strengthen the role of the dollar, the *New York Times* left no doubt that, in matters related to international finance, the Treasury Secretary *is* the Administration.

---

[10] "Rubin to Press Central Banks to Disclose Financial Data," *New York Times*, September 19, 1997, p. D5.

[11] A few years earlier, an ex-CIA official had explained why the agency could not be a player in global high finance: "Tracking global capital flows or predicting currency crises is beyond the agency's ability, said ... a former CIA official: 'We don't have the resources, we don't have the expertise,' he said. 'To develop understanding of the people who trade currencies, their motivations, their lifestyles, you'd have to send your people to Harvard, Stanford and Wharton for years. Currency traders keep secrets very, very well [!], and to penetrate that would be the equivalent of cracking the operational code of the Politburo or all the Japanese codes in World War II.'" "Emerging Role for the CIA: Economic Spy," *New York Times*, October 15, 1995, p. A1.

His [Rubin's] first move was to impose an ironclad rule that he would be the only one in the Administration even to talk about the dollar, the loquacious president included … Mr Rubin had a free hand in fighting the dollar war; the President almost never got involved.[12]

During the 1997 crisis in Southeast Asia, matters got considerably more complicated and the President's involvement became necessary. Still, no one failed to see the source of the administration's views:

As Asia's financial crisis has deepened, President Clinton has become personally involved in the efforts to persuade Asian leaders to follow American-designed plans to stabilize their economies … But one South Korean official said that some in the Government had "resented the use of Presidential pressure," especially because they believed – largely accurately – that some of the toughest elements of the economic prescription were being drafted by Mr Clinton's Treasury Secretary, Robert E. Rubin.[13]

Speculative capital and the IMF

In discussing the expansion of speculative capital, we must take special note of the role of the International Monetary Fund.

The IMF was created in the Bretton Woods as a lender to sovereigns for their balance of payments problems. From the start, its agenda had a political undertone. The British delegation had proposed the idea of a fund as a "neutral" international clearing house. The US rejected that proposal, insisting instead on an institution which would lend only if the economic policies of the borrowing sovereign were in line with the principles of free markets. In the midst of debate over the pros and cons of the Bretton Woods agreement, Harry White (1945, p. 209) candidly expressed that point:

Primarily, the Fund is the means for establishing and maintaining stability, order and freedom in exchange transactions. The resources of

---

[12] "An Old Wall Street Pro's Voice in the Campaign," *New York Times*, September 22, 1996, Section 3, p. 1.

[13] "Clinton's Personal Touch in Asian Rescue," *New York Times*, December 18, 1997, p. D8.

the fund are only for the purpose of helping countries to adopt and keep such policies.

After the collapse of the Bretton Woods system, the IMF was side-lined for a while. Its role, defined in the context of fixed exchange rates, seemed outdated. As late as 1995, at the height of the Mexcian peso crisis, the Fund had but a marginal role:

> [In Mexico's] 1982 debt crisis ... the IMF and the World Bank led efforts to rebuild international confidence ... Now [1995], [they] have neither the money nor the clout to make that kind of difference. ... The markets have now become the policeman, holding the carrot and stick "that used to be in the hands of the World Bank and the IMF."[14]

Then, in 1996, the IMF was reinvented by the US Treasury Department.

Several factors contributed to the interest of the Treasury in the IMF. First, the Treasury came under sharp attack from the conservatives for its orchestration of the Mexican bailout. Had Mexico failed to pay back the money lent to it, there is little doubt that the Secretary would have been forced to resign. The experience must have vividly brought the difference between private and government money to Rubin's attention.

Furthermore, the Treasury Department is an arm of the US government. For obvious political reasons, it cannot too overtly be used to influence other countries, especially because such direct involvement, for reasons that we will discuss shortly, is strongly opposed at home. Thus, in its incursion into new territories, speculative capital was in need of a supra-national organization that would provide a cover of internationalism and independence. The IMF fitted that bill. One of the first signs of the Fund's revival came in early 1996, when the member countries agreed to shore up its reserves for dealing with financial crises:

> The big industrial nations agreed today with a group of smaller countries to double the money available for dealing with a severe international financial crisis, to $50 billion. The agreement comes a year and half after the global economic system was shaken by the near collapse

---

[14] "Peso Crisis Highlights Diminished Roles of IMF, World Bank in Latin America," *Wall Street Journal*, January 17, 1995, p. A13.

of Mexican peso, and is intended to provide more firepower in keeping acute, destabilizing financial problems in one country from spreading to others. The money would be lent to the International Monetary Fund rather than directly to a country in crisis.[15]

For over a quarter of a century, the IMF had been the instrument of stability of the exchange rates. In the post-Bretton Woods era, since the IMF could not beat speculative capital, it came to join it: "For the IMF, rebuilding financial markets is a new job ... The change in mission was helped along by the urgings of [deputy Treasury Secretary] Mr Summers, Treasury Secretary Robert Rubin and Federal Reserve Chairman Alan Greenspan."[16]

> *In the post-Bretton Woods era, since the IMF could not beat speculative capital, it came to join it.*

So the IMF became the lightning rod for the opponents of speculative capital.

Finance capital and the Federal Reserve

Finance capital goes to work to earn a profit. Naturally it wants – demands, if you will – an environment that will preserve the value of that hard-earned profit. The amount of profit that finance capital can generate is a complex function of many factors. This analysis falls out-side our subject. Suffice it to say that one important factor is labor cost. That explains why finance capital supports all the efforts to contain it. But because it does not directly confront labor, it is less aggressive on that subject and more compromising than industrial capital. At times, it can even support a modest rise in wages, a position which puts it in the liberal camp.

What finance capital will not and cannot compromise on is the "environment," on which it proves itself greener than the Greens. The envi-

---

[15] "A Fund to Bail Out Countries in Crisis Is Doubled, To $50 Billion," *New York Times*, May 24, 1996, p. A9.

[16] "Clinton's Personal Touch in Asian Rescue," *New York Times*, December 18, 1997, p. D8.

ronment of interest to finance capital, however, is an economic one, where the "healthy" is defined and measured in terms of the absence of inflation.

Finance capital materializes itself in "paper assets." The value of these assets is derived from profits but is measured in money. If the supply of money grows without a corresponding growth in profits, more money will be equated with a given value, with the result that the price of the paper assets will decrease. That would mathematically diminish finance capital and actually lessen it. The obsession of finance capital with inflation is thus easy to understand: it is a matter of survival. That is specially true of the credit component of finance capital, where the yields are fixed and therefore the vulnerability to inflation is much greater.

Finance capital goes to work to earn a profit.

What causes inflation and how can it be brought under control? Like many other economic phenomena, the causes are many and varied. Finance capital, however, has little patience for, or interest in, comprehensive analyses. As it sees it, inflation exists because someone prints money. That "someone" is the Federal Reserve. So through Milton Friedman, it declares that "inflation is always and everywhere a monetary phenomenon." It then moves to set things right.

Friedman's uninspired observation about inflation, akin to saying that over-population is always and everywhere a sexual phenomenon, serves a useful purpose. It shifts attention from the complexities of the issue toward a single organ: in the case of inflation, the Federal Reserve. Inflation exists because the Fed prints too much money. Why? Because the politicians are forcing it to, either by pursuing an expansionary fiscal policy or by saddling it with extra and impertinent burdens. The conclusion shapes the mission statement of finance capital, which is to make the Federal Reserve "independent" by taking politics out of the Fed's way and certainly out of the Fed itself. The game plan calls for opening three fronts.

The most important front is curtailing fiscal policy, the planned spending by government. It purports to stimulate the economy by administratively allocating resources. Such programs cost money. If the government follows ambitious social spending programs, it becomes impossible for the Fed to keep a tight money supply. For monetary policy to have the desired effects, fiscal policy must be reduced in size and scope. It must be exiled to the political wilderness. So finance capital pushes various legislative initiatives that, under the banner of "containing government spending," "reducing the budget deficit," "balancing the budget," "automatic spending cutbacks," etc., serve to push fiscal policy to the sidelines. Monetary policy, and with it the Federal Reserve, move to center stage.

> *For monetary policy to have the desired effects fiscal policy must be exiled to the political wilderness.*

Second, the Fed's decision-making body, the Board of Governors, must be sold on the idea of fighting inflation to the exclusion of other considerations. This phase of the action plan is also in place. The Fed's zeal to "fight inflation" – i.e., to raise interest rates at any hint of a rise in labor costs – is "universally" acknowledged and admired. Even mild critics of the policy, if they are accidentally tossed into the Board, are in due time ejected, as the case of Alan Blinder demonstrated.[17]

Finally, there is the Humphrey–Hawkins Act, which finance capital considers the most egregious example of the intrusion of politics into the affairs of the Federal Reserve. The official name of the Act, Full Employment and Balanced Growth Act, succinctly captures its purpose, which is "to translate into practical reality the right of all Americans who are able, willing, and seeking to work the full opportunity for useful paid employment at fair rates of compensation."[18]

The Act mandates the Fed to balance its arsenal for fighting inflation against employment and economic growth. More accurately, it forbids

---

[17] Alan Blinder was appointed vice chairman of the Federal Reserve in 1994 and forced out two years later. Reporting on his decision not to seek reappointment, the *Wall Street Journal* wrote: "Federal Reserve Vice Chairman Alan Blinder is expected to announce today that he won't be seeking reappointment when his term ... expires ... Mr Blinder has drawn attention, and occasional criticism, for his candor in his two years as a Fed governor. A liberal of the Keynesian school of economics, Mr Blinder has emphasized the Fed's dual responsibility for promoting economic growth and resisting inflation." "Blinder Will Leave Fed At the End of Term Late This Month," January 17, 1996, p. A4.

[18] Pub. Law 95–523, 92 Stat. 1887.

the Fed to fight inflation by a sharp increase in rates which could lead to recession and unemployment. Such overt political intervention in the Fed's decision-making process is intolerable. The Act must go. That is why demands for its repeal appear in the *Wall Street Journal* with celestial regularity:

> It would be much easier for the Fed if it could focus solely on achieving and maintaining a stable price level, eliminating other goals now assigned by the Humphrey–Hawkins Act.[19]

> Currently, the Humphrey–Hawkins Act dictates that the Fed must promote growth when the unemployment rate rises ... The act should be repealed.[20]

> The solution for this turmoil [stock market volatility] ... is for the Fed to declare that its job is to stabilize the general price level, period. Congress could certainly help by legislating precisely this; ... Relieved of the inflation-unemployment trade-off specified by the current Humphrey–Hawkins Act, the Fed would be free to specify some intermediate targets.[21]

> Congress should ... repeal the Humphrey-Hawkings Act, which purports to govern monetary policy.[22]

Etc.

The Humphrey–Hawkins Act has so far managed to remain on the book, though the Federal Reserve all but ignores it. There is little doubt that in coming years it will be repealed; at a minimum, it will change beyond recognition. In that regard, the die is cast.

The drive beyond the home turf: speculative capital as the invisible hand of "global finance"

Speculative capital must constantly increase in size to compensate for

---

[19] "Agenda '95–97': A Single Goal for Fed," *Wall Street Journal*, November 16, 1994, p. A28.

[20] "Get Fed Out of the Trade-Off Game," *Wall Street Journal*, October 3, 1995, p. A20.

[21] "The Delphic Dollar," *Wall Street Journal*, December 10, 1996, p. A22.

[22] "Let the Market Set Interest Rates," *Wall Street Journal*, May 20, 1997, p. A18.

falling spreads. In that regard, Karl Marx's observation that expansion of capital is a condition for its preservation is particularly pertinent.

From the viewpoint of this constantly expanding force, the size of the world seems to be shrinking. It becomes a "village." In this village, of course, there are numerous national boundaries, sovereigns whose laws might inhibit speculative capital. So speculative capital moves to "open up" these markets, i.e., eliminate laws and regulations which hinder its access to them. Such a move requires contending with the various political and social systems across the globe, all of which, if speculative capital has its way, must gradually be brought under its orbit. The euphemism "global markets" or "global finance" is used to describe this push of speculative capital to eradicate regulation and open up international markets.

The efforts of speculative capital to influence governments has not gone unnoticed. That something is happening in the "global markets" or through them is a topic that occupies the attention of the best and brightest in the press, academia and the policy-making bodies. Writing in the *New York Times Magazine* under the heading "The Nuke of the 90's," an awestruck former Treasury official, Roger Altman (1998, p. 34), thus compares global markets to nuclear weapons and concludes: "The global markets are the most powerful force the world has ever seen, capable of obliterating governments almost overnight." That is hyperbole. Speculative capital does not obliterate governments overnight. It has neither the means nor the reason for it. But the very comparison of "global markets" with nuclear weapons shows that the force behind the phenomenon is felt even if its causes are not understood.

Freeing all central banks from politics

The expansion of speculative capital takes it to sovereign lands where it faces the same regulatory hurdles it faced at home. Thus begins its anti-regulatory campaign on the road. And because this form of capital is a skilled campaigner, it begins the initial legs of the campaign with the friendly territories, where a home-grown finance capital has already taken hold and agitates for joining the global economy. Combining forces, they replay the script of central bank independence and soon score a hit. *The New York Times* was attuned to this development and in an editorial in 1994 endorsed it: "central bankers are gaining more authority domestically. Elected politicians ... are increasingly granting their central bankers the stature and independence they need to fight the inflation."[23]

In May 1997, shortly before the French election, the paper revisited the subject and under a descriptive heading, "Divorcing Central Banks and Politics: Independence Helps in Inflation Fight," wrote:

> In granting more independence to the Bank of England, the new British Government is a later entrant in a trend that has seen nations give increasing autonomy to their central banks, distancing monetary policy from direct political control. The practice has spread across the globe in response to demands from investors in financial markets for proof that governments will remain committed to inflation fighting ... The trend toward independence is rapidly eroding the practice, common only a few years ago in nearly all nations except the United States and Germany, of regarding monetary policy as the responsibility and right of the government of the day.[24]

So controlling the supply of money and rate of interest is no longer deemed to be the responsibility of governments.

The direction of developments in Europe mirrors that of the US. Indeed, one aspect of the drive for the institution of European Monetary Union was the establishment of independent central banks across Europe: "In Europe, the move toward central bank independence is being speeded by plans for monetary union among the members of the European Union."[25] European finance capital is aware that an aggressive monetary policy is an effective tool for containing labor costs, a prerequisite for bringing price-competitive new products into international markets. Again, the *New York Times* explained:

> Less than 15 months from the creation of a single currency, Europe's central bankers have sent a sobering message to its politicians: You can

---

[23] "Role Shift for Central Banks," *New York Times*, November 15, 1994, p. D1.
[24] *New York Times*, May 7, 1997, p. D7.
[25] Ibid.

no longer use monetary policy to cushion economic shocks … With reduced influence on credit policy, politicians will have to undertake fundamental changes if they want to create the flexible labor markets that would allow their nations to compete better internationally … And that would require the courage to initiate such unpopular moves as making it easier for employers to lay off workers, keeping a ceiling on minimum wages and removing obstacles to part-time work and flexible working hours.[26]

Central bank independence, as we said earlier, is not in itself sufficient. For monetary policy to succeed, fiscal policy must also be curtailed. So the prospective members of the European Union had to devise a matching fiscal policy. The Maastricht Treaty was a step in that direction. It limited, among other things, the government budget deficit of nations wishing to join the European Union to 3 percent of gross domestic product.

The agenda set by finance capital is so entrenched in Europe that even a major change in the government has little impact on it. In the summer of 1997 the Socialist Party and its communist allies won a decisive victory in the French election on a platform of jobs and employment. Yet, despite his strong mandate, Prime Minister Jospin could do no more than extract minor concessions about increasing Maastricht-imposed government spending limits. Robert Hormats, the vice chairman of Goldman Sachs International, accurately summed up the options of European governments within the confines of the European Union: "There are no easy ways out any more. They can't bet on lower interest rates, they can't devalue and they can't raise spending. So that leaves the labor-market reform."[27]

> *The agenda set by finance capital is so entrenched that even a major change in the government has little impact on it.*

Thus, we see that an event such as the European Union that appears as a purely political matter is at core but a subject in finance; we arrived at it from analyzing speculative capital. It could not be otherwise.

---

[26] Bankers' Discipline," *New York Times*, October 23, 1997, p. D21.
[27] "Bankers' Discipline," *New York Times*, October 23 1997, p. D21.

Regulation and politics deal with the details of dividing the money. To understand them, we must "follow the money." Only then will they begin to make sense.

> Money, money, money, money ... Politics is mostly about which part of the electorate gets the money. Saying so is usually said to be cynical, but this is one of those periodic times in American history when the question of who gets the money is too blatantly in the open to be ignored. (Baker, 1996, p. A19)

Penetration of emerging markets

Europe is a special case, where events are driven by a local finance capital strong enough to sway the laws in its favor. In the majority of countries, the home-grown finance capital is not sufficiently developed to challenge the "status quo." The status quo in these places is typically a manufacturing-based economy where the laws greatly favor industrial capital to the detriment of local and international finance and speculative capital. Speculative capital thus begins the second phase of its campaign, in which it aims to open these markets, or to help them "join the global economy." These are the "emerging markets," whose very name signals the subordination of the political entity "country" to a financial one, "market."[28]

The emerging-market countries are diverse. Their economic power and their political and social systems vary greatly from one to another. Whenever possible or feasible, speculative capital uses individually tailored approaches to penetrate these markets. In the case of China, for example, one leg of the strategy is the familiar "independence" of the central bank:

> Underscoring the urgency of financial reforms, China is reshaping its central bank along the lines of the US Federal Reserve ... "The Goal is to increase the People's Bank's [China's Central Bank] independence and reduce interference by provincial governments in monetary policy," said an official.[29]

---

[28] That is, similar to "citizens" becoming "consumers."

[29] "China Models Central Bank on US Fed," *Wall Street Journal*, April 7, 1998, p. A15.

But the quickest and most cost-efficient way to gain access to the emerging markets is to approach them *en masse*. That was precisely the idea behind the agreement in the World Trade Organization signed in December 1997. The agreement eliminated numerous barriers to movement of capital among countries. The *New York Times* reported:

> Under the darkening clouds of Asian financial crisis, the United States and more than 100 other countries signed a global trade agreement ... to open up the world's financial markets. The agreement ... commits countries to dismantling hundreds of barriers and admitting foreign banks, insurance companies and investment firms to their markets.[30]

After the initial opening up, the second phase of the operation, the push for transparency gets under way.

Transparency

Opening up closed markets allows speculative capital to come ashore. But that is merely a first step. Speculative capital has not landed to enjoy the scenery. It is there to arbitrage. That will be possible only if it can determine the arbitrage opportunities. And it can do so only by looking at data. If data is not available, all the opening up efforts will come to naught. So it begins the push for the local financial institutions to open their books, to become "transparent." It insists on everything being put on the table.

The part of local capital that comes under attack resists this latest demand. It knows that, in terms of sheer size, it is no match for the foreign Goliath. So it adopts the time honored strategy of the weak against the strong: it wages a "guerrilla war," using the accounting and legal terrains as its natural allies. A corrupt accounting system which reflects very little in the way of what actually takes place and the authority of the local government to simply refuse to divulge the information become very handy in this war. If the books are indecipherable or simply are withheld, the attack of speculative capital can be deflected.

---

[30] "Accord Is Reached to Lower Barriers in Global Finance," *New York Times*, December 13, 1997, p. A1.

Speculative capital is aware of this old trick and will have none of it. It moves to force the enemy into the open by leveling the terrain. First, it demands that all parties agree to accepted accounting practices. This call is difficult to resist. It is in the spirit of openness and the bookkeep-

Speculative capital moves to force the enemy into the open by leveling the terrain.

ing operation of the local capital is generally a sham.

At the same time, there is a call for openness (of books) on the part of all participants in financial markets. Thus begins the transparency war, captured in all its details in a *New York Times* story:

> The American [transparency] initiative … stems from the discovery that Thailand's central bank kept secret data that would have warned international investors of the country's impeding crisis. But several Asian leaders have disagreed and argued that the crisis was precipitated by currency speculators, many of them from the United States, and it is likely that they will oppose disclosure requirements that would embolden such speculators to make new assaults on the value of the currencies.[31]

Local capital objects to the imposition of firm regulation because it is happy with the existing lax system that greatly benefits it and keeps outsiders at bay. Imposition of firm regulation can be devastating. A local Thai banker explains, while complaining: "'I do not oppose the new rules in principle,' said [the banker]. 'But when they push all these new requirements on us all at once, well, you are simply pushing all the Thai banks into foreign hands.'"[32]

A few months later, a bank executive interjects the word "political" into the topic. The issue is no longer only financial: "Mr Stent said that as the crisis has dragged on, some people here are coming to believe that

---

[31] "Rubin to Press Central Banks to Disclose Financial Data," *New York Times*, September 19, 1997, p. D5.

[32] "Thai Troubles Drive a Dynasty To Sell Its Crown Jewel Bank," *New York Times*, April 16, 1998, p. A1.

Thailand's political and financial institutions are not strong enough to tolerate the pressures of being fully open."[33]

But the die is cast and there is no turning back on transparency and disclosure issues. The experts weigh in with their comments. Stuart Kessler, chairman of the American Institute of Certified Public Accountants, takes a hard line:

> The argument over whether to bailout ailing Asian economies has diverted attention from more basic, if less seductive, issues: the need for transparency in international transactions and the critical role that financial accounting standards play in meeting that role ... adherence to internationally accepted financial disclosures should be a condition for any bailout.[34]

Kessler will probably be surprised to see his comments in this book in the context of the push of speculative capital to conquer new markets. He would protest: "I have never even heard of such a thing as speculative capital. I do not know what it is. I would not recognize it if I saw it. How could I be its 'agent?'" His protestation would be quite sincere. As the chairman of the AICPA, he *always* supported transparency. It could not be otherwise. But that is precisely the *modus operandi* of the invisible hand: it sets the *agenda* and then uses the existing structures, norms and conventions to institutionalize it. That is why its "agents" remain all but oblivious to it; the spring of 1998 just seems an opportune moment for airing one's long-held views.

Robert Hormats, vice chairman of Goldman Sachs International, takes up the same issue from a more ambitious beginning:

> America's resilient financial system owes much to James Madison and his colleagues at the Constitutional Convention. They created a system that discourages concentration of power ... and promotes an environment in which the public ... insists on accountability by business as well as government. In much of Asia, information accountability – financial transparency – has not kept pace with the requirements of an

---

[33] "Rubin Defends IMF Policies and Continues His Asian Tour," *New York Times*, June 30, 1998, p. A12.

[34] "One Set of Rules, Please," *New York Times*, March 8, 1998, Section 3, p. 13.

international market dominated by large pools of highly mobile, institutionally managed, leveraged funds.[35]

While not everyone would agree that the US Constitution points to the need for transparency in Asian markets, Hormats's remark on the reason for that need is right on the mark: the requirements of large pools of highly mobile, institutionally managed, leveraged funds. There is no talk of "investors."

If the intellectual persuasions do not work, there is the more direct threat of sanctions. Treasury Secretary Rubin puts those who resist transparency on notice:

> In a move aimed at pushing developing countries to strengthen their economies, Treasury Secretary Robert Rubin suggested that major financial powers block the expansion of foreign banks whose home nations have weak banking regulation. Under such a plan, regulators in the US, the United Kingdom and other financial centers would use the threat to pressure developing nations to tighten their regulations. The US and the International Monetary Fund contend that the Asian financial crisis was caused, in part, by lax regulation.[36]

And the battle goes on.

An accounting house-cleaning of some magnitude is on the cards for the financial institutions in the emerging markets. Furthermore, as time goes by, the scope of transparency, in terms of both the information and the countries it covers, is bound to increase. The positive aspects of this trend should not be overlooked.

The Southeast Asian monetary crisis: a case study in deregulation

International agreements are of use if they are honored. Governments have a wide leeway in the way they honor an agreement or carry out its provisions. They can procedurally and administratively slow down the implementation of treaties for years, even decades. They can ignore or

---

[35] "James Madison's Example for 'Tigers,'" *Wall Street Journal*, April 2, 1998, p. A22.
[36] "Rubin Urges Foreign-Bank Crackdown," *Wall Street Journal*, April 15, 1998, p. A2.

refuse to enforce crucial aspects of the agreements at the request of a strong local interest group. Some renegade countries might refuse to join the global economy or otherwise accommodate the deregulatory forces.

Speculative capital cannot let arbitrage opportunities be squandered due to bureaucratic foot dragging. It calls its troops and storms the barracks of the resistance.

The monetary crisis that hit the Southeast Asian countries in mid-1997 provided some of the most fascinating examples of the operation of speculative capital, of the kind it would have been impossible to see in calmer times. The Southeast Asian crisis acted as an eclipse under whose cover one could see the hard-to-perceive politics of high finance. We can-

> *Speculative capital cannot let arbitrage opportunities be squandered due to bureaucratic foot dragging.*

not leave this part without providing some of that evidence. The material is quoted from the daily reports of the *New York Times* and the *Wall Street Journal*.

We begin with South Korea, where the size of the economy and the scope of its problem gave the first hints to politicians and regulators of the seriousness of the problem: "Messrs Rubin and Greenspan spent the Thanksgiving [1997] holiday helping to press the IMF to stick to tough conditions and to press the Koreans to accept them."[37] Why is the influence of Messrs Rubin, Greenspan and Summers over the IMF so openly acknowledged, even leaked to the press?

One reason is internal politics. The Treasury Department is aware that Congress opposes the IMF funding. By heralding their influence over the Fund, the Treasury officials hope to soften Congressional opposition. That is why at times they seem to go out of their way to emphasize reshaping the IMF in the US-desired image.

The other reason is to ensure that all intended parties do know on whose behalf the IMF acts. In that way, the Fund's recipes carry extra

---

[37] "Clinton's Personal Touch in Asian Crisis," *New York Times*, December 18, 1997, p. D8.

weight. Whether or not the over-bluntness was necessary, the message did get across: "One Korean newspaper ... complained in an editorial that the US was using the IMF consultations as an opportunity to take advantage of Korea's problems and 'further its own interests.'"[38]

The foreign policy establishment criticizes this loud approach to international affairs, believing it to be a sign of clumsiness which could jeopardize US interests. Its spokesperson airs his displeasure: "Former Secretary of State Henry Kissinger warned that the US-backed austerity being imposed by international financial institutions could trigger a wave of anti-Americanism."[39]

But the bluntness Kissinger sees and does not like is the *modus operandi* of speculative capital which *must* act "loudly" and forcefully, never gingerly or incrementally.[40] The loudness impresses itself upon the New Age diplomacy and the language and conduct of its administrators. Secretary of State Albright's celebrated "bluntness" is a case in point. Even "polite-to-a-fault" politicians are not immune to this pressure. In an almost unbelievable breach of diplomatic and social protocol, Vice President Al Gore used the occasion of an economic summit in Malaysia to call for the ouster of the host, Prime Minister Mohathir Mohamad, while he was listening a few feet away! This happened after the Malaysian government had instituted currency controls in the aftermath of financial crisis in Southeast Asia. The *New York Times* interpreted the episode to its readers:

> Polite-to-a-fault Al Gore used his visit to Malaysia for an Asian economic summit meeting to throw American support behind protesters calling for ... dumping Mr. Mohathir ... Mr. Mohathir ... is a prime

---

[38] "Asia's Financial Foibles Make American Way Look Like a Winner," *Wall Street Journal*, December 8, 1997, p. A13.

[39] "Asian Woes Cause Headache for US Foreign Policy," *Wall Street Journal*, January 13, 1998, p. A24.

[40] Observe the introductory comments in a technical document analyzing the deregulation of the Japanese financial industry: "The total repeal of foreign exchange controls does not allow for gradual financial reform, because such gradualism places Japanese financial institutions at great disadvantages when it comes to competing with foreign institutions. Thus, big bang should inevitably mean radical deregulation." "A Brief Outline of the Japanese Big Bang," The Nikko Research Center, 1997.

example of how opposing Washington's political and economic agenda for an interconnected world can move a leader from the list of authoritarians whom Washington tolerates to the list of authoritarians who have outlived their usefulness.[41]

The *New York Times*'s own foreign policy/global markets columnist had already felt the need to be harshly frank:

> The hidden hand of the global market would never work without the hidden fist. And the hidden fist ... is called the United States Army, Air Force, Navy and Marine Corps (with the help, incidentally, of global institutions like the UN and the International Monetary Fund).[42]

These are the conditions on the ground: Country X, say, South Korea, that never truly opened its markets, is now in dire straits. The country's large corporations and the government itself need immediate, urgent short-term financing. Under these conditions, there is very little to negotiate. If South Korea wants money, it must sit and listen to the conditions of its bailout.

> In order to receive the loans, South Korea must undertake a sweeping reform program ... It includes opening the short-term bond market to foreign investors, closing insolvent financial institutions and decreasing the economic growth rate to 3% next year, from an estimated 6% this year [1997]. The government also said that it will increase the limit on foreign ownership in the stock market ... to 50% ... from the current 26%, allow foreign banks to own larger stakes in Korean banks ... and increase interest rates.[43]

What if the government, or the opposition, does not agree with this pre-

---

[41] "Tongue-Lashing And Backlashes," *New York Times*, November 22, 1998, Section 4, p. 5. While imposition of currency controls was no doubt the prime factor in Vice President Gore's attack, the manner in which it was carried out had probably to do with Prime Minister Mohamad's criticism of the role of "Jews" in the Southeast Asian crisis and Vice President Gore's particularly intimate relations with the American Jewry. Otherwise, removing the prime minister did not seem to be a goal of the US government.

[42] "Techno-Nothing," *New York Times*, April 18, 1998, p. A13.

[43] "IMF Help for Seoul Gets Mixed Response," *Wall Street Journal*, December 5, 1997, p. A15.

scription? South Korea, Thailand and Indonesia provide examples of the way speculative capital handles that contingency.

First, there is the threat of cutting off the flow of money: "Stanley Fischer, the first deputy managing director of the IMF said ... that without 'rigorous implementation' of the [IMF-proposed] plan, the flow of money [to South Korea] ... would stop."[44] But speculative capital is not so crude as to exclusively rely on direct force. It can influence "politics," which it knows is the cheaper and more pleasant way of achieving the same result. In South Korea, the presidential election was held in the midst of the crisis. The *New York Times* reported:

> *Speculative capital is not so crude as to exclusively rely on direct force.*

> None of the three contenders [in the presidential election] has given a very credible explanation of how he would manage the economy. Two have even said they would renegotiate the International Monetary Fund bailout ... although they have since been backtracking. This has alarmed investors and foreign governments, particularly because each candidate had signed a pledge agreeing to go along with the bailout.[45]

Just who requested the presidential candidates in South Korea to sign such a pledge, the *New York Times* did not mention. But speculative capital is the product of hedging. It knows how to hedge its bets.

After the election, the worries of investors and foreign governments proved groundless. The newly elected president set aside the campaign scruples and stuck to his pledge:

> During the campaign, Mr Kim attacked the IMF agreement, in part because it would lead to takeovers of Korean Companies ... But on Dec. 19 [1997], the day after he was elected, Mr Kim declared: "I will

---

[44] "Terms of Bailout Vague on How Reluctant Koreans Will Enforce It," *New York Times*, December 6, 1997, p. D1.

[45] "Who Can Lead South Korea Out of the Quagmire," *New York Times*, December 13, 1997, p. A1.

boldly open the market. I will make it so that foreign investors will invest with confidence."[46]

One of his aides elaborated further: "'No longer will there be discrimination against foreign products, companies and capital,' says an aide [to Korea's newly inaugurated president]. 'Korea now recognizes that capital has no nationality and welcomes foreign investors.'"[47] The Korean bailout then proceeded as planned.

The mechanics of the bailout were also interesting. Briefly, the plan called for converting the private debt of Korean companies to government debt. The Korean government balked at the idea. Then, on January 9, 1998, the *Wall Street Journal* reported that the government officials had a change of heart: "Korean officials, having first resisted the plan's premise that the government issue bonds to replace commercial bank debts, now appear receptive to the idea."[48]

What prompted this change of position? On the previous day, Deputy Treasury Secretary Summers was reported to have said "that the United States would not provide $1.7 billion in speed-up aid to South Korea ... until the [US] commercial banks agree on extending payments for about $25 billion in short-term loans to South Korean banks."[49]

Events in a nutshell are as follows: the US commercial banks demand that the Korean government issue bonds to replace – meaning guarantee – the private debt of the South Korean companies. The Korean government refuses on the ground that the private debt of private corporations is not the responsibility of the government. The Deputy Treasury Secretary announces that until the US commercial banks agree to extend their loans, the US government will not release the bailout funds. And banks will not agree to extend their loans unless the South Korean government agrees to their terms. Such is the "interweaving" of private and public interests in the age of speculative capital.

---

[46] "Korean Companies Looking Ripe for Sale," *New York Times*, December 27, 1997, p. D3.

[47] "Korea's Kim Shifts Focus to Fixing Economy," *Wall Street Journal*, February 25, 1998, p. A14.

[48] "US Bankers Bring Plenty of Savvy to Korean Crisis," *Wall Street Journal*, January 9, 1998, p. A10.

[49] "US Warning to Indonesia: Comply on Aid," *New York Times*, January 8, 1998, p. D1.

That is no revelation. The *New York Times* had brought the nature of this orchestration to the attention of those readers who had the patience to follow the story in detail: "The fact that the meeting ... [between South Korean officials and the US and Japanese bankers] took place at the New York Federal Reserve ... seemed to emphasize that the whole package of government and private aid was being carefully orchestrated."[50] The *Times* might have added that the baton remained firmly in the hands of the Treasury Department.

In Thailand, too, whose economic problems early in 1997 signaled the ensuing crisis, the IMF agenda met the resistance of a "weak" cabinet and also ran foul of the Country's constitution. Both had to be replaced:

> With a nudge from Thailand's enlightened King, the Parliament overwhelmingly passed the new Constitution in September – with the support of the army ... "The new Constitution was born out of the idea that to participate in the global economy you have to have a well-managed country and [therefore] we need democracy and political reforms to manage things better," said an editor.[51]

The *New York Times* "global market expert" elaborated:

> The dominant response in Thailand so far is to answer the currency crisis with deeper political and economic reforms. If this trend spreads around the region ... Southeast Asia could eventually emerge from this crisis with not only more efficient economies, but with more liberal-democratic policies.[52]

A few months after the new constitution, a new Thai cabinet adopted the changes demanded by the IMF: "Administration officials say that while Thailand agreed to the IMF package last summer, it did not begin to honor the terms until November, after a weak and divided cabinet was replaced."[53]

---

[50] "In a Shift, US Aid Will be Sped to South Koreans," *New York Times*, December 25, 1997, p. A1.

[51] "Thailand's New Songs," *New York Times*, December 15, 1997, p. A23.

[52] "Thailand's New Songs," *New York Times*, December 15, 1997, p. A23.

[53] "With the Focus on South Korea, Thai and Indonesian Aid Falters," *New York Times*, January 7, 1998, p. A1.

In Indonesia, where a strong man could not be swayed or a weak cabinet replaced, the familiar demands were followed by increased arm twisting which ultimately led to the ouster of President Suharto. The demands on Indonesia were the familiar ones:

> It will be crucial for Indonesia to carry through on policy commitments it has made in the context of the IMF program," Lawrence H. Summers, the Deputy Treasury Secretary and a central figure in the American efforts to contain the Asian financial crisis, told reporters late today. Mr Summers specifically pointed to "measures to reform and clean up the financial system, to adjust monetary policy, and to control public infrastructure spending.[54]

The same scenario was repeated with variations in Malaysia, the Philippines, Singapore and to a lesser degree in Hong Kong, and to a still lesser one in Taiwan.

Watching these events, it must have been logical for Prime Minister Mahathir Mohamad of Malaysia to conclude, as he did, that a US – hatched conspiracy was behind the troubles in the region. In the summer of 1997, he accused currency speculators of plotting with the US government to destroy the Southeast Asian economies. He even mentioned George Soros by name and went on to call him a "moron!"

It is true that the Treasury Department and the Federal Reserve orchestrated the bailout effort with private banks. It is also true that the Treasury and the IMF were, in the words of the *Wall Street Journal*, in "cahoots." It might even be true that some branches of the US government tried to exploit the crisis to further "national interest." But these were all after-the-fact events. There was no conspiracy in the sense of consciously planning the crisis and causing it. There could not have been, because none of the players understood the dynamics of events unfolding before their eyes. What the players in the crisis did was to react to the turn of events as they were occurring. The assertion by George Soros that he was in fact "long" on Malaysian currency is believable. As a speculator, he probably bought it after its initial fall, hoping for a rebound.

---

[54] "US Warning to Indonesia: Comply on Aid," *New York Times*, January 8, 1998, p. D1.

The conspiracy theory ignores the strong opposition in the US to the involvement of the Treasury Department and the IMF in Southeast Asia.

That the main players in the crisis did not understand the nature of the problem must be clear by now.

We cannot dismiss Congress's repeated rejection of funding requests for the IMF or the vehement anti-Treasury, anti-IMF editorials which preceded and followed each vote as a sideshow. These clashes are unheard of in the calls for repeal of the Glass–Steagall and Humphrey–Hawkins Acts.

That the main players in the crisis did not understand the nature of the problem must be clear by now. It will become clearer still when we take on the subject of systemic risk in the next chapter. But what is the source of the opposition to the expansion of speculative capital? Why does a savagely anti-regulatory newspaper such as the *Wall Street Journal* criticize currency trading and call for the establishment of fixed exchange rates? Our theory of speculative capital must explain these seemingly incoherent positions.

Opposition to the international expansion of speculative capital

Speculative capital is first and foremost *capital*. It everywhere stands for, and supports, improving the rate of return of capital and containing labor costs. Secondly, it is *finance* capital. In that form, it struggles for causes dear to finance capital, chief among which, we saw, was the independence of the central banks. Industrial, commercial and credit capital then settles down to enjoy the fruits of victory: interest and dividends in a "low inflationary environment."

But speculative capital is also *speculative*. It cannot sit still. Idleness produces the same strain as holding one's breath. It must constantly arbitrage and, because doing so eliminates the arbitrage opportunities, it needs to bring new territories under its domain of operation. It needs to expand.

The expansion demands ever larger quantities of dollars, the medium of choice in which speculative capital embodies itself. The quantitative increase of dollars undermines the tight monetary policy that other forms of capital have fought so hard to win. Their mouthpiece, the *Wall Street Journal*, complains: "[The dollar] being the world's dominant reserve currency gives the US government the privilege of issuing billions of IOUs that remain permanently in float around the world."[55] They rise to oppose speculative capital. The disciplined parents confront their unruly offspring. The trade finance departments of the banks object to proprietary trading.

This battle between speculative capital and its rivals is fought at the highest levels of government and well beyond the authority of local regulators. So it takes a political guise. The interweaving of interests in this drama at times gets complicated. Temporary alliances are made and, having accomplished their purpose, broken. Interests are pulled in different directions, forcing painful choices. A short-term gain is sacrificed for a long-term benefit. Or vice versa. Occasionally in times of crisis, like a boat caught in a storm that must head to shore but is temporarily forced to turn to sea, they take positions that are contrary to what is expected. In general, though, the participants play their role according to the script they are assigned. The compass of self-interest which guides the parties actions in the battle is remarkably steady.

On its home turf, speculative capital is strongest. Its expansion seems to be a part of the natural state of affairs against which everything else must be measured. When Citicorp and Travelers, for example, merge, the merger is applauded as being good for "consumers."

> Some consumer advocates oppose the merger [between Travelers and Citicorp] because, they fear, financial behemoths inevitably threaten ordinary customers. But one-stop financial shopping could actually protect naïve investors ... An institution that sells [different] products can steer customers toward the product that best serves their needs[!].[56]

The relation of the merger with the driving force behind the deregulation of the financial industry goes unnoticed and unmentioned.

But theoretical deficiency does not impair the instinct of speculative

---

[55] "Mothra and Godzilla in Jakarta," *Wall Street Journal*, February 17, 1998, p. A22.
[56] "A Monster Merger," *New York Times*, April 8, 1998, p. A18.

capital's rivals to recognize the threat to their interests. They move to counter its expansion by a combination of defensive and offensive strategies.

As part of the defense, they prepare plans for the day the dollar might completely fall into the orbit of speculative capital. The plan revolves around the euro, which the rivals designate as their backup currency, a refuge of a sort, if you will. The policies that drive the European Union and the creation of the euro are replicates of the policies they have championed in the US. They aggressively support the common currency of Europe even though it presents a clear threat to the dominance of the dollar.

> *But theoretical deficiency does not impair the instinct of speculative capital's rivals to recognize the threat to their interests.*

Norbert Walter, chief economist at Deutsche Bank Research, cannot or does not want to explain the complex situation. So he is forced to offer a bizarre "consumer"-based explanation: "The euro will be to the dollar what Airbus is to Boeing [!] ... We have better airplanes as a result ... and euro will give us better [!] reserve currencies."[57]

Another euro supporter goes as far as claiming that the dominance of the dollar is unhealthy even for the US: "It is no longer necessary or even healthy for the US or the rest of the world to rely solely upon the dollar."[58]

Speculative capital knows that the euro reduces the number of currencies available for arbitrage. But that is a long-term issue in which it has no immediate interest. For the time being, the euro is yet another currency to be played against the dollar, yen, peso, etc., so it does not oppose the creation of the euro either.

As speculative capital attempts to spread its influence into the government machinery, legislative branch, judiciary and then across borders, resistance grows stronger. Internationally, the source of resistance is the local populace:

---

[57] "11 Nations Taking Next Pivotal Step Toward the Euro," *New York Times*, April 26, 1998, p. A1.

[58] "The Case for the Euro – II," *Wall Street Journal*, March 25, 1998, p. A22.

Stunned by the economic crisis, many Asians are concluding that glob-
alization is stacked in favor of the West, and they are looking to some
surprising new models, including the semi-closed economies of China
and India. Alternative ideas including ... a focus on agricultural ...
self-sufficiency, are being discussed.[59]

But these countries are already under the influence of speculative capital. Given that, the farm-based self-reliance solutions last as long as the
proverbial snowball under the summer sun.

But on the home front, rivals are strong. They also know that speculative capital is weakest in the merging markets when it is stretched thin.
So they take the fight there. That is how, starting in the second half of
1997, the Southeast Asian countries became the battleground between
speculative capital and its rivals. Speculative capital marched under the
banner of "rooting up crony capitalism and nepotism," "imposing international accounting standards," "insisting on transparency." Its rivals
criticized "throwing good money after bad" in foreign ventures or
throwing the "taxpayers' money" down the "rate hole" by financing the
IMF. They organized their forces and opened up with both barrels, one
directed at the Treasury Department, the other at the IMF. The two sides
knew each other's command centers.

First, they subjected the Treasury Department to harsh criticism for
helping to bail out "foolish investors." The *Wall Street Journal* chastised the Treasury Department for its involvement and the methods of
operation in South Korea:

> The US Treasury has by various accounts helped strong-arm Korea's
> creditor banks to the bargaining table – in what amounts to a quid pro
> quo for the bailouts these same banks are getting, via Seoul, from the
> IMF. It is worth asking whether any government treasury should be
> much involved in talks on private debt.[60]

---

[59] "Distrust of Western Economics Grows in Thailand Amid Crisis," *Wall Street Journal*, January 20, 1998, p. A14.
[60] "Banking in Korea," *Wall Street Journal*, January 27, 1998, p. A22.

Then came the attack on the IMF:

> The question is how the IMF – a secretive body whose methods and goals remain a mystery – came to play the role of chemotherapist in a country [Indonesia] where the wrong dosage will kill the patient ... there is reason to suspect that the Administration of President Bill Clinton is the prime force behind the IMF's decision to play hardball with Mr Suharto. That they are in cahoots is clear.[61]

Even the ever so balanced *New York Times* had to reflect the voices of opposition:

> A growing number of critics in the United States and across Asia argue that the IMF is not only acting at Washington's bidding but that it is protecting foreign investors, including many American banks and businesses, that made foolish investments in Asia.[62]

Knowing words alone could not win the battle, opponents of speculative capital moved to cripple the IMF's operations in the region by cutting off its financial lifeline; they opposed the administration's $18 billion funding request for the IMF on the ground that the Fund was responsible for the crisis in the first place. The *Wall Street Journal's* editorials were relentless:

> What caused the Asian crisis? ... While seeking another $18 billion from the US and total resources of $285 billion to handle this and future crises, the IMF has been puzzling for months over the question of causes ... We suggest Mr. Camdessus [IMF's managing director, the "socialist from France," according to Trent Lott, the Senate majority leader] consult the mirror on the wall.[63]

In an attempt to deny or at least delay the funding, the conservative members of Congress had tied the funding request for the IMF to various issues, including a promise of a cease and desist in anti-abortion

---

[61] "IMF Diplomacy," *Wall Street Journal*, March 10, 1998, p. A27.
[62] "Clinton's Personal Touch in Asian Rescue," *New York Times*, December 18, 1997, p. D8.
[63] "The IMF Crisis," *Wall Street Journal*, April 15, 1998, p. A22.

activities by the international agencies. The *New York Times*, with strong ties to the Treasury Department, criticized the linkage:

> House Republican leaders flaunt their disregard for America's broader interests by letting anti-abortion crusaders hold up funding for the International Monetary Fund ... The $18 billion for the IMF is meant to replenish its reserves after the recent bailouts of Thailand, South Korea and Indonesia ... America's trade interests and even the health of the economy could be jeopardized by delaying this funding.[64]

But the most telling battle erupted over a plan by Indonesia to introduce a currency board which would tie its currency, the rupiah, to the US dollar. Under a currency board, a country sets its currency at a fixed exchange rate with the dollar. Maintaining that relation then becomes the guiding light of the country's monetary and fiscal policies. It cannot, for example, issue any local currency

Speculative capital cannot live with "fixed" arrangements.

unless it is 100 percent backed by dollars in the central bank. The currency board's appeal to finance capital is clear: the board operates on the basis of a strict adherence to fiscal and monetary discipline; no spending beyond one's means. The currency board is the gold standard except that gold has been replaced with the dollar. All parties in the US except speculative capital enthusiastically support the idea.

Speculative capital cannot live with "fixed" arrangements. It needs to expand, which means that it constantly needs more rupiahs, dollars, marks and yen. In the fight over the currency board in Indonesia, the *Times* and *Journal* pulled out all the stops. The *New York Times*, having run out of ideas as to why Indonesia should not adopt a currency board, opposed it on the grounds that it would be a bad and "reckless" policy for Indonesia!

> The advocates of an Indonesian currency board point to its successful application in Hong Kong and Argentina ... Indonesia fits neither circumstance. For it to relinquish control over its monetary system amounts to reckless policy disarmament[!] ... Fortunately, the mone-

---

[64] "Foreign Policy Held Hostage," *New York Times*, March 16, 1998, p. A24.

tary fund has threatened to cut off the money if Mr Suharto proceeds with his foolhardy idea. The dictatorial Indonesian leader has the power to impose his irresponsible will on his countrymen. But the fund must tell him the West will not be complicit.[65]

The *Wall Street Journal*, noting that President Clinton had called President Suharto to dissuade him from implementing the currency board, went on the offensive:

> There can be no doubt that Indonesia's sovereign authority is under sustained assault. [The] International Monetary Fund … threatened to pull down what remains of Indonesia's economy unless Mr Suharto abandons a plan to establish a currency board … what is one to make of an American president pushing another country not to link its currency to the US dollar?[66]

Despite these protestations and gestures of support, Indonesia yielded to pressure and had to scrap the plans for a currency board. The *New York Times* celebrated the news, taking time to point out that there really was no other option:

> Pressed by foreign governments and by the power of the international marketplace, Indonesia retreated today from a highly criticized plan to strengthen its ravaged currency … Indonesian analysts said the Government's concession to international pressure was a painful acknowledgment that the nation was no longer free to determine its economic policy independently of the will of foreign markets. … Since the rupiah began its slide in July, Indonesia's economy and politics have increasingly been influenced by foreign investors' sentiments and the dictates of the IMF.[67]

The losing side was not pleased. A few days later, The *Wall Street Journal* lashed out at such blatant interference with the affairs of a sovereign nation:

---

[65] "Currency Boards Are No Elixir," *New York Times*, February 18, 1998, p. A22.
[66] "Mothra and Godzilla in Jakarta," *Wall Street Journal*, February 17, 1998, p. A22.
[67] "Under Pressure, Indonesia Halts Currency Plan," *New York Times*, February 21, 1998, p. D1.

> Freighted with an aging dictator, crony corruption and the worst crisis
> of all Asia's battered economies, Indonesia would seem to have trou-
> bles enough. Nope. It is now besieged by President Clinton, Treasury
> Secretary Rubin and their front men at the International Monetary
> Fund, mobilizing to stop President Suharto from adopting a currency
> board ... For Indonesia [the currency board] could spell the beginning
> of salvation ... But recent weeks have found Treasury Secretary Rubin
> attacking plans for an Indonesian currency board with every weapon
> he's got, including phone calls to Mr Suharto from Bill Clinton.[68]

The difficulty of determining who would come out on top in speculative capital's battle with its rivals presented some politicians with difficult choices. One such politician was the House Democratic leader and
presidential hopeful, Richard Gephardt. Earlier, he took a position
against speculative capital and was branded an isolationist. After the initial success of speculative capital in Southeast Asia, he adjusted his
position and in a trip to New York became an IMF supporter. The *New
York Times* covered his trip:

> Declaring that he had been "misunderstood and misrepresented" as a
> protectionist and isolationist last year, the Democratic leader of the
> House, Richard A. Gephardt, yesterday threw his support behind the
> Clinton Administration's efforts to win $18 billion in new financing for
> the International Monetary Fund ... His appearance in New York
> seemed part of his efforts to repair ruptured relations with foreign pol-
> icy specialists and major players – and donors – on Wall Street, whom
> he met over a private lunch.[69]

A few months after this meeting, the IMF opponents in Congress suc-
ceeded in dropping the administration's IMF funding request from the
authorization bill. Sensing a shift in the balance of power, Gephardt
moved to distance himself from the losers:

---

[68] "Rubin's Rupiah," *Wall Street Journal*, February 27, 1998, p. A18.
[69] "Saying He's No Isolationist, Gephardt Backs New Aid to IMF," *New York Times*,
March 4, 1998, p. A15.

The House Democratic leader and five other senior democrats threatened today to withdraw support for President Clinton's request for $18 billion in new financing for the International Monetary Fund ... if the Administration did not stop pressing for the fund's plan to enhance the unrestricted movement of investments in and out of countries.[70]

The interesting part of the story is Gephardt's condition for securing his support for the IMF funding, which shows the real reason for the fighting: "Unrestricted movement of investments in and out of countries."

That was not the end of the story. A few months later, under the headline "G.O.P., In Switch, Backs More Funds to Shore Up IMF," the *New York Times* reported:

House Republicans took the first step today toward approving all of the added money requested for the International Monetary Fund ... Representative Dick Armey of Texas, the majority leader and a harsh foe of the IMF, virtually conceded the fight. "In the end, I suppose they will probably get about as much money as they're looking for," Mr. Armey said.[71]

As to why the foes of the IMF funding had suddenly seen the light, the same article provided a clue: "With the Asian financial crisis deepening ... Wall Street's anxiety is rising and building pressure on House Republicans to drop their objections to the fund."[72]

The terms under which the Republicans agreed to funding were also quite amusing. It showed the internationalist proponents of speculative capital could outsmart their provincial opponents:

In order to approve the IMF package, congressional Republicans are demanding ... that the Treasury secretary and the Federal Reserve Board chairman certify that other major IMF shareholders ... have agreed to endorse the US-backed reforms before Congress releases portions of the funds.[73]

---

[70] "Democrats Threaten to Oppose IMF Bill," *New York Times*, May 2, 1998, p. A7.
[71] *New York Times*, July 16, 1998, p. A1.
[72] Ibid.
[73] "IMF Is Likely to Accept US Conditions," *Wall Street Journal*, October 13, 1998, p. A2.

The reforms were: shortening the maturity of loans and increasing their rates to three percentage points above the market rates and requiring "borrowing countries to set schedules for liberalizing trade, eliminating government-directed lending and okaying bankruptcy laws" – in short, exactly what speculative capital had always demanded. Little wonder that the spokesperson for the administration was jubilant: "'Most of the reforms that members of Congress are pushing for are things we've been pushing for a long time,' the Administration's delegate to the IMF said."[74]

The role of the Federal Reserve

By far the most precarious position in the battle between speculative capital and its rivals is that of the Federal Reserve. In the inter-family fight between the various forms of finance capital, the Fed must walk a tightrope. The Fed chairman knows that his job hangs in the balance but not in ways that monetarist economists imagine or advocate.

The chairman laughs at the naiveté of Milton Friedman and like-minded economists when they suggest that the Fed should be replaced with a computer. These economists reason that the sole duty of the Federal Reserve should be – and soon *would be* – to raise or lower interest rates according to readings from one or more indexes. That function cries out for automation. A computer could be programmed to raise or lower short-term rates if, say, the consumer price index rose above or fell below a preset number. That would leave little else for the Fed to do. Like other casualties of automation, it would declare itself redundant and go out of business. The central bank independence which the chairman avidly supports, paradoxically, seems to mean no Federal Reserve.

In the inter-family fight between the various forms of finance capital, the Fed must walk a tightrope.

The Fed chairman knows that, in reality, his importance as a regulator outweighs his role as an adjuster of interest rates. But the regulatory

---

[74] IMF Is Likely to Accept US Conditions," *Wall Street Journal*, October 13, 1998, p. A2.

power of the Federal Reserve, like that of the other central banks, is of a quite different kind than say, the SEC or CFTC. These latter agencies regulate the events or the conduct of individuals *in isolation*. The mechanics of an initial public offering, the responsibility of insiders in merger discussions, whether or not a specific derivative falls within the scope of the Commodities Exchange Act, these are the types of issues that the SEC and the CFTC deal with. The Federal Reserve, by contrast, regulates the system – more precisely, the *working of the system*. It supervises the *process*. The process we are referring to here is the process of the circulation of capital – the very finance itself.

Circulation of capital is not analogous to the flow of a river or working of a machine. The river flows naturally due to gravity. The working of a machine is also "natural" in the sense that it relies upon, and follows from, the laws of nature. A machine can be set on "autopilot" precisely because we trust the laws of gravity, electromagnetism, optics, etc., to carry it through its functioning. It is taken for granted that all the components of a machine will work in unison with one another and in accordance with the laws of nature. It would border on madness if it were otherwise.

The process of circulation of capital, by contrast, is driven by the profit motive of competing forms of capital, each fighting against all others for a bigger share of the profit pie. If commercial capital increases its share, everything else being constant, the share of industrial capital must decrease. And if the share of credit capital increases, the share of all the others will decline.

As the regulator of the process, the Fed must constantly juggle the competing demands of its constituents locked in the struggle. In the pre-speculative capital days, the task was relatively easy. It consisted of controlling the money supply and the interest rates with the dual purposes of sustaining industrial growth and keeping inflation in check. As finance capital grew in influence, the Fed's focus shifted to fighting inflation, which, if anything, was even easier. Industrial capital dissented every now and then, but those folks in the Midwest never understood the fine points of finance anyway.

The rise of speculative capital presented a challenge. Speculative capital needs to expand. Expansion requires fresh sources of credit capital, which a tight monetary policy precludes. How could the Federal Reserve meet the demands of speculative capital without straying from the tight monetary course prescribed by the credit and commercial capital?

The Fed Chairman finds his answer in that mystical source of power and wealth increase – credit. So while holding a tight grip on interest rates and money supply, he facilitates the expansion of speculative capital by unleashing fresh sources of credit in ways which few notice, much less object to. In doing so, he helps accelerate speculative capital's self-destructive movements which could lead to a system-wide collapse. That is the systemic risk.

> *How could the Federal Reserve meet the demands of speculative capital without straying from the tight monetary course prescribed by the credit and commercial capital?*

References

Altman, Roger C. "The Nuke of the 90s," *New York Times Magazine*, March 1, 1998, p. 34.

Baker, Russell (1996) "Used to Talk, Now Shrieks," *New York Times*, June 29, p. 19.

Volker, Paul and Gyohten, Toyoo (1992) *Changing Fortunes*, New York: Times Books.

White, Harry (1945) "The Monetary Fund: Some Criticisms Examined," *Foreign Affairs*, Vol. 23, No. 2 (January), pp. 195–210.

6

SYSTEMIC RISK

What is the "system" in systemic risk? • Interaction of speculative and credit capital • Basis risk • Build-up and materialization of systemic risk • Consequences • Countermeasures • The role of derivatives

Introduction

Systemic risk is the risk of a chain-reaction of bankruptcies which then disrupt the process of circulation of capital.

In a pamphlet published by the Federal Reserve Bank of New York, Gerald Corrigan (1987, p. 16) then president of the bank wrote:

> The hard fact of the matter is that linkages created by the large-dollar payments systems are such that a serious credit problem at any of the large users of the system has the potential to disrupt the system as a whole.

Corrigan was specifically writing about a "gridlock" problem in CHIPS, the interbank clearing system in New York.[1] That is what he meant by the "large-dollar payments systems." He was concerned that the default of a major bank with myriad of large payments could cause a chain reaction of defaults in CHIPS. The term systemic risk he is said to have coined referred to the risk arising from such cross-defaults. It was the risk of disruption in the clearing system.

That is a narrow understanding of systemic risk. It is on the same footing as regarding finance as the study of cash flows; it reduces diverse aspects of the subject into a quantitative flash point. The problem so narrowly delineated is easily solved. But for that very reason, the cause of the problem escapes scrutiny, with the result that it surfaces more menacingly at a higher level.

The cause of the problem escapes scrutiny, with the result that it surfaces more menacingly at a higher level.

That is precisely what came to pass with regards to the systemic risk. The potential problem of chain defaults in CHIPS was resolved by establishing credit lines to cover the payments of a defaulting bank. CHIPS has now sufficient funds to cover the oblig-

---

[1] CHIPS is the acronym for Clearing House Interbank Payment System. Banks settle their large payments, mostly the dollar legs of foreign exchange transactions, through CHIPS. The average gross daily volume in CHIPS is presently over $1 trillion, with the net debit standing around $50 billion.

ation of its two largest net debits. But the systemic risk did not go away. In September 1998, the Federal Reserve organized the rescue of Long Term Capital Management (LTCM), a hedge fund on the brink of collapse. In defending the intervention against critics, the Fed chairman cited the danger of the systemic risk, which he defined as the risk of the collapse of financial systems. Despite the notable expansion of the definition of systemic risk – from a gridlock in CHIPS to financial systems – the prescription for the problem was exactly what it had been in CHIPS: saving the first "domino" from falling so the others would not fall. The justification for the intervention – how the Fed knew the bankruptcy of LTCM might result in chain defaults – was strictly of a "trust me" kind.

It is impossible to understand systemic risk without knowing speculative capital and understanding the financial, regulatory, legal and political aspects of its operation. Systemic risk is the culmination of contradictions in these arenas as they relate to speculative capital. Having studied speculative capital in some detail, we now ready to explore the systemic risk. To that end, we must answer the following questions:

- What is the "system" in systemic risk?
- How does the systemic risk take shape?
- How does the risk spread throughout the system?
- What is the "peril of systemic risk? That is, what are the consequences of materialization of systemic risk?

What is the "system" in systemic risk?

The system in systemic risk is the process of circulation of capital *and* the markets which form the circuitry of the process – the course of its movement. Alternatively, we can say that the system is a web of markets "linked" together by the thread of speculative capital. Thus, the "system" has two components: process and markets.

A system defined by such terms as circuitry and flow lends itself to superficial analogies. Often, electrical circuits are used to depict it. Occasionally, one hears of traffic systems and "gridlock." Writing in the *Wall Street Journal*, the financier George Soros gave it a human touch and compared it to the body's blood circulation system – with the US, naturally, being the heart.

But the system of concern to us is a social one; it has little in common with physical or biological systems. The "market" component of the system varies greatly in size, from a stock exchange in a country to the country's national economy. The strength of the market's linkage to the system is shaped by its size, regulatory structure, the political environment in which it functions and the country's proximity to existing centers of international trade and finance. There are numerous secondary factors as well, which, sometimes reinforcing and sometimes offsetting each other, further contribute to shaping the characteristics of the system.

While speculative capital exerts enormous influence on the financial, legal and political structure of countries in its orbit, its dominance has not yet reached a point where all the markets in these countries – fixed income, currencies and equities – move synchronously all the time. As we saw in the previous chapter, strong forces stand in the way of such dominance. The current size of speculative capital also precludes its simultaneous engagement in all the markets. For that, speculative capital must grow many more times in size. For these reasons, the scope of the systemic risk is "local," meaning that it is limited to a segment of the global markets. That "local" could encompass a cluster of Southeast Asian countries or be limited to the stock and futures markets in the US.

Speculative capital exerts enormous influence on the financial, legal and political structures of countries in its orbit.

Needless to say, the larger systems have a more complex structure. A systemic failure besetting the Southeast Asian economies must be analyzed in terms of financial, as well as political and legal issues. A meltdown in the US stock market due to the influence of stock index futures trading and portfolio insurance strategies can be explained in terms of purely financial parameters. In all events, systemic risk is born from the movements of speculative capital: "The heart of this current crisis [in Southeast Asia] … is the surge of capital flows. The surge is followed by a precipitous flow out. Few countries, no matter how strong their financial institutions, could have withstood such a turnaround,"[2] declares the chief economist of the World Bank.

This is a description of the movement of speculative capital without knowing speculative capital. Capital inflows, followed by precipitous capital flows, do not in themselves cause a crisis. If every country in the world received $100 billion in the morning and remitted $100 billion in the afternoon, there would be no systemic risk; the net effect of the transactions will be zero. Likewise, the CHIPS manager who proudly announces the establishment of credit lines to cover the failure of its two largest net debits must ask himself this question: under what conditions would the two largest net debits in CHIPS – say, J. P. Morgan and Chase – fail? What would *cause* such failures? That is the question that we answer in examining systemic risk. Systemic risk is a technical concept and must be explained as such; generalities do not suffice.

How does systemic risk take shape?

Systemic risk comes into existence as a result of formation of basis risk in leveraged positions. To understand systemic risk, we need to understand basis risk and the role of leverage.

Basis risk is a concept inherent to arbitrage trading. In several places in previous chapters, we mentioned basis risk and pointed out that simultaneous positions established in arbitrage are not, as generally assumed, "risk free." In this chapter, we must delve deeper into that subject. We begin our analysis of systemic risk, however, with looking at leverage – the relation between speculative and credit capital.[3]

Interaction of speculative and credit capital

Webster's definition of leverage as "increasing means of accomplishing some purpose" in finance refers to increasing the rate of return of capi-

---

[2] "US and IMF Made Asia Crisis Worse, World Bank Finds", *New York Times*, December 3, 1998, p. A1.

[3] Leverage arises from interaction of credit capital with all forms of capital. Our focus here is on its interaction with speculative capital.

tal through the use of credit capital. Such increase, when credit capital interacts with industrial or commercial capital, is always modest because the amount of credit capital available to a factory owner or a wholesaler is limited by their equity. That is why some factory owners and wholesalers can avoid debt "as a matter of principle." One could say that these businessmen have the mentality of pre-capitalist peasants; they have not grasped the advantages of borrowed capital. But more to the point, they can *afford* to have that mentality because the contribution of credit capital to their bottom line is modest.

No manager of speculative capital, on the other hand, can avoid leverage. With regard to speculative capital, credit capital is more than an booster of returns. It is a vital component of support, an engine of sorts, without which speculative capital cannot operate. This new role develops logically and naturally, and in consequence of the real-life conditions under which speculative capital operates.

In real life, the arbitrageable spreads yield returns which are considerably below the average rate of return of capital. It would be an unimaginably gross inefficiency of the markets were it otherwise. The very operation of speculative capital further tends to decrease these spreads, diminishing its rate of return. The small-time speculator – a pit

No manager of speculative capital can avoid leverage.

trader in a futures exchange, for example – compensates for the narrowness of the spreads by trading constantly and incessantly. The *mass* of speculative capital cannot act in that way. It is impossible to turn over the multi-billion dollar portfolio of a hedge fund many times a day or even a week. So speculative capital searches for venues which will allow it to increase the monetary value of its return without increasing its size. One such venue is through enlisting the aid of credit capital. (The other is through the use of derivatives, as we will see shortly.) Acting as a lever, credit capital raises the return to levels which speculative capital in itself cannot produce. The mathematics of leverage is widely known in the market:

> Before [February 1994], speculators had been borrowing at a short-term rate of like 3% and buying five-year Treasury notes yielding around 5%, a gaping spread of two percentage points that enabled some

to double their money in a year. The math was tantalizing. Using leverage, an investor with $1 million could borrow enough to acquire $50 million in five-year Treasury notes. And the spread of two percentage points could generate about $1 million in profits on the $1 million investment, as long as rates remained stable or declined.[4]

Without the leverage of credit capital, the $1 million in question would have generated $20,000 in return, hardly sufficient to cover the expenses of running a fund. With the help of credit capital, the return is increased 50 fold, to $1 million. That was precisely the game that the treasurer of Orange County and many fund managers were playing prior to 1994, albeit with lower leverage ratios. While fund mangers are aware of the role of credit capital, few of them fully grasp the vital role of "borrowed money" in arbitrage situations.

A few months after the troubles at Long Term Capital Management became front page news, the *Wall Street Journal* ran a lengthy article on the rise and fall of the firm. It described one episode involving a botched sales presentation at Conseco Capital where Myron Scholes, a partner at LTCM, was explaining the firm's strategy:

> The fund, Mr Scholes said, would leverage its capital to take advantage of pricing "anomalies" in global markets. "You are not adding any value," interjected Andrew Chow, the Conseco vice president in charge of derivatives. He added: "I don't think there are that many pure anomalies that can occur."[5]

According to the *Journal*, in response, Scholes derided the Conseco vice president, saying that "as long as there continue to be people like you, we'll make money." Needless to say, the presentation failed to raise funds.

Had Myron Scholes known of the relation between speculative and credit capital, he may have been able to save the day and counter the valid point of Conseco's vice president by responding in the following manner:

---

[4] "Drop in Rates Doesn't Mean Repeat of 1994," *Wall Street Journal*, October 16, 1995, p. C1.
[5] "How Salesmanship, Brainpower Failed at a Giant Hedge Fund," *Wall Street Journal*, November 16, 1998, p. A1.

"I interpret your comments as meaning that arbitrage opportunities, while many, are mostly too narrow to yield acceptable levels of return. That is indeed a very correct observation. But the emphatic point of my comments, Mr Chow, was *leverage*, not *anomaly*. Specifically, we plan to identify an arbitrage situation of say, 15 or 20 basis points and then increase the absolute size of the return by leveraging the position by a factor of 30, 40, 50 or more. Of course, that kind of leverage involves risk. That is why I did not originally emphasize the point; that would have been poor salesmanship. But sir, there you have it. We are going to generate good return through leveraged arbitrage."

At the time the troubles at Long Term Capital became public, the firm's leverage ratio was reported to be around 50.

To a bank loan officer who lends on the traditional criteria, that leverage is incomprehensible, almost madness. No business could generate sufficient profits to service a debt 50 times the owner's equity. But arbitrage is no ordinary business. In fact, it is not even a business. It is a refined version of banks' own practice of borrowing low and lending high, so the banks readily recognize it. The strategy is "refined," because now the profits are guaranteed to be riskless "no matter what happens to interest rates."

That is why and how speculative capital comes to depend on credit capital for survival. The expansion of credit capital becomes a condition for its own expansion. Credit capital, too, assumes a support function unlike any it had before. It becomes imperative for it to "be there," when called upon and follow speculative capital to new arbitrage ventures such as leveraged finance, leveraged buyout and junk bonds. These markets are the manifestation of the incestuous relation between credit and speculative capital: they revolve around credit capital, but without speculative capital in the lead, they could not have been developed.[6] In the speculative frenzy of the 1920s,

Speculative capital comes to depend on credit capital for survival.

---

[6] The fall of Michael Milken did not end the junk bond market. Quite the contrary. It signaled the beginning of the institutionalization of junk bonds, which could begin only if the crude serfdom established by Milken were to be dismantled.

for example, the role of credit capital did not go beyond the traditional boosting of returns through margins because the independent form of speculative capital did not exist.[7] Just how closely the junk bond market is associated with speculation can be seen from the following technical comments of a trader:

> "High-yield bonds should outperform during the next six weeks, but in the next six months, I'd concentrate on higher-quality bonds because I'm still worried about corporate earnings next year," says Joseph Balestrino of Federated Investors.[8]

Prior to the advent of speculative capital, bonds of all kinds were purchased and held for years, even decades. Mr Balestrino's horizon, when speaking of junk bonds, is six weeks.

The most important aspect of the relation between credit and speculative capital is the quantitative one. Because speculative capital constantly expands, credit capital, too, must expand. The expansion brings about an increase in the leverage which can best be seen in the light of comparison. When National Can was acquired in 1985, it had $100 million in equity and was saddled with $565 million in debt. Nelson Peltz, who acquired National Can through junk bond financing, boasted that he had pulled a fast one on the market by arranging a deal with the leverage ratio of 11 to 1. "We put the $100 million in the sub [the subsidiary formed for the buyout]. But it was all debt! We called it equity here but it was debt over there. Do you understand the leverage in this deal? It was eleven to one!" (Bruck, 1988, p. 109).

Eight years later, the venerable firm of Kidder–Peabody had managed to raise its leverage ratio to 94 to 1: "Kidder is Wall Street's most highly leveraged firm; it held $94 in bonds, stocks and other assets for every $1

---

[7] The massive borrowing of the US government beginning in the 1980s also helped to spearheaded the advance of speculative capital. We cannot delve into that subject here. We merely note that while the policies which transformed the US from a creditor to a debtor country in a stunningly short time were driven by various political and social forces, Ronald Reagan was as much instrumental in the institutionalization of speculative capital as Michael Milken. Both were the products of their time.

[8] "To Some, Junk Bonds Are Undervalued," *Wall Street Journal*, December 1, 1998, p. C1

in equity at year end."[9] With that, the firm pulled a fast one on itself. It suffered heavy losses in fixed income trading and a few months later was sold to a rival.

Where does the credit capital for sustaining such colossal expansion come from? The ambiguity and apparent subjectivity of the word "credit" at times make it seem that it is created out of thin air. The practice of banks in creating credit money further reinforces that illusion.[10]

In reality, "credit" is credit capital. Its creation, expansion and movement have their own laws and are governed by a complex set of rules. Their detailed analysis is beyond the scope of this book. Here, we are only concerned with the source of expansion of credit capital and the consequences of that expansion. The source of the expansion of credit capital is the easy credit policy of the Federal Reserve. The "easy credit" involves more than reducing interest rates. It also includes technical rule changes which provide fresh sources of credit. In April 1996, for example, the *Wall Street Journal* reported: "The Federal Reserve moved to ease scores of regulations affecting margin requirements, calling it 'one of the most significant reductions in regulatory burdens on broker-dealers since 1934.'"[11]

Apparently unconvinced of the significance of the Fed's announcement, the *Journal* relegated the story to page 18. It said, in part:

> The final rules ... will eliminate restrictions on a broker-dealer's ability to arrange for an extension of credit by another lender; let dealers lend on any convertible bond if the underlying stock is suitable for margin; increase the loan value of money-market mutual funds from a 50% margin requirement to a good faith standard ... and allow dealers to lend on any investment-grade debt security ... the Fed will allow the lending of foreign securities to foreign persons for any purposes against any legal collateral ... It will also expand the criteria for determining which securities qualify for securities credit, a change that

---

[9] "Fired Kidder Aide Tells US He Acted On Orders, Firm Violated Capital Rules," *Wall Street Journal*, July 26, 1994, p. A2

[10] A bank creates money by debiting "loan asset" and crediting "customer account." The practice creates money – credit money – by mere bookkeeping entries.

[11] "Fed Acts to Ease Many Regulations Affecting Margin," *Wall Street Journal*, April 25, 1996, p. C18.

will sharply increase the number of foreign stocks that are margin-eligible.[12]

The changes described in the article were too technical to be individually analyzed here. (That is probably why the news received very little attention.) The important point is the purpose of the rule changes: to open the floodgates of credit capital. The Fed was correct about the significance of the decision.

As one example, the new rules allowed the money market mutual funds "to be treated like their underlying securities for margin purposes." The US Treasury bills in such funds could be purchased with a 90 per cent margin. When the mutual fund itself is treated like its underlying security, its shares can in turn be pledged as margin for buying securities 10 times their value. The result is a leverage ratio approaching 100 to 1.

Rule changes by the Federal Reserve do not take place on a whim. In fact, they never take place without a strong impetus: in this case, the pressure of speculative capital whose expansion called for ever larger amounts of credit capital. In the familiar scenario of speculative capital forcefully breaking down the regulatory walls, the Fed had to give room and reduce the "regulatory burdens."

> *The result is a leverage ratio approaching 100 to 1.*

An unrelated *Wall Street Journal* article, published a few weeks after the rule changes were announced, told of the source of the pressure:

> Everyone who has even thumbed casually through the books of securities firms recently agrees they are more highly leveraged than ever ... It is [the] matched-book portion of firms' balance sheets, where assets and liabilities are paired ... that has soared in recent years ... [two] consultants ... have suggested that the bloating of the industry's asset-liability structure reflects an unprecedented and somewhat involuntary commitment to "yield arbitrage," or the practice of taking advantage of small differences in interest rates ... Securities firm executives insist and analysts generally agree that this business generates little market

---

[12] Ibid.

risk, just a dollop of credit risk and perhaps more operations related risk than anything else.[13]

The two consultants quoted in the article noticed the role of yield curve arbitrage in increasing the leverage of the securities firms. Their observation that the firms' commitment to this strategy is "somewhat involuntary" is specially perceptive. Of course, speculative capital engages in a great many arbitrage opportunities; yield curve arbitrage is only the most readily recognizable one.

The leverage surpasses all historical levels in the bond market: "The demand for financing, and for leveraged purchases of bonds, has reached a ridiculous level."[14] Yet the Federal Reserve had to loosen the rules even further:

> The Federal Reserve Board proposed new capital guidelines ... that would provide the biggest break to banks that sell triple-A rated asset-backed securities. Currently, banks ... are assessed an 8% capital charge on the security's full value. Under the proposed guidelines, the 8% charge would be ... [reduced to] an effective [rate of] 1.6% ... a Fed financial analyst who helped write the proposed rules [said]: "This rule will fit in nicely with the way the market is moving."[15]

The analyst is right on the mark. In fact, he is more right than he could suspect. In saying that the rule changes "fit in nicely with the way the market is moving," he has in mind the general deregulatory trend and the need of banks for constantly increasing amounts of credit capital. But there is one other, more fundamental movement in part of the market which is not readily discernible. That movement is the gradual advancing of the markets toward a sudden disruption. The anatomy of one component of that movement – the spiralling leverage – is now laid bare before us:

● A financial institution with $2 in equity and $8 in liabilities ventures

[13] "Securities Firms' Leverage Stirs Debate," *Wall Street Journal*, May 6, 1996, p. B6B.
[14] "Fizzle, Bond Rally May Some Fear, *Wall Street Journal*, August 12, 1996, p. C1.
[15] "Fed Board Proposes New Rules for Banks," *Wall Street Journal*, August 22, 1997, p. A2.

into arbitrage trading. The firm's assets, the sum of its liabilities and the owners' equity is $10, as shown by the fundamental accounting equation:

$$A \text{ (assets)} = L \text{ (liabilities)} + OE \text{ (owners' equity)}$$

in this case:

$$10 = 8 + 2$$

The firm's leverage ratio – the ratio of liabilities to owners' equity – is 4.

• The firm locks its speculative capital in various arbitrage activities. This is "matching of assets and liabilities." If the size of the matched position is 50, the balance sheet takes the following form:

$$52 = 50 + 2$$

The leverage ratio increases to 25.

• The firm needs more arbitrage positions. It has found an ideal situation where it can lend $30 to a customer and then lock in a profitable spread by taking an opposite position in Treasury notes. But the customer only holds grade C bonds – one level above "junk." The regulation prohibits lending on such collateral. So the firm – and many other firms in its position – pressures the Fed to change the regulation. The Fed "allow[s] dealers to lend on any investment-grade debt security." The transaction takes place and the balance sheet looks as follows:

$$82 = 80 + 2$$

The leverage ratio is now 40, having increased tenfold from the starting point.

• The cycle continues.[16]

---

[16] The pressure on the Federal Reserve system to accommodate the needs for ever greater amounts of credit capital is incessant. Witness the following: "Government-bond dealers are urging the Federal Reserve Bank of New York to buy government-sponsored enterprise debt as part of its open-market operations…The bond group's pitch was that such a move would benefit the Fed's portfolio management." "Bond Dealers Urge Fed to Resume Buying 'Agency' Securities Such as Fannie Mae's," *Wall Street Journal*, November 2, 1998, p. A31A. That is quite a daring pitch, selling "portfolio management" to a Federal Reserve bank.

Basis risk

In this example, the leverage progressively increases, but assets and liabilities always remain "matched," meaning that decline in the value of one position is expected to be offset by an equal rise in the value of the other. For that reason, the matched positions are thought to be "risk neutral," which explains why they are assumed to generate "little market risk [and] a dollop of credit risk," the latter referring to the possibility of counterparty default.

Unfortunately, the events in the market do not always bear this out. Sometimes the two sides of a matched position move unequally, the loss surpassing the gain. Or one position suffers a loss while the other does not produce any gain. Worse yet, both positions suffer a loss! Even prior to the watershed year 1997 which witnessed the financial crisis in Southeast Asia, firms which had incurred losses in their matched positions were legion. In 1994, for example, Banc One lost $235 million in what it said was "balance sheet management:"

> Banc One was sitting on $18 billion in net received fixed rate swaps …
> As interest rates rose, Banc One's spread on swaps turned negative …
> [the bank's chairman] said that Banc One, which used swaps to hedge
> its balance sheet, was likely to wind down its use of such derivatives.
> "Using derivatives for balance sheet management has extracted a toll
> on shareholders," [an analyst] said.[17]

Even the "rocket science" of bond arbitrage did not seem immune to unexpected turns:

> The poor performance by Salomon's high-flying proprietary operations are particularly disturbing, investors say. The losses, which people at the firm estimate as much as $100 million before taxes, were concentrated in the elite US bond arbitrage group.[18]

---

[17] "Banc One Will Take a $235 Million Charge," *New York Times*, November 22, 1994, p. D5.

[18] "As Markets Boom, Salomon Losses Return," *Wall Street Journal*, July 12, 1995, p. C1.

Traders are aware of the danger of the uneven movement of the matched positions; they call it the basis risk. The name has its origin in the US Treasuries market, which, until the rise of speculative capital, was the only one in which traders could systematically take simultaneous long and short positions in different maturities.[19]

Textbooks in finance by and large sidestep basis risk because it is fundamentally irreconcilable with the theories of modern finance. Basis risk cannot exist in efficient markets. The value of derivatives is also derived from the implicit assumption that there is no basis risk. The authors who choose to even allude to the subject find themselves trapped in obvious contradictions. John Hull (1997, p. 32) describes the source of the basis risk in futures:

Textbooks in finance by and large sidestep basis risk because it is fundamentally irreconcilable with the theories of modern finance.

> There are a number of reasons why hedging using futures contracts works less than perfectly in practice. 1. The asset whose price is to be hedged may not be exactly the same as the asset underlying the futures contract … These problems give rise to what is termed *basis risk.*

In this passage, Hull implies that if the asset whose price is to be hedged is *exactly the same* as the asset underlying the futures contracts, the hedge would be "perfect" and there would be no basis risk. But the point is precisely that even if the futures and its underlying asset are the same, basis risk is still present. Every trader can tell of days when the spot prices moved sharply up or down without a corresponding move in the futures. Or vice versa. Hull must have known that. Two pages later he adds: "Note that basis risk can lead to an improvement or worsening of a hedger's position. Consider a short hedge. If the basis strengthens unexpectedly, the hedger's position improves." In explaining the basis risk, standard finance has hit a wall: this *risk* can *improve* a hedger's position!

Basis risk is a difference risk. It is the risk of *change* in the *difference* between two variables. The word "risk" pertains to the change in the

---

[19] The concept of basis risk in the futures market existed ever since the futures contracts began trading. But trading which *focused* on basis began with the Treasuries.

basis and not its direction. A favorable change to one party is as much in need of explanation as an unfavorable change to another; they are the two faces of the same coin. The question before us is this: Why does the basis risk exist?

The simple answer to that question is that the basis risk is the omnipresent market risk, only that it has assumed a slightly different form. It exists because it was always there and never went away.

To elaborate this point, let us consider the quintessential hedger of finance textbooks – a farmer who sets out to protect himself against a drop in the price of whatever commodity he happens to produce. If he produces wheat, corn or soybeans, he sells wheat, corn and soybean futures, respectively.[20] In so doing, he locks in a specific price and insulates himself against future price fluctuations. Should a corn farmer, whose production cost is $3.00, sell corn futures at $3.20, he would be locking in a profit of $0.20 per bushel. That profit is guaranteed regardless of corn

> *Hedging no more eliminates price fluctuations than buying flood insurance eliminates floods.*

price fluctuations in the future. That is the much touted benefit of futures as an insurance vehicle.

The phrase "regardless of corn price fluctuations" describes the position of the farmer. In adroitly shifting the focus from the market to the farmer, standard finance is able to pass over the subject. But it is clear that hedging no more eliminates corn price fluctuations than buying flood insurance eliminates floods. It merely insulates the farmer against them. And it does so at a definite cost. By choosing to hedge, the farmer trades the market risk for the basis risk.[21] Otherwise, the same factors

---

[20] Technically, farmers use the OTC forward market. For the purpose of our present discussion, the difference is immaterial.

[21] In futures, the basis is defined as the difference between the spot and forward prices of the underlying:

$$\text{Basis} = \text{spot price} - \text{forward price}$$

Let us assume that S_0 and S_T are the spot price and the price at time T of the underlying, respectively. In the open position, the risk is $S_T - S_0$, with S_T unknown. If the position is hedged with a futures contract whose spot and time T prices are F_0 and F_T, respectively, the risk becomes:

which influences the price of corn remain unaffected and could change the basis in unpredictable ways. If, in our example, the corn price increases to say, $4.10, the farmer must deliver it at the contract price of $3.20 and forego the additional $0.90 profit. That is the basis risk, whose source, like that of the market risk, is price fluctuations.

What are the factors which cause the price of corn to fluctuate? A partial list might include: the seasonal change in demand for corn, new producers in the market, an increase or decrease in the substitutability of other agricultural products for corn and vice versa, advances in genetic engineering, the imposition and relaxation of government subsidies, exceptionally good weather, floods, drought and other meteorological factors, the actions of speculators, wars, etc. The economists' expedient short form for them is "supply and demand" factors.[22]

Many of the factors are social in nature and do not lend themselves to quantification. Each factor influences the corn price in a certain manner, different from others. And the influences interact, sometimes reinforcing and sometimes offsetting one another. These effects, furthermore, are "local," meaning that they are specific to the corn market and corn prices. The outbreak of war or a severe drought affect the prices of all agricultural products. But their impact on corn prices is never quite the same as say, on soybeans. That simply follows from the fact that corn is a specific commodity unlike any other. The net effect of these influences on the hour by hour or day by day price of corn is impossible to quantify.

Our simple answer" is that basis risk exists because of the interaction of numerous, impossible-to-quantify variables. That is the economists' familiar supply and demand "answer." It is not wrong. But pointing to supply and demand as the cause of the basis risk is akin to blaming gravity for the cause of a plane crash. It is too general an answer to be of use

---

$$(S_T - S_0) - (F_T - F_0) \qquad or \qquad (S_T - F_T) - (S_0 - F_0)$$

The term $S_0 - F_0$ is the current basis, which is known. The remaining risk is the basis at time T, $S_T - F_T$, which is unknown. By hedging, the price risk $S_T - S_0$ is replaced with basis risk, $S_T - F_T$.

[22] We repeat that "supply and demand" determine the fluctuation *around* the value and not the value itself. Here, our concern is precisely with fluctuations.

in a specific investigation. In asking "Why does the basis risk exist?" we wanted to find out why two matched positions result in either a profit or a loss. That is, we wanted to know: why does the difference between the two matched positions fluctuate?

"Matched positions" could describe wildly different scenarios, including cases outside finance. We see that the source of the ambiguity and the reason our initial inquiry went astray is structural: a matched position is defined as two positions where the loss in one is expected to be offset by a gain in the other. But the problem is precisely the break-down of that definition: the positions, which were matched with the expectation of changing equal and opposite amounts, change an unequal amount. In that case, they could not have been "matched," although that is how they must have appeared to the arbitrageur at the time the posi-tions were taken. So the answer to our problem must lie at the point of formation of basis risk, where the farmer first used futures to hedge his corn. Let us return there and follow the developments closely.

Basis risk in arbitrage

When the farmer hedges his corn, the basis risk is inconspicuous, almost hidden. That is because he owns the deliverable commodity. Ownership acts as a protective cushion against price shocks, and also as a cover for concealing the cost of hedging. If the price of corn declines, the farmer will be happy at having sold it at a higher price. If the price increases, it appears to him as an opportunity cost. His practical mind sees it as a pointless "what might have been" speculation. Under no condition, however, does he risk being ruined. He has eliminated that risk by agree-ing to limit his potential profit.[23]

When we move from hedging to arbitrage, the nature of the game changes drastically. The arbitrageur does not own the corn or any other commodity. His game is to lock in a profitable spread between *any two* positions. If the spread moves against him, he incurs a loss. The loss is

---

[23] The heavy losses farmers suffered from the so-called hedge to-arrive futures came about precisely because they had sold more futures than they could deliver.

no longer a matter of lost opportunity but a very real one. Replace the farmer in our example with an arbitrageur. He will be "long" the spot and "short" the corn futures. That amounts to being short the basis. If the basis increased above its original value of $0.20, the arbitrageur would have to pay the difference. For example, if futures rise to $4.10, he loses $0.90 (4.10 – 3.20) per bushel. The change in basis which was of little consequence to the farmer can make or break the arbitrageur. The ante is upped considerably.

That is not all. Along with an increase in risk, the margin for error is reduced. That follows from the nature of the basis risk which arises from the difference between two values. The numerical value of the change in the basis is the result of the permutation of changes in two variables. The arbitrageur must calculate them both.

To illustrate this point, let us assume that F and S are two values whose difference, $D = F - S$, is the basis risk an arbitrageur faces. If D decreases, he would incur a loss. The loss will materialize if:

- F remains constant, S increases.
- F increases, S increases still more.
- S remains constant, F decreases.
- S decreases, F decreases still more.
- F decreases, S increases.

These conditions do not exist in the case of a single position. Holders of a stock, bond or currency will profit if the value of their holding increases by a however small an amount. The arbitrageur, on the other hand, could be right in the *direction* of one or even both his trades and still incur a loss because he was wrong in the *size* of the price movement. That is, it is not sufficient for him to be right. He has to be right by the right amount.

How does the arbitrageur select his targets? That question does not arise for the farmer. Because of the historical circumstance of being a corn farmer, his choice of hedge vehicle is limited to what is offered to him. The arbitrageur does not have that limitation. He is free to choose. But his freedom means little and could in fact bring about his ruin unless he can select the arbitrage targets in a logical way. Could he arbitrage the spread between pork bellies in the US and the French stock index

CAC-40? Of course, he could – if we take "could" to mean the actual possibility of doing it. But then he would have no capital and no job. And that is no freedom. *Would* he arbitrage the pork bellies and CAC-40? He intuitively answers "No" to the question and he would be right. That is because his free choice is formed – nay, dictated – by the hidden dynamics of speculative capital which creates the arbitrage opportunities at the same time as it lures the arbitrageurs towards them. "One senior Wall Street executive with responsibility for the matched book said that with regard to the genesis of balance sheet inflation, a fine line exists: 'Did it happen to me or did I make it happen?'"[24] The answer to this hapless executive is: you were forced to do it! Like Oedipus, this deed is inflicted upon him rather than committed by him.[25]

> *But his freedom means little and could in fact bring about his ruin.*

We are running ahead of ourselves. Let us return to the arbitrageur and look more closely at his actions, options and the circumstances surrounding them.

The arbitrageur must buy low and sell high. If he buys low in one location and sells high in another, he would be a merchant. If he buys low now and sells high later, he would be a wholesaler or a retailer. So when Samuelson and Nordhaus (1995, p. 181) write that "speculative markets serve society by moving goods from abundant times or places to those of scarcity" they are precisely wrong on both accounts. An arbitrageur must buy low and sell high *at the same time in the same place*.[26] Obviously, he cannot do that with the same commodity. That would entail the presence of an infinite supply of rich fools. Instead, he must

---

[24] "Securities Firms' Leverage Stirs Debate," *Wall Street Journal*, May 6, 1996, p. B6B.

[25] Even the holder of an option – that much heralded "right but not the obligation" – has no option. This point will become clear in Volume 2, Chapter 2, when we examine the risks of options.

[26] Buying a currency in Tokyo and selling it in New York constitutes buying and selling at the same location because the executor of the strategy, a trader in an international bank, has simultaneous access to both markets. The function of the real-time quotation systems is precisely eliminating the geographical differences.

buy (or go long) one position and simultaneously sell (short) an *equivalent* position. In this way, he matches his positions, which are qualitatively different. The heart of his game plan is beginning to emerge: to arbitrage the deviation of qualitative differences of equivalent positions so as to profit when the difference is returned to normal.

We now see something which, even if we implicitly understood it, was never explicitly clear: the arbitrageur's initial simultaneous purchase and sale do not end his exposure to the markets. Rather, they open it. This situation does not exist in the textbook examples of arbitrage. If I buy 1000 shares in IBM for 160 at the New York Stock Exchange and sell them at 160¼ at the Pacific Stock Exchange, the realization of ¼ point profit is instantaneous. The selling closes my exposure to IBM. But such examples do not exist in real life. Even in SOES trading, pure arbitrage does not exist. There, the time span between the purchase and sale of a stock is short. In that regard, the transactions approach arbitrage. But conceptually, SOES trading is no different than ordinary buying and selling of stocks. A SOES trader needs only *two trades* to close his exposure and realize his profit or loss. He buys and sells. Or vice versa.

The arbitrageur needs a minimum of *four* trades: buy and simultaneously sell the equivalent positions. But the *equivalent positions* are not the same as the *same positions*. They do not cancel out each other the way purchase and sale of the 1000 IBM shares do. Buying corporate bonds and selling Treasuries at the expectation of a decline in the spread between the two leaves the arbitrageur exposed to both markets. Those are the initial two trades. Later, he must unwind the positions – sell corporate bonds and buy back the Treasuries. It is after the completion of these trades that his exposure ends. By establishing the initial positions, the arbitrageur in fact sets a trap in the hope of catching the anomalies. Sometimes, he finds himself inside the trap, caught by the anomalies! In all events, the inexorable laws of finance exert themselves, creating amusing ironies.

One irony is that the arbitrageur uses his ingenuity to eliminate the risk by eliminating the time between his purchase and sale, only to find himself holding *two* positions and facing a time of uncertain duration! Another irony is the nature of the methods by which the arbitrageurs choose their targets. The equivalency of positions and the deviation of their difference from the "norm" are established through either the theory of finance or statistical analysis. Both methods are utterly unsuitable for the

> **We have before us the fundamental conflict between an arbitrageur's business and his tools of trade.**

business in hand. In these methods, in fact, we have before us the fundamental conflict between an arbitrageur's business and his tools of trade. His business is quantifying qualitative differences. His tools of trade are purely mathematical, void of any qualitative content. It is that conflict which brings him to the gallows. *There would never be an arbitrage related loss, much less systemic risk, if the relation between the markets were purely mathematical and could be determined as such.* Positive economics – "scientific" and free of social factors – finally comes home to roost.

Let us begin with the theory.

Theory of finance

Arbitrage argument is one of the main pillars of modern finance from which the law of "same price" is deduced. The law states that "similar" products must trade at the same price, otherwise the arbitrageurs will buy the lower-priced, and sell the higher-priced product and, in doing so, lock in a riskless profit. But we saw that "similar" cannot mean "same." It would be absurd to say that 100 IBM shares must trade at the same price as 100 IBM shares. "Similar," rather, connotes equivalent. Equivalent means the *equality of certain aspects* of *two qualitatively different* things. In geometry, for example, a circle and a square are said to be equivalent if they have equal areas.

The thing that is equal in arbitrage is the cash flow of the positions. Cash flows is the focus and subject of arbitrage. (That is why finance is "thought" to be the discipline of studying cash flows.) But the positions themselves are qualitatively different. That difference is the source of arbitrageur's profit and root of basis risk.

The quality of a position or a security is assessed by its credit rating. The assessment is partly based on hard facts such as such sales figures, revenues and profit margin of the company in question. But there are also many subjective factors which are sometimes captured and some-times escape the attention of analysts. The collapse of the Soviet Union and its impact on defense companies in the US, for example, was not easy to foresee. That is why rating agencies use a lettering system. Let-ters provide a uniform basis of comparison without creating a false sense of mathematical exactness. That approximation is sufficient for the purpose the ratings serve: providing a measure of the ability of a company to service debt. IBM and General Electric both have well-known products, established markets and strong finances which enable them to service their bond issues without any significant danger of default.

But markets, which must also grapple with the issue of quality, can-not take refuge in the vagueness of letters. They need numbers. No two qualitatively different entities can be exactly the same. The difference might be small and negligible, but it is never zero. There is no escaping the fact that IBM is *not* GE. That is why GE and IBM stocks trade at dif-ferent prices and P/E multiples. And that is why, even though both com-panies have the same rating, their bonds sell at different prices. The prices reflect the quality of securities, not only in absolute terms, but also relative to the overall quality of market, the latter being an average of sorts of the quality of all securities.

Market constantly compares and judges the quality of a security against that of the overall market and reflects the difference in price. "Liquidity," that vague concept frequently used by traders and never mentioned in finance, is the gauge of this conversion of qualitative dif-ference to quantitative values. It serves the same purpose as the rating. But unlike the appraisal of rating agencies, which is focused on compa-nies and securities alone and with regard to some fixed criteria, liquid-ity is a function of the quality of both: the product and the market. The higher the difference between the quality of a product and the overall market, the greater the illiquidity of product and, thus, the lower its price.[27]. In the extreme case of a completely illiquid product, its market

---

[27] Lack of liquidity translates to lower price, not widening the bid/asked spreads. The claims of Nasdaq market makers who widen the bid/asked spread of "illiquid" secu-rities on the excuse of accounting for illiquidity are baseless.

price drops to zero.[28] The social recognition of the value of a security all but vanishes.

> Paine Webber told regulators that it had not been able to get any other investors to bid on the bonds. Why? "It turns out kitchen sink bonds are so complicated and backed by so many pieces of collateral that they are not nearly subject to analysis," said … chief investment officer [of an asset management company]. "We just aren't going to be able to figure this out if we look at it for the rest of our lives."[29]

Theory of finance cannot account for these crucial points because it has washed its hands of qualitative elements. That is its great betrayal of arbitrageurs: luring them to markets with the promise of riskless profits only to leave them in the cold with no more than their "gut feeling" to lean on.

The Black–Scholes model is a case in point. It values options by equating them to an equivalent leveraged position in the underlying stock. Its assumptions eliminate the possibility of a qualitative difference between the two positions, meaning that the idealized value of an option and its market price are always assumed to be the same. But a leveraged position in a stock is not the *same* as an option on that stock. The writer of an option might default. An exchange traded option might be halted. Or more complicated scenarios might emerge. The victims of option valuation method are legion. Witness the reason for the loss of the following trader – a "rocket scientist," judging from the complexity of his position – as described in the *Wall Street Journal*:

> A [Morgan Stanley] trader took a $25 million loss … on a position in Office Depot Inc. convertible bonds … [The trader] tried to hedge the … bond position by selling short … a mix of Office Depot common stock and call options … Office Depot reported worse-than-expected … earnings, sending its common stock tumbling 23% the next day. The trouble was that the convertible bonds fell more than expected, amid mounting concerns about the company.[30]

---

[28] To be deemed illiquid, a product must have *some* value but command no price in market. A product with no value and no price is not illiquid; it is worthless.

[29] "Kitchen Sink Bonds: Paine Webber's $180 Million Misstep, *New York Times*, July 26, 1994, p. D1.

[30] Bond Hit At Morgan: $25 Million, *Wall Street Journal*, October 18, 1996, p. C1.

The convertible bonds falling more than expected is the basis risk – the risk arising from the difference in quality between the positions – which neither the theory of finance nor the Black–Scholes model can account for.

The trader's error in this example is worth a brief comment. He must have known that options could be replicated by a leveraged position in their underlying. His trades were designed to synthetically create an option and then arbitrage its difference with market prices. His error was using the company's own bonds for creating the synthetic option. But in that context, only Treasuries should be used.

Arbitraging synthetic options against the real options on the strength of the Black–Scholes model is incorrect. It yield profits only by accident.

Arbitraging synthetic options against the real options on the strength of the Black–Scholes model is a common pastime of the quantitatively oriented hedge funds. Long Term Capital had several such positions. But even when done correctly, the practice is incorrect. It yield profits only by accident.

Statistical analysis

The relation between two random variables is studied through various statistical methods, the most common of which is correlation analysis. The technique shows what percentage of the change in one variable could be "explained" by a change in another. For example, the death toll on highways is correlated with driving speed. As the speed increases, the death toll rises. Or, there is a high correlation in the US between the month of January and the US stock indexes. In January, the stocks, as measured by popular indexes, tend to rise.

Arbitrageurs use the correlation analysis and graphs of the movement of the two variables to detect anomalies and arbitrage opportunities.

Correlation, as statisticians are quick to point out, in not causation. Its "explanation" of the strength of the synchronous movement between two variables is a reporting of the "what is" kind, without delving into the causes of the phenomena. If two variables happen to move in tandem randomly, correlation analysis would still show that one variable largely explains the other. On the other hand, a logical historical correlation between the two variables might be interrupted due to the influence of outside factors. The death toll on US highways, for example, is currently declining despite a creeping up of the speed limits, largely because of the technical improvements in cars' safety features and an aggressive campaign against drunk driving. So a gambler who noticed the trend in the rise in speed limits and who bets on a rise in highway deaths on the strength of charts alone, would lose.

Arbitrageurs use charts in a fundamentally different way than day traders. For a day trader, the charts provide critical "buy" and "sell" signals. He does not have to think for himself. He buys at "valleys," sells at "peaks." That is his discipline, of which he is thoroughly proud and whose virtues he preaches to anyone willing to listen.

For an arbitrageur, charts show the anomaly and therefore, provide the signal for opening the "matched" positions. But the signal for closing them does not come from charts; it is already implied in the original position. The arbitrageur will unwind his trades when the spread between the positions has returned to "normal." Unfortunately, the time it might take for this return to normalcy is not known. It could be one week. It could be many months. Or, as in the case of the US stock market, there could be a complete departure from the past norms. Despite their reputation as being rapid-fire traders, arbitrageurs might be "in it" for a long time. In that regard, an adjective such as "long term" is an accurate description of the investment horizon of funds employing speculative capital.

> *Every losing arbitrageur considers himself a martyr of finance: he would have done well only there was not enough time.*

The danger facing the arbitrageur is now clear: while waiting for normalcy, the spread might move against him and wipe out his equity. In that case, he would be out of the game. Even if the spreads returned to normal, it would be too late for him. That is why every losing arbitrageur considers himself a martyr of finance: he would have done well – he *had* to do well – only there was not enough time. Less than a year after Orange County's bankruptcy, its portfolio was sold at a hefty profit. The intervention of the Federal Reserve on behalf of Long Term

Capital was also partly intended to "buy time." Within a few months, the hedge fund's positions had substantially improved.

Intrusion of social factors into arbitrage decisions

Unfortunately, capital cannot be locked in a position for long, as it would see its rate of return drop. That eventuality must be avoided. That is why arbitrageurs cannot make their trading decisions on the evidence of charts alone; they need to know the "story" behind the charts as well. That "knowing the story" is fundamental analysis, which involves accounting for all the hard-to-quantify, social factors. So after protracted attempts to reduce finance to quantifiable elements – one by-product of which is modern finance – the arbitrageurs come full circle, finding themselves exactly where they had begun: wondering how to account for the social aspects of finance. But they are neither trained nor conditioned to analyze them.

This latter statement should not be taken to mean that arbitrageurs are incapable of thinking in non-mathematical terms. That would be a gross underestimation of the skills of this generally sharp crowd. The Morgan Stanley trader in the above story lost $25 million because of his technical error, but his targeting of Office Depot was right on the mark: the company was about to release crucial information. Likewise, no trader would attempt to arbitrage the US pork bellies against the prices in Paris Bourse even if the analysis showed a correlation between the two and charts revealed an anomaly. They know that the two markets are not currently linked by speculative capital. Furthermore, the interaction of social factors and their final impact on prices could be very complex and thwart the more "logical" scenarios.

As an example, let us put ourselves in the position of the manager of Long Term Capital Management. He counts the central bank of Italy among his investors.[31] Perhaps on the strength of that relation, he knows with more conviction that the interest rates in Italy will decline faster

---

[31] That the central bank of Italy had invested $100 million in Long Term Capital was the most curious piece of information to come out of the hedge fund's troubles. What the bank planned to do with the profits – and just what "profit" means for a central bank – remained a minor mystery.

than in, say, Germany. That might even be a requirement for Italy joining the *euro* club. The course of action is now obvious: buy Italian bonds, sell German bonds. Half-audaciously, half-naively, he calls the strategy "convergence trade," faintly implying a mechanical force bound to bring the yield in two countries together in the time horizon suiting Long Term Capital.

Then the Russian government defaults on its bonds, creating a panic in the European bond market and the "flight to quality" towards German bonds. The convergence trades diverge. The *Wall Street Journal*, describes one of the firm's many bets which had gone bad:

> Also, the fund's "convergence" trades – bets that government securities of growing European nations, like Italy, would outperform the securities of safer European nations, such as Germany, making their yields converge – have suffered."[32]

Such losses are common in trading. A Morgan Stanley trader loses $25 million on the bet against Office Depot. Long Term Capital loses a few billions on the wrong bet in various strategies. And a Barings trader brings down the house playing with futures on the Japanese stock and bond markets. As long as the loss occurs in the course of miscellaneous

A financial resonance is created which has the potential to disrupt the system.

strategies – as in these examples – the risk remains confined to immediate parties involved.

Sometimes strategies coincide. Speculative capital is directed from all sides to a few markets. As a result, a financial resonance is created which has the potential to disrupt the system. The source of the risk is the basis risk which now, thanks to the involvement of large pools of leveraged speculative capital, is metamorphosed into systemic risk.

> The same force that crushed Long Term Capital – investor stampede
> into US Treasury and other safe securities that pushed down their

---

[32] "Diverging Yields Challenge Hedge Fund," *Wall Street Journal*, October 5, 1998, p. C1.

yields while driving up yields on riskier bonds – also is depressing the earnings of securities firms, pushing them to trim their balance sheets by unloading risky securities. Until the market turmoil of the past several weeks, securities firms had been building up their balance sheets … Without the increased leverage, those firms probably wouldn't have generated the same kind of earning growth.[33]

The build-up of systemic risk

The mass of capital, whether speculative or otherwise, has its own dynamics, apart from what one can learn from analyzing the decisions of individual managers of capital. A matter-of-fact description of conditions in the junk bond market by two Wall Street executives succinctly captures that point:

> "There is nowhere else for the money to go." That's … [the] chief of high-yield research at Merrill Lynch & Company, explaining the rush of billions of dollars this year [1997] into C-rated and nonrated bonds, the bottom of the junk bond heap … Chief global fixed-income strategist at Lehman Brothers, thinks a "fundamental shift" is pushing money managers to take more risk. "You've got to have more of this lower-quality stuff," he said, or you cannot perform well anymore.[34]

The "money" Merrill's high-yield chief is referring to is the mass of credit capital. This money is different from what the individual traders might throw into the various arbitrage ventures. It is measured in billions and is directed toward a single market. "You" as in "You've got to have more of this lower-quality stuff" refers to the fixed income fund managers. They need to produce attractive returns. That is not possible with the low yield of the Treasuries and A-rated corporate bonds. To "perform well," they have to direct their capital to high-yield bonds. Their combined actions move the market toward the lower quality secu-

---

[33] "High Leverage Isn't Unusual On Wall Street," *Wall Street Journal*, October 13, 1998, p. C1

[34] "Junk Here, Junk There: Hey, That's Big Money," *New York Times*, August 31, 1997, Section 3, p. 1.

rities and tend to lower the spread between the junk bonds and the Treasuries.

All hedge fund managers are aware of this condition. They, too, begin buying junk bonds. But they must do more, else they would be indistinguishable from the fixed income funds. A return of 8 per cent is excellent for a fixed income fund, but dismal for a hedge fund. So in addition to

The build-up of risk in the system is in full swing.

buying junk bonds, they also short Treasuries. If the Fed increases the rates, as insiders say it might, the short Treasury positions would generate profits. As for the Fed lowering the rates, that is a remote possibility under existing conditions. In this way, the speculative capital enters into the market to arbitrage the high quality and no-quality bonds. Highly leveraged positions are now locked in spreads between Treasuries and junk bonds. The build-up of risk in the system is in full swing.

This real-life example is not an isolated case. It is how speculative capital operates in all the markets. Julian Robertson, the manager of a large hedge fund, explains his strategy in the stock market:

> "Our basic business," Mr Robertson explained … "is buying the best 200 stocks in the word and shorting the worst 200 … The trouble arises, however, when the improbable occurs and the worst stocks do better than the best. Unfortunately, this happens more frequently than we would like, particularly in international markets."[35]

The "trouble" to which Robertson is alluding is the narrowing of the spread between the best and worst stocks, with devastating consequences. According to the same article:

> October [1998] was a cruel month for hedge fund manager Julian Robertson … Mr Robertson told investors that [his] fund had lost 17%, or about $3.4 billion … wiping out all their gains for the year. The October losses came on top of $2.1 billion of losses in September.

---

[35] "Robertson's Funds Become Paper Tigers," *Wall Street Journal*, November 2, 1998, p. A3.

Why does the improbable occur (more frequently than anybody likes) and the worst stocks do better than the best?

It would be naive to think that the fault lies with the stock picking skills of fund managers. They are professional traders and spend hours scrutinizing companies. The culprit, rather, is the speculative capital, which enters the game of arbitrage with a heavy baggage of its characteristics and alters the historical relation between the best and worst stocks. We explain.

> *Why does the improbable occur and the worst stocks do better than the best?*

Speculative capital is massive in size. It grazes on the spreads and brings volatility to markets. Because the speculative capital is hidden from view, the cause of volatility remains a mystery. Markets seem increasingly irrational.

> What can you really know about a stock when its value seesaws 10% or 15% in the space of a week or less for no apparent reason? Not much, say some perplexed investors. With the stock market embroiled in some of the most volatile moves in years, it is getting increasingly difficult for money managers to plan and execute their strategies.[36]

and:

> Rising volatility is worrisome, if only because people who are paid to study such things have no clear answers as to why it is happening now.[37]

Nevertheless, fund managers must deliver results. Staying on the sidelines on account of volatility is not an option. What can they do if stocks are volatile and drop for no apparent reason? The answer is that they discover "relative value" trading. A news story in the *Wall Street Journal* captured this crucial shift in stock trading strategy:

> [Mr Schermerhorn, who manages $4 billion for Federated Investors in Pittsburgh] also scorns the growing emphasis on "relative" valuation,

---

[36] "Sharp Swings in Stock Prices Are Making It Tougher for Managers to Plan Strategies," *Wall Street Journal*, November 24, 1997, p. C1.

[37] "Reassurances, Despite a Bouncing Bull," *New York Times*, August 31, 1997, p. F4.

comparing a company's P/E ratio with those of other companies in the sector, rather than absolute valuations or historical levels. But other investors concede they are reluctantly having to pay more attention to relative valuation. "Lately, if you'd used almost any kind of absolute-valuation guidelines, you'd have kept out of this market altogether, and missed a lot of the bull market," sighs Mr Jandrain [who manages a stock fund for Banc One]. "The reality is that we're still at record [valuation] levels historically by nearly every measure, and you have to look for pockets of relative value."[38]

"Relative value" trading – comparing one stock against similar stocks – is arbitrage trading. Banc One's Mr Jandrain might not be aware of this, but his journey is not dissimilar to the experience of Citibank which we saw in Chapter 3. He is being forced to disregard forecasting, i.e., individual stock analysis with an eye to estimating its future growth, in favor of buying relatively undervalued or selling relatively overvalued stocks. He calls that "looking for pockets of relative value." But arbitrage by any name is arbitrage. In his quest for pockets of relative value in the equities market, Jandrain has assigned his fund to the ranks of speculative capital, thus guaranteeing that relative value trading, and, with it, the volatility of the stock market, will increase. "Sector rotation has been a hallmark of the bull market of the last three years. But traders and investors say these swings seem more violent and more short-lived than before."[39]

Such is the impact of speculative capital on financial markets: fund managers reluctantly joining a trend which they abhor and whose dynamics they do not understand. In the process, they push the stock market even higher. Those traders who position themselves to profit from a decrease in the P/E ratios get clobbered.

The culmination of the relative value trading is the creation of trading houses such as the one covered in the *Wall Street Journal*:

---

[38] "Sharp Swings in Stock Prices Are Making It Tougher for Managers to Plan Strategies," *Wall Street Journal*, November 24, 1997, p. C1.

[39] "Market Is Diagnosed As Manic-Depressive," *Wall Street Journal*, February 23, 1998, p. C1.

At BNP/Cooper Neff, stocks aren't companies in the industry sector. They are "mathematical objects." ... [The company's president] thinks studying news and financial reports ... is a waste of time ... And the only way to beat the market ... is to trade thousands of stocks, by the millions of shares, in search of tiny inefficiencies ... he sees the world as 7,000 stocks to trade against one another in one gigantic hedge fund.[40]

Julian Robertson wonders why his short sales increase in price more than his long positions. The reason is that what he considers 'worst stocks' are undervalued "mathematical objects" worth snapping up in the eyes of BNP/Cooper Neff, whose president speaks as if possessed by speculative capital: "The only way you can know anything about value is how the market tries to find an equilibrium. That's all the market is – a big feedback mechanism trying to find equilibrium."[41]

This shows that speculative capital is highly adaptable and changes its methods of operation to suit the specifics of each market. In the stock market, it cannot directly challenge the strict 50 per cent margin requirement. Instead, it circumvents the rule by a design of its own: pushing the stock prices constantly higher. As a result, the same effect as high leverage is achieved through high P/E ratios in the stock market. A 50 per cent equity position in a stock with the P/E ratio of 200 could be at a greater risk of being wiped out than a 10 per cent equity position in a bond. In all events, it is the logical consequence of the operation of speculative capital and not any irrational exuberance which propels the stock market to new heights. All the while, the risk of a sharp decline in the market increases because stock prices do not reflect the value of their

It is the logical consequence of the operation of speculative capital and not any irrational exuberance which propels the stock market to new heights.

---

[40] "Trading Vast Volumes, Stock Firm Consults Only Its 'Black Box,'" *Wall Street Journal*, December 16, 1997, p. A1.

[41] Ibid.

companies: "'This hasn't been an environment in which values means much,' says Nola Kulig ... a portfolio manager."[42]

After a major loss, financial firms trim their balance sheets and pronounce a new policy of emphasizing less risky, free-generating business. The latest such episode occurred in Goldman Sachs in early 1999, where the firm's co-chairman who came from the trading side was forced out and an executive from the investment banking side took over. The new chairman, according to the *New York Times*, had "pushed for a reduction in the amount of money that Goldman devoted to trading."[43]

The trouble with free-generating activities is that they do not generate nearly enough revenues to sustain the expenses of large financial firms. The desires to reduce trading are expressed in earnest but also in ignorance of the dynamics of the financial markets. Goldman Sachs retrenching from trading is no more plausible than Citigroup becoming a neighborhood bank. The present situation has come to pass precisely because the financial institutions could not help from being drawn into trading.

The materialization of systemic risk: the trigger

Systemic risk begins to take shape when the mass of speculative capital is locked in a particular arbitrage position – say, between Treasuries and junk bonds. These fully loaded positions are arrived at by way of consideration of financial factors. But, because of the social nature of finance, they remain highly vulnerable to political and social events. And frequently, the "trigger" events are social and political. The Russian government, for example, defaults on its bond obligations. The general credit in the market deteriorates. The spreads between junk and US Treasury yields increase and individual funds suffer losses. They must

---

[42] "Robertson's Tiger Heads Funds are Bloodied By Market's Current 'Momentum' Approach," *Wall Street Journal*, February 12, 1999, p. C2.
[43] "This Time, Shared Reins Didn't Work at Goldman," *New York Times*, January 13, 1999, p. C1.

either provide additional equity capital or be liquidated. But they have no equity capital; recall that they are highly leveraged. In this way, they are liquidated and the pool of speculative capital *as a whole* incurs loss. That is systemic risk.

Under these conditions, the extent of the damage to the system is a function of two factors. One is the size of the adverse move: the more volatile the markets, the bigger the moves and the greater the amount of equity that is lost. The other is the leverage ratio of the individual funds: the higher the ratio, the lower their margin of tolerance to market swings. With the operation of speculative capital constantly increasing the volatility, and the need for comparable returns pushing towards higher leverage, the momentum of the markets dominated by speculative capital is towards the greater risk of bankruptcy. In other words, it is not the failure of one or a few firms, but the *common strategy*, which triggers systemic risk.

> *The momentum of the markets dominated by speculative capital is towards the greater risk of bankruptcy.*

Of course, the smaller pools of speculative capital are the most vulnerable to unexpected turns of events. The proprietary trading desk in Citigroup and a hedge fund such as Long Term Capital Management might both be long junk bonds and short Treasuries. But their source of income and percentage of equity capital devoted to that arbitrage position would be markedly different. Citigroup's portion is a relatively small percentage of the mammoth organization's equity. Its activities across the spectrum of finance create a well-diversified source of income which acts as a cushion against shocks in any one particular area.

Long Term Capital, by contrast, has no other source of income except trading profits. Its equity capital, furthermore, is pitifully small compared with Citigroup's. As a result, although both firms might be engaged in the same arbitrage positions and both suffer the same magnitude of losses, the amount of loss in relative terms would be much greater for Long Term Capital.

But even Long Term Capital discovered that unwinding its positions pushed the markets in precisely the opposite direction, further exacerbating its problems:

Long Term Capital bought a number of Treasury futures to liquidate one side of a huge trade. The buying moved the spread between the futures and the so-called cash market in that particular issue by one-quarter of a point, an enormous move in the world's deepest, most liquid securities market.[44]

The reason was simply the fund's own positions:

What is worse for Long Term Capital is that since the bailout was agreed to, prices of the riskier bonds it had made massive bets on – including junk, emerging-markets and commercial mortgage-backed securities – have fallen even further behind Treasuries, weighed down by fears that the fund will have to dump its portfolio sooner rather than later.[45]

But the damage of unwinding the positions goes far beyond the individual firm. It reverberates throughout the system because many others are also locked in the same positions. The actions of a single fund to unwind its positions moves the spread precisely in the opposite to what tens of billions of dollars in speculative capital have bet. In this way, the individual problem of the basis risk turns into the general problem of systemic risk.

It was precisely this fear of exacerbating the problem that compelled the Federal Reserve to engineer the bailout of Long Term Capital: if the losing positions could be sustained through the infusion of additional equity capital, there was a chance that the situation might improve. But the commitment of "healthy" firms to a bailout increases their risk profile and makes the system as a whole more vulnerable.

To illustrate this point, take five hypothetical firms which have committed capital to engage in a similar arbitrage action. Again, we can assume that they arbitrage the spread between Treasuries and junk bonds. Table 6.1 shows the equity capital of each firm earmarked for arbitrage, its total equity capital, the leverage ratio and, finally, the size

---

[44] "New York Fed Assists Hedge Fund's Bailout," *New York Times*, September 24, 1998, p. A1.
[45] "Bond Market Still Punishes Hedge Fund and Investors," *Wall Street Journal*, October 5, 1998, p. C1.

of arbitrage positions. Except for the leverage ratio, all figures are in billions of dollars

Table 6.1 Capital structure of hypothetical firms engaged in arbitrage

Firm	Equity Capital	Size of Arbitrage Position	Leverage Ratio
1	20	100	5
2	2	80	40
3	10	40	4
4	4	160	40
5	20	60	3

Let us now assume that the adverse movement in the spreads results in a 5 per cent loss for all the positions. Table 6.2 shows the amount of loss and total equity capital left to each firm.

Table 6.2 Remaining equity capital after 5% loss

Firm	Total Equity Capital	Loss	Remaining Equity Capital
1	20	− 5	+15
2	2	− 4	− 2
3	10	− 2	+ 8
4	4	− 8	− 4
5	20	−3	+17

We see from Table 6.2 that firms 2 and 4 have negative equity capital. They have lost all their equity and are further in debt for a total of $6 billion. To avert a panicky unwinding of their positions, a deal is made so that the healthy firms take over their positions. Each healthy firm contributes $2 billion and assumes an equal part of the bankrupt firms' positions. After this arrangement, the picture is as shown in Table 6.3:

Table 6.3 New positions after the takeover of bankrupt firms

Firm	Equity Capital	Size of Arbitrage Position	Leverage Ratio
1	8	180	22.50
3	6	20	20
5	15	140	9.33

Firm 1, for example, had an original equity capital of $20. It lost $5 in arbitrage trading. Then it took in a third of the losses belonging to firms 2 and 4. So its equity capital is reduced to 8. Meanwhile its size of arbitrage position has increased to 180, being the original 100 of its own position plus a third of the combined position of bankrupt firms 2 and 4.

Compared with Table 6.1, the vulnerability of each firm in the system has now increased. If there is an additional 5 per cent loss in the positions, firms 1 and 3 would be out of business.

This example exaggerates the impact of the bailout on the risk profile of the remaining firms. In real life, taking over the positions of a firm such as Long Term Capital would add very little to the total exposure of giant institutions such as Merrill Lynch or Goldman Sachs. What is not exaggerated is the size of the market fluctuations. The operation of speculative capital could produce losses many times more than our 5 percent example. Under those conditions, the number of bankruptcies would rise drastically.

The consequences of systemic risk

Systemic risk is a category in finance. Its rise is tied to the rise of speculative capital. One can directly trace systemic risk to the Bretton Woods conference. It was there that the search for an answer to the problem of balance of payments was directed from policy planning to the realm of foreign exchange and, from there, to the supremacy of the dollar. That is why, unlike in a recession, which begins with the industrial corporations, systemic risk first hits the financial institutions. Its impact, depending on the circumstances and the severity of the losses, could be confined to financial sector or spill over to entire sovereign economies.

The extent of the influence of finance capital over the economy is not widely understood. In the midst of the financial crisis in Southeast Asia, two Harvard economists wrote: "the currency upheavals probably reflect short-run financial considerations rather than a long-term crisis of regional growth ... And as we are seeing, governments and private markets cannot be unravelled in the real world."[46]

Setting aside the utter misreading of the crisis, the word "unravel" these economists use needs an explanation. A nation's wealth, as measured by the value of what it produces through economic activities cannot vanish. In that regard, governments and markets cannot be unravelled the way an ill-conceived plot could. But in the tail-wagging-the-dog state of affairs characterized by the supremacy of finance capital, the impact of financial crises on the economy is very real as it wipes out equity or "wealth." For private parties, the loss of wealth is expressed in their local currency. When the sway of systemic risk reaches beyond private parties to national economies, the loss of wealth takes the form of devaluation of the currency.

The devaluation of a currency is the declaration of a partial bankruptcy at national level.

The devaluation of a currency is the declaration of a partial bankruptcy at national level. Its impact hits all aspects of a nation's commercial and economic life. Here is an example of that impact on Thailand, as described by the *New York Times*:

> Since the Thai Government freed the baht from a dollar-linked trading band early in July, the currency has lost 30 percent of its value, jolting

[46] "Fail-Safe Strategies in a Market Era," *New York Times*, January 4, 1998, Section 4, p. 1.

Asian foreign-exchange and stock markets and leaving a mound of financial wreckage. The banks are not lending, bills are going unpaid, interest rates are sky-high for those who can manage to borrow, and bankruptcies are spreading for those who can't. Unemployment is climbing, and workers are protesting that they must bear the brunt of the costs.[47]

In a system dominated by dollar-denominated speculative capital, countries go bankrupt not because they run out of "wealth," as measured by the value of goods and services, but because they run out of dollars. That is why, in the aftermath of such bankruptcies, barter trading grows:

> With national and corporate coffers from South Korea to Indonesia depleted of foreign exchange, companies looking to sell their goods in Asia are being offered everything from tea to textiles instead of cash. Southeast Asian leaders are calling for regional trading programs that avoid the mighty US dollar, or any other currency for that matter. Because credit is unavailable to many Asian companies, their trading partners and bankers are chasing ways to keep commerce flowing.[48]

The US cannot run out of dollars because it can print them. That gives the country a tremendous advantage, making it the *de facto* central bank of the world. At times, it even creates an illusion of invincibility at home.

Alas, the Federal Reserve can no more escape the laws of finance than the artful arbitrageurs could. As the size of speculative capital grows, its tendency to direct itself to dead-end positions surpasses the power of authorities. Gradually and subtly, signs are emerging that the mass of speculative capital might have stopped responding to the commands of the Federal Reserve. Worse yet, it has begun to interpret them to its own liking, as it sees fit! The bond

> *The US cannot run out of dollars because it can print them.*

---

[47] "A Domino Effect in Thailand," *New York Times*, September 21, 1997, Section 3, p. 2.

[48] "Asia's Credit Crunch is Sending It Back to the Age of Barter," *Wall Street Journal*, April 6, 1998, p. A10.

market, for example, all but ignored the rate cut by the Fed in November 1998. Instead, the stock market used the occasion to push itself to record highs. The chief investment strategist for Merrill Lynch observed:

> The stock market has seen its capitalization increase by at least $1.5 trillion in the last two months [October and November 1998]. You can't do that with normal savings. There is something powerful underneath this thing, and I would argue it is the Fed ... The Federal Reserve [threw] a tremendous amount of money at the capital markets. It is that liquidity that is helping stocks ... The Fed has now reflated the equity market bubble. The risk is that next spring they will be looking at an even bigger bubble.[49]

In recent years, after every decline, the US stock market has rapidly rebounded. This is attributed to "bottom fishing," or the investors using a "buying opportunity." Such rebound is in fact due to the existence of arbitrage relations which, by nature, pull in both directions. That is why the emergence of this phenomenon coincides with speculative capital finding its way into the stock market. The danger of systemic risk is that, at some point, the fall in prices would be sufficiently severe to rupture the arbitrage relations. If such a condition were to come to pass, its consequences would go beyond anything seen in Southeast Asia or anywhere else. "'What is hard to measure after a period of sustained bull market activity is whether the amount of hedging has built up to a degree that it would significantly accelerate decline in the market,' [says a securities lawyer]."[50] The lawyer quoted here, speaking about the role of dynamic hedging strategies in the market decline, mistakes arbitrage for hedging, but otherwise his comments are right on the mark.

We see that systemic risk is the culmination of the contradictions in the arenas of finance, law and politics as they relate to speculative capital. This complex hybrid does not lend itself to easy solutions. A detailed analysis of the conditions which would gauge the risk in a given system and determine how close it is to the trigger point requires access

---

[49] "The Bubble is Back, Compliments of Fed," *New York Times*, December 6, 1998, Section 3, p. 6.

[50] Changes Minimize Risk of Crises, *Wall Street Journal*, August 25, 1997, p. C1.

to a vast array of data. A large part of such data is proprietary information and is not even reported.

Fundamentally, though, any solution must include hampering speculative capital. And speculative capital aggressively resists such attempts. In short, the problem of controlling systemic risk is that the risk, like dangerous waste, is the by-product of the operation of speculative capital. And speculative capital insists upon operating unfettered.

In real life, when the chain reaction of bankruptcies spreads, the affected entities, be they private markets or sovereign states, take steps to mitigate the damage. After the crisis in Southeast Asia, there have also been proposals for preventing systemic risk from occurring. We briefly comment on these measures.

Countering systemic risk

The most intuitive response to systemic risk is to shut off the operation of speculative capital in places it causes stress. For sovereign states, the vulnerable market is the local currency market. So they impose currency controls. The Malaysian government imposed such controls in the September 1998 and was able to stabilize the ringgit.

In theory, the controls could be applied in the early stages of the detection of the problem. In practice, they are always implemented after the damage is done and little recourse remains. This is due to the two-sided nature of arbitrage relations, which keeps alive the hope that the tide might be turned.

In a small system, controls take the form of "circuit breakers" which kick in to halt trading after a sharp rise or fall in prices. There are circuit breakers in the US stock and futures markets. The rules for the engagement of circuit breakers were recently loosened. But they continue to draw fire from critics, who, speaking on behalf of speculative capital, object to any "intervention" in the markets.

The difference between currency controls and circuit breakers lies in their duration. Circuit breakers expire after a period ranging from an hour to a day. Currency controls have no set duration. Their lifting is left to the discretion of local officials who immediately come under attack

> *The movement of speculative capital cannot be restricted through partial measures.*

for having instituted the controls – recall Vice President Al Gore's call for the ouster of Prime Minister Mohathir of Malaysia after the Prime Minister had instituted currency controls.

Then there are those who propose to avert the risk by "reforming" the system. Some of them call for the creation of an international agency of sorts to "allocate capital" to countries. Others, the World Bank among them, want to create "some systems" which will limit the movement of short-term capital.

The good intentions of the concerned parties notwithstanding, the movement of speculative capital cannot be restricted through partial measures. To avert systemic risk, the currencies must be fixed against each other, entire deregulation of financial markets rolled back and trade liberalization treaties annulled. It goes without saying that such "turning back the clock" is presently a pipe dream.

> Federal Reserve Chairman Alan Greenspan rose to the defense of global currency traders, saying they help lift living standards around the world ... Mr Greenspan acknowledged that the huge expansion of global financial markets has created "mechanisms for mistakes to ricochet throughout the global financial system" with increasing speed. "Why not then, one might ask, bar or contain the expansion of global finance by capital controls, transaction taxes, or other market-inhibiting initiatives?" Mr Greenspan asked aloud ... Because, he replied ... "We cannot turn back the clock on technology – and we should not try to do so," he added.[51]

Short of being pushed back into the bottle by means of a global treaty, speculative capital always finds ways to flow to profitable spreads. And as we saw, it generally does so by "pushing the envelope" of the existing system. The multi-trillion dollar swap and the OTC derivatives markets, for example, rose from the back-to-back and parallel loans which

---

[51] "Greenspan Defends Currency Traders, Asserts They Help Living Standards," *Wall Street Journal*, October 15, 1997, p. A2.

were created in the 1970s to circumvent the currency controls in Great Britain. Speculative capital even circumvents a strict rule such as prohibition against short selling stocks in a "down tick:"

> Traders ... are dusting off an old trading strategy ... which allows investors to bet on a stock's decline even if the stock is caught in a freefall. The strategy, which involves a complicated trading technique called "married puts," is especially alluring in a volatile market ... because it allows the traders to sidestep rules that prevent short sales, or bets that a stock will decline, when the stock's share price already is falling.[52]

The Federal Reserve is the sole institution which has at its disposal two ways of cutting the flow of fuel to speculative capital: by a reduction in leverage and increasing interest rates. Neither is particularly easy to implement. Requiring financial institutions to reduce their leverage by increasing reserve requirements will immediately cut into their profits and, thus, will be vehemently opposed. The current trend is towards loosening the requirements.

That leaves the Fed with the only tool over which it has some autonomy and through which it can hamper speculative capital and reduce systemic risk: raising interest rates. The IMF and US Treasury officials must have had some inkling about the role of interest rates in dampening the expansion of speculative capital. That is why they advise countries afflicted with the consequences of systemic risk to raise interest rates. This advice generally leads to further worsening of the situation because the interest which must be raised is not on the local currency but on the US dollar. Speculative capital is denominated in US dollars. It is only through increasing the interest rates *in the US* that the dollar shell of speculative capital begins to squeeze it and retards its movement. Otherwise raising interest rates locally only exacerbates the shrinkage of credit and the spread of bankruptcies.

---

[52] 'Bullet' Strategy Makes Comeback as Traders Find Ways to Skirt Rules on Short Selling," *Wall Street Journal*, September 14, 1998, p. C2.

The role of derivatives

Speculative capital needs to arbitrage various markets. It needs to do so with a high degree of leverage. And it must do so at a minimum cost, preferably at no cost. The structure of derivatives offer all these opportunities. Thus, speculative capital discovers derivatives. But because this abstract force is hidden, the rise of derivatives is attributed to an inexplicable bolt of financial innovation having suddenly struck Wall Street.

At times, product designers outdo themselves in creating complex derivatives. But ultimately, every derivative is a bet on the direction of a market or the spread between two variables. The "5/30" swap which

Thus, speculative capital discovers derivatives.

became the subject of a lawsuit between Procter & Gamble and Bankers Trust, for example, involved a payment that was determined by the difference between the price of the long (30-year) bond and the yield of the five-year Treasury note, hence the name "5/30." Stripped out of its silly complexity, the swap was designed to arbitrage the spread between the yield of the 30-year and five-year Treasuries, a strategy the treasurer of Orange County would have readily recognized.

The leverage in derivatives is "attached" to their structure, meaning that, unlike in regular transaction where leveraging is voluntary, in derivatives the mere use of the product entails leveraging. The buyer of a bond or stock can choose not to use leverage. A party to a derivative has no such option; the leverage is already built into the structure of the product.[53] The extension of credit in derivatives is thus implicit rather than explicit.

While no one would have difficulty in understanding the necessity of paying back the interest and principal on a sum borrowed from a bank, the notion of "paying back" for the leverage used in derivatives is not universally understood. Nick Leeson, the Bearings' trader whose large positions in futures went sour and drove the firm to bankruptcy, proved

---

[53] The buyer of an option can only lose his premium. But the premium is subject to a higher risk of loss because an option is a leveraged position in the underlying.

a case in point. In referring to his amassing 60,000 futures contracts in the Japanese stock and bond market, he remarked: "As stupid as it may sound, none of this is really real money; it's not as if you have cash sitting in front of you."[54]

Whether traders understand it or not, taking part in buying and selling a $100 commodity with only $2 in equity capital has its perils. Traders and the financial press use the term "control" for such scenarios; the trader with $2 "controls" a $100 contract. But that is a poor choice of word, as in "controlling" a beast by grabbing its tail. The consequences are generally predictable:

> Hawaii's insurance officials seized Investors Equity Life Insurance Co. of Hawaii late last month when it became evident that the company was deeply in the red from a strategy that involved trading billions of dollars of Treasury-bond futures … The losses are particularly eye-opening given that the company … reported just $16 million in net worth at year-end, while its total assets amounted to $186.8 million … Company officials have told regulators they controlled $800 million to $1 billion of futures contracts … through leveraged purchases.[55]

The low cost of derivatives is another aspect which appeals to speculative capital. Derivatives require an infrastructure in the form of staff and systems, but otherwise they have very little cost capital terms. That point is crucial for increasing the return of arbitrage operations, which is why speculative capital aggressively resists moves to increase the cost of trading derivatives:

> The Securities and Exchange Commission, responding to brokerage-industry complaints about the loss of derivatives business to foreign markets, is re-evaluating its rules on how much capital securities firms must set aside to cover trades they make … Net-capital rules are

---

[54] "Barings Trader Questions Monitoring By His Superiors, *New York Times*, Sep 11, 1995, p. D4.

[55] "Tiny Hawaii Insurer Makes Wrong Call Using Derivatives, Is Seized by the State," *Wall Street Journal,* July 20, 1994, p. C1.

becoming increasingly important as securities firms delve deeper in the trading of exotic securities that often require hefty capital levels.[56]

A derivative such as an interest rate swap, furthermore, is by nature a "matched" transaction. That is because its notional amount is recorded both as a credit and a debit. The "exposure" of the firm does not seem to be affected. Hence, swaps become the ultimate tool of speculative capital. They are low cost. They can be used to arbitrage all the markets. And they are recorded as matched transactions, thus meeting "risk management" requirements.

To academics, these relations appear completely upside down. So, instead of leveraged tools which allow for "controlling" large positions with a small equity capital, derivatives appear as a substitute for equity; using derivatives one can somehow bypass the need for equity!

> In this sense [speaking of companies with no debt], risk management can be viewed as a direct substitute for equity capital. That is, the more the firm hedges its financial exposures, the less equity it requires to support its business. Or to put it another way, the use of risk management to reduce exposure effectively increases a company's debt capacity. (Stulz, 1996, p. 24)

The errors in this single paragraph – where credit capital, equity capital, derivatives, hedging and risk management are thrown into a confused mishmash – are industry standard when it comes to derivatives. In the context, the bizzare conclusion that follows is also natural. No other subject in economics and finance has generated so much incorrect theorizing and hypothesizing. But because these errors in derivatives are the norm, debunking the errors and showing the risks of derivatives cannot be done in a chapter or two. They require a book of their own. That is the subject Volume 2 of *Speculative Capital*.

> *The errors in this single paragraph are industry standard when it comes to derivatives.*

---

[56] SEC Reconsiders Its Net-Capital Rules Due to Widespread Use of Derivatives, *Wall Street Journal*, November 8, 1996, p. A6.

References

Bruck, Connie (1988 *The Predators' Ball*, New York: The American Lawyer/Simon & Schuster.

Corrigan, E. Gerald E. (1987) "Financial Market Structure: A Longer View," *Federal Reserve of New York*, January.

Hull, John C. (1997) *Options, Futures and Other Derivatives*, Upper Saddle River, NJ: Prentice-Hall.

Samuelson, Paul and Nordhaus, William (1995) *Economics*, 15th edn, New York: McGraw-Hill.

Stulz, Rene M. (1996) "Rethinking Risk Management," *Journal of Applied Corporate Finance*, Vol. 9, No. 3, pp. 8–24.

INDEX